Healthy Dogs

A Handbook of

Natural Therapies

Dr Barbara Fougère
BSc BVMS (Hons)

HYLAND HOUSE

First published in Australia in 2003 by
Hyland House Publishing Pty Ltd
PO Box 122
Flemington, Victoria 3031

National Library of Australia
Cataloguing-in-publication data:

Fougère, Barbara.
Healthy dogs: a handbook of natural therapies.

Bibliography.
Includes index.
ISBN 1 86447 056 9.

1. Dogs – Health – Handbooks, manuals, etc. I. Title.

636.7083

Edited by Nerissa Greenfield
Layout and Design by Rob Cowpe Design
Printed by Griffin Press, Australia

Contents

Preface   vi

Acknowledgments   vii

PART 1
DIET AND NATURAL THERAPIES—AN OVERVIEW

1   **A Tale of Three Dogs**   1

2   **Health and Disease**   4

The Energy View • Domestication • The Modern Dog and Free Radicals • Stress • Nutrition • Parasites • Life-style • Breeding • A Dog's Home Is His Castle • Exercise • Environment • Veterinary Care • How healthy is your dog?

3   **What Do Dogs Eat?**   13

A Natural Diet • The Correct Way to Feed • Commercial Dog Foods • Selecting a Good Quality Dry Food • Selecting Canned Foods • Bones • Home-made Diets

4   **What Do Dogs Need?**   19

How much do you feed? • Changing Dog Foods • Guidelines for Feeding Puppies • The Pregnant Dog • Feeding During Lactation • Adult Dogs • Senior Dogs • Protein Requirements • Fat • Carbohydrates • Dietary Fibre • Water • Vitamins • Minerals • Balance

5   **Home-made Diets for Dogs**   27

Food Types • Cooked versus Raw Foods • Organic Foods • Recipes • Recommended Supplements • Alternatives

6   **Supplements**   42

Vitamins • Minerals • Essential Fatty Acids • Fibre • Probiotics • Prebiotics • Antioxidants • Carnitine • Coenzyme Q • Dimethylglycine • Enzymes • Honey • Bee Propolis • Liver • Bioflavinoids • Grape Seed Extract • Garlic • Glandular Products • Glucosamine • Glutamine • Green Foods • Kelp • Lecithin • Perna Mussel • Shark and Bovine Cartilage • Shitake, Maitake and Other Mushrooms • Choline • Wheat Germ • Yeast

7   **Medicinal Herbs**   64

8 Acupuncture   **77**

Some of the Major Indications • Muscle and Bone Problems • Nervous System and Spinal Problems • Skin Disorders • Digestive Tract Disorders • Heart Disorders • Behavioural Problems • Immune Disorders • Cancer • Reproduction • Respiratory Disorders • Urinary Tract Problems • Eyes and Ears

9 Bach Flower Remedies   **87**

10 Homeopathy   **97**

Nosodes • Schüssler Biochemic Salts

11 Aromatherapy   **103**

12 Chiropractic, Physical Therapy and Massage   **106**

Chiropractic • Subluxation • Physical Therapy and Massage • Heat as a therapy • Cold as a therapy • Stretching • Massage

13 Tellington Touch and Hands-on Healing   **110**

Tellington Touch • The Ear Ttouch • The Tail Ttouch • The Mouth Ttouch • The Belly Lift • Hands-on Healing

PART 2
RECOMMENDATIONS FOR SPECIFIC HEALTH CONDITIONS AFFECTING YOUR DOG   116

14 Chronic Disease   **119**

Toxins • Diet • Leaky Gut Syndrome • Dysbiosis • Vaccination • A Naturopathic Approach to Chronic Disease • Detoxification • Basic Detoxification Program

15 Skin and Coat   **127**

Chronic Skin Problems • Allergic Skin Disease • Atopy • Chronic or Recurrent Skin Infections • Bacterial Skin Disease and Hotspots • Yeast or Malassezia Dermatitis • Dry Skin and Dandruff • Hair Loss and Shedding • Anal Glands • Lick Granulomas • Doggy Odour • Demodectic Mange

16 Digestive System   **142**

Gum Disease and Periodontal Disease • Bad Breath • Acute Diarrhoea • Chronic Diarrhoea • Food Allergies • Coprophagy • Constipation • Flatulence • Chronic Vomiting • Liver Disease • Pancreatic Problems • Exocrine Pancreatic Insufficiency • Pancreatitis • Diabetes

17 Ears and Eyes   **157**

Ear Infections • Middle and Inner Ear Problems • Deafness • Aural Haematoma • Eyes • Cataracts • Eye Irritation • Conjunctivitis • Dry Eye • Glaucoma

18 The Immune System   **164**

Stress • Immune Support • Allergies • Elimination Diet/Low Allergy Diets • Autoimmune Disease • Cancer • Lymphatic System and Spleen Health • Infections and Antibiotic Use

19 Glandular Health 179

Adrenal Gland Health and Stress • Addison's Disease • Cushing's Syndrome • Corticosteroid Use • Thyroid Health and Disease

20 Pain and Inflammation 184

Wounds, Stings and Trauma • Snake Bite • Recovery from Surgery or Hospitalisation

21 Muscles, Bones and Joints 190

Arthritis, Osteoarthritis, Degenerative Joint Disease and Osteochondrosis • Hip Dysplasia • Lyme Disease • Trigger Points • Leg Injuries • Spinal Problems • Disc Disease, Protrusion; Prolapsed, Slipped Disc • Cervical Disc Disease • Thoracolumbar Disc Disease • Wobbler Syndrome, Cervical Vertebral Instability • Degenerative Myelopathy

22 The Cardiovascular System 203

Heart Disease • Heart Worm Prevention • Anaemia • Hyperlipidaemia

23 The Nervous System, Epilepsy and Strokes 207

Head Tilt and Ataxia • Vestibular Syndrome in Old Dogs • Nerve Paralysis • Facial Paralysis • Epilepsy and Seizures • Head Injuries and Brain Problems

24 The Respiratory System 211

Nasal Discharges and Sinusitis • Bronchitis • Pneumonia

25 Behavioural Problems 216

Nervousness and Anxiety • Barking • Separation Anxiety • Fear • Thunder and Loud Noises • Aggression • Obsessive–Compulsive Disorders • Urinating Inappropriately

26 Urinary Tract 224

Bladder Infection—Cystitis • Bladder Stones—Urolithiasis • Incontinence (Bladder) • Kidney Disease

27 Reproductive System 231

Female Reproduction • Maintaining a Healthy Pregnancy, Whelping and Lactation • Female Infertility • False Pregnancy • Mastitis • Pyometra or Infection • Male Infertility • Prostate Disorders

28 Health Maintenance 237

Guidelines for Vaccination • Alternatives to Conventional Vaccination • Worming Your Dog • Flea and Tick Control • Ageing • Weight Control

Further Information
Useful Contacts 249
Further Reading 250

References 252

Index 261

Preface

I graduated in 1986 and was introduced to complementary therapies in my final year of veterinary school. My first few years as a graduate were very much about putting into practice all the conventional medicine and surgery I had studied over the years. As time went on the limited range of options available for chronically unwell dogs frustrated me. Antibiotics, corticosteroids and non-steroidal anti-inflammatory drugs were the mainstay of therapy and generally not ideal for long-term use. I recalled my final year study of complementary medicine and decided to explore in more detail the therapies I had been introduced to. Since then I have undertaken post-graduate studies in medical herbalism, human and veterinary homeopathy, environmental and nutritional medicine, veterinary acupuncture, Reiki and other approaches to health. I have also tried to keep abreast of the plethora of advances in veterinary medicine and have spent several years working in the veterinary pharmaceutical and pet food industry.

I wrote this book with the intention of sharing my experience and information, hoping that you too will explore the options available to you in helping the dog or dogs you are caring for, when conventional approaches are frustrating you. You may be a veterinarian interested in other health approaches to offer your clients, a naturopath working with dogs, a veterinary nurse, a dog breeder or a concerned dog owner. The aim of the book is to provide some guidelines and directions for complementary medicines and alternative approaches for particular problems. The argument that complementary and alternative veterinary medicine is largely not substantiated by the 'scientific method' is acknowledged. Nonetheless, my observations over countless cases leads me to conclude that as long as we do no harm, natural therapies can and indeed do, help many dogs to lead healthier lives with greater well-being.

If your dog is unwell or you are interested in maintaining your dog's good health, this book also suggests natural therapies that you might not have considered for your pet. It is intended to complement but not replace the advice of your veterinarian. Your veterinarian cares about your dog's well-being and can assess how serious a problem is and detect subtle changes and symptoms that may not be obvious to you. While your vet may not be trained in the use of complementary therapies, he may be willing to try some of these suggestions. Because complementary medicine is mainly 'unproven' in the eyes of conventional medicine, your veterinarian may, however, feel ethically bound not to recommend or try these other approaches. They may in this case assist you by supporting your desire to explore other options by locating a holistic veterinarian whom you can both work with.

While this book doesn't cover the very vast spectrum of all alternative medicines and therapies, it is intended to bridge the gap between conventional veterinary medicine and some of the more widely available natural therapies for dogs. Conventional medicine has valuable strengths and helps many animals but it also has some limitations, especially with long-standing (chronic) disease. It is my wish that this book helps you to work with your veterinarian towards the very best health for your dog.

Acknowledgments

This book is dedicated to Diana and Peter Fougère for your love and support.

I would like to acknowledge my colleagues and teachers in the evolving science and art of complementary veterinary medicine. They include Drs Clare Middle, Vivien Harris, Chris Piper, Susan Wynn, Pam Short, Lyndy Scott, Steve Marsden, Doug Wilson and members of the Australian Association of Holistic Veterinarians. It takes courage to move beyond convention.

Thanks to Balmain Veterinary Hospital and Dr Andrew Dargan in particular for facilitating my work within your exceptional practice. Dr Sue Hunter, Danielle Parkinson and Melanie Scalone – thank you for reading and rereading this manuscript and for all your enthusiasm in everything we do; it is a pleasure working with you.

Thanks also to Rosalind Donald and Anne Raymond for your photography and assistance; to Christine Fougère, Terri Grow, Peter and Cathy Lawson for your friendship and encouragement; and, finally, to the wonderful dogs (and their people) who have had to put up with acupuncture needles, yucky herbs, pills and strict diets but who never complain. They have shown me the power of healing. I love my work.

P A R T **1**

DIET AND NATURAL THERAPIES
—AN OVERVIEW

A Tale of
Three Dogs

Max

Max is an eight-year-old English Sheep-dog with horrible, smelly, bad skin. And for as long as Lisa, his owner, can remember he had always had rashes. The rashes start quite small then Max literally tears himself apart trying to relieve the itch. For over five years now he has been regularly treated with antibiotics, prednisone and antihistamines and a series of immunotherapy injections that did help the itch but didn't stop it coming back.

Rosie

Rosie, a little cross-breed is just four years old and has literally been given a death sentence. Her blood tests and biopsy show severe liver disease. Understandably Rosie's owner Jenny is devastated. The specialist has told her that there is nothing more that they can do in hospital and the medication and fluid therapy may or may not help. For now Jenny can only wait, and hope.

King

And then there is King, once an active German Shepherd, who is now resigned to a retirement of chronic pain in his hips due to arthritis. He has trouble getting up, but more distressing for Mark, his owner, is that he simply doesn't appear to be enjoying life. Mark has tried the latest anti-inflammatory medications and they help a little but King is still very debilitated.

Michael the Veterinarian

Michael has cared for these dogs for several years and is just as frustrated and concerned as the owners of Rosie, Max and King. He is frustrated because no matter how hard he has tried, and despite referrals to specialists there appears to be nothing more that can be done for these three dogs. A chance meeting at a veterinary conference opened Michael's eyes to other options. He met Anne, a veterinarian who practises acupuncture, herbalism and other natural therapies. It seemed there was something else that could be tried.

Modern medicine meets complementary medicine

Michael didn't need to persuade his clients about trying something new. So they made appointments to see Anne. Anne examined each dog and questioned their owners in depth about their pet's personality and habits, their diet, other pets in the house, environment, and general history. This process helped Anne to detect patterns to each dog's health problems that were not considered vital to conventional medicine. She searched for underlying causes and factors that contributed to the poor health of each of these dogs.

What happened?

So King with severe arthritis was treated with a series of acupuncture sessions, and herbs. His diet was adjusted, supplements were added and exercise was gradually built up over about six weeks. Over that time, his regular medication was also reduced. The acupuncture relieved the pain, but both Mark and Michael observed other changes. King's coat improved, his breath was much better and his stools improved too. The most important thing was that King was enjoying life again, which was an excellent outcome.

Now poor Rosie with severe liver disease would be lucky to make it through the next few days. Anne and Michael discussed Rosie's problems, and then with Jenny and the specialist, they decided that Rosie should stay at home in her own environment rather than in hospital. Rosie was started on a herbal tonic, nutritional supplements and broths. Much to Anne and Michael's surprise (given the usual course of liver failure), and to Jenny's absolute relief, little Rosie made a slow but steady recovery. Three months later Rosie still has a way to go, but blood tests show that her liver is recovering and she is getting better every day.

And what about Max? Michael had referred him to a veterinary dermatologist where he was diagnosed and treated for atopy (allergies) a couple of years ago. And yes, Max was allergic to just about anything you could care to imagine, grasses, fleas, dust mite and pollens amongst others. He did respond to the series of injections at first but then they were back to the corticosteroids to manage the persistent scratching. So Anne devised a plan with Lisa to start Max on a detoxification program, altering the diet, adding vitamins, oils and herbs and increasing fluids. Three weeks later the corticosteroids were gradually reduced. He came off them six weeks later, still a little itchy, but not bad. Then Lisa selected a homeopathic remedy for Max. Soon after his scratching had stopped. Max is almost symptom free twelve months later.

Your Dog

So what about you and your dog? Maybe you recognised similar problems in your dog. Maybe you are frustrated because your dog is never really healthy. And maybe you are wondering if there is more you can do. Perhaps you are concerned about the side-effects of some of the drugs your dog is taking. And perhaps like many others you are open to natural remedies to complement the care your veterinarian provides. If you are a veterinarian you are probably thinking that these dogs might have got better anyway, perhaps with different medications and that may be true. What is also true is that a different approach in each of these cases was able to support the animal in getting better in a relatively short space of time with an absence of side-effects.

Your dog may be perfectly healthy and you just want to keep him that way. You may be interested in diet and nutrition and natural health care to help him live a long, active life.

Well, there are many alternative and complementary therapies that can contribute to the care and well-being of animals. Your dog is special and his health is important. So too are your choices. I want to encourage you to work with your veterinarian to go beyond conventional medicine if it isn't providing the outcome you want. The key to the success with natural therapies is to understand when and how they should be used and to know that they do not act to cure your dog, but can activate and support your dog's own healing ability. More importantly we need to understand the continuum of health and disease, and how we can optimise the chances for a long, healthy life for our dogs. So let's start here first.

Health and Disease

Bob

The first time I met Joanne and her Blue Heeler Bob, it was clear that both were in bad shape. Joanne appeared to be very anxious and restless and Bob was just the same. Joanne had brought Bob to me because of a long-standing skin problem that she hoped could be helped because the prednisolone medication Bob was taking was no longer controlling his symptoms and he was considerably overweight. I called Bob's usual vet and we went through his medical history in some detail. Poor Bob had suffered fits several years ago, an allergic reaction to an injection, occasional neck pain, chronic skin problems, a huge blood blister in his ear (called an aural haematoma), and several bouts of diarrhoea—all in the past six years.

With such a complicated background, Joanne and I sat down and tried to unravel what had been going on. Why was Bob always unwell? He had been a healthy pup right up until he was two when Joanne was forced to move from a small country town into a tiny two-bedroom, third floor apartment in the city. That's when all Bob's problems had seemingly started.

When I examined Bob he was quite overweight. He had a red itchy rash all over his back and underbelly; he had cataracts in his eyes and a wagless tail. His diet was home-made, with plenty of fresh vegetables, grains and legumes, as well as fresh meat and bones. His heartworm prevention medication and worming were up to date, and he had always had his yearly booster vaccination. Joanne tried to take Bob for a twenty-minute walk each evening after work.

What could we do to improve Bob's skin condition, his general health and well-being and hopefully prevent further problems? Firstly we needed to uncover the underlying factors that were contributing to his problems and possibly acting as obstacles to his own self-healing mechanisms.

The Energy View of Health and Disease

In several systems of medicine besides conventional Western medicine, such as Traditional Chinese Medicine, disease is said to occur where there is stagnation or blockage of energy in the body. The body is regarded as more than simply physical. It is also a body of energy (at an atomic level all our cells are comprised of atoms and even the cells manufacture energy in their mitochondria). We can observe that anything that affects our energy is reflected in our physical body, and visa versa. Health and vitality are always mirrored by our energy levels. You know intuitively when you are not well or stressed, or when your dog isn't well, because the first thing you are aware of is a drop in energy.

It takes energy to keep the body in peak health. If that energy becomes depleted, stagnant or reduced for some reason, the body becomes vulnerable. Energy is needed by all living cells to bring in nourishment and get rid of wastes. If your dog's energy is just a little low, he may be simply tired or a little stressed and he might be a little more susceptible to minor infections. If his level of energy is low over a period of time, any minor problem can become more entrenched in the form of chronic disease. When energy is low, the cells of the organs or tissues simply are unable to function properly and disease is possible.

This is one simplified view. If your dog has a long-standing problem, think back to when it first began. What happened? Was there anything going on that might have upset your dog's balance in life, his energy? Were there a number of minor problems such as an ear infection, or perhaps a small rash, a stomach upset perhaps, which over time have been replaced with something more chronic? Bob had had a long history of problems, which all seemed unrelated, but in fact they were all signs of a body out of balance. Bob the dog was definitely low in energy. And his excess weight and sedentary life-style weren't helping him to get better.

Domestication Has Come at a Price

Wild dogs roam in packs. However, our pet dogs often spend all day by themselves. Wild dogs are free to mate and the strongest survive, but domestication and selective breeding of dogs has brought with it genetic conditions and inherent weaknesses. Where wild dogs hunt or scavenge and are occupied with survival, the indoor pooch is provided for, and fed anything but the carcasses of prey or scavenged food. Our dogs have come in from the wild, to be loved and adored.

As dogs have become domesticated, they have been subjected to an unnatural state of being. And while our domesticated dogs certainly live longer lives[1] (compared to 70 per cent of wolves that die each generation), they are now prone to the scourges of modern living and degenerative diseases like arthritis, heart disease, cancer, allergies and chronic skin disease. Dogs can no longer be compared to their wild counterparts. They have been changed radically. They no longer have the same color, markings, shape, body size, anatomy, physiology and behaviour[2] as their wild cousins do.

The Modern Dog and Free Radicals

In our own modern lives there are many life-style factors that affect our health. We constantly hear of the dangers of a poor diet, not enough exercise, too much alcohol, smoking, drugs and stress. It may not surprise you to know that your dog is very much like you. She is affected by many of the same things you encounter in your daily life. These are life 'forces' that can deplete her energy, and another viewpoint of disease in our modern lives is the idea of 'free radical' exposure.

So one of the simplest reasons dogs get sick is because they are domesticated and live in urban (and often stressful) environments. In today's urban environment our dogs are exposed to free radical attack from many sources (including naturally occurring sources of free radicals during normal metabolism in the body). Free radicals cause damage to cells and lead to disease in a very insidious way. UV radiation from the thinning of the ozone layer, radiation, microwaves, x-rays and magnetic fields build up over time. Furniture and coverings on the walls and floors of homes are constantly emitting free radicals due to the degradation of residues of the chemicals used in their manufacture. (Chemical sensitivity can occur after renovation.) Cigarette smoke contains a multitude of chemical compounds, some of the densest free radical sources. And like us, our dogs breathe in traffic fumes and industrial pollution, which are also rich sources of free radicals. And even a long hard run or a general anaesthetic can boost naturally produced free radicals in the body.

The accumulation of free radical exposure (also called oxidative stress) has been implicated as an underlying and important contributor to many diseases, especially degenerative diseases such as arthritis and heart disease as well as disorders of the skin, eyes, digestive tract and the immune system.[3]

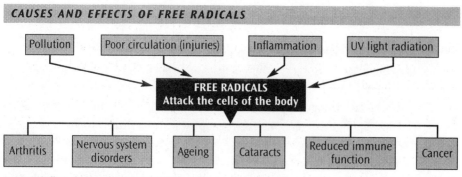

Causes and Effects of Free Radicals (Machlin 1993)[4]

While our dogs are young, their natural antioxidant enzymes and molecules are high enough to absorb and counteract most free radicals in the body. However, with ageing, the effectiveness of these protective systems slowly wears down. More and more free radicals survive and cause damage to tissues and over time they wear out the body. It is the life long exposure to free radicals that causes the degenerative or 'wear and tear' changes associated with ageing.

All this is compounded by the fact that our dogs, like many people, usually eat too much, have little stimulation, too little exercise and many eat poor quality diets.

Stress

Probably the most overwhelming influence on dogs' health is stress. Stress is a normal response to extra demands, be they physical or emotional. Like people, a dog's body will adapt to stress via the nervous and hormonal systems. Stress causes release of hormones from the brain, adrenal glands and pancreas to enable the body to respond appropriately.

Good stress such as exercise and play can enliven and enhance life energy. However, chronic stress or distress can build up over time,[5] leading to depletion of hormones and life energy that eventually debilitates the body. On the other hand repeated good stress (like play and exercise) can help a dog to adapt to prevent distress and disease.

Emotional Stress

Do dogs think and have emotions? There is solid evidence that animals experience fear, depression, anxiety, frustration, boredom, isolation, loneliness, separation, con-flict and helplessness, and its logical that they experience positive emotions such as pleasure, joy, love and happiness.[6] For anyone who understands his or her dog, the answer is obvious. In my experience dogs experience a wide range of emotions and feelings. From grief at the loss of an animal friend or their owner, to jealousy of another pet or person, as well as anger, fear and terror, loneliness and depression and many others. Today, many dogs suffer separation anxiety when their owners leave them alone for the day while they go to work. Many dogs are very fearful or timid. If any of these emotions is extreme, or persists, and the dog cannot adapt, their health can be compromised.

When I asked Bob's owner Joanne what happened when she moved to the city, she told me that Bob had spent most of his puppyhood on a farm with her partner John. Bob was very attached to John. And when they left, Joanne recalled that Bob had been very upset and had pined for several months afterwards.

If your dog has a chronic problem, think back to when it started. Was there anything significant happening in your life, your family, your home or the life of your dog which may have been particularly stressful? A word of advice though. It is really important not to attribute any blame or cause to yourself or anyone else if your dog is unwell. The reaction your dog has to emotional stress is his own, and varies considerably from dog to dog just as it does with people. In some ways our dogs actually mirror what is going on for us in our lives too. If you are particularly stressed then there is a reason-able chance your dog will be too.

Nutrition

Nutrition has such an impact on the health and well-being of your dog, that the next few chapters are devoted to the subject. Needless to say, that the ability of a dog to cope with stress, and function optimally is going to be influenced by the quality of his food and the availability of nutrients and energy. Good nutrition (correctly balanced home-made diets, the best quality premium foods and combinations) contributes greatly to the vital energy of the body, helping it to keep in balance.

When I asked Joanne about Bob's diet, it sounded great. It was natural and fresh. But on closer analysis the diet was low in some key nutrients including vitamin A, fatty acids and zinc. These deficiencies were not only affecting Bob's ability to cope with his life-style but were also affecting his immune system and the health of his skin.

Parasites

Fleas and internal parasites are a natural part of most dogs' lives. Generally a healthy dog will be able to cope with a small natural burden of parasites. But a dog that is already depleted in energy will be less able to cope. A constant burden of fleas or worms will add to his woes. So parasite control is very important. We'll talk about it some more later.

We took a sample of Bob's stool to check for parasites, which was negative. However, we could see flea dirt in his coat, so we knew that this was definitely a contributing factor to his itchy skin.

Life-style

Poor Bob. He had once enjoyed the life of a farm dog. There were so many interesting things to chase, things to smell and space to run. Now his life revolved around the inside of a third floor apartment and a twenty-minute walk once a day. His life-style was not suited to his needs.

More so, it didn't suit Joanne either. And one of the first things we discussed was making more time for outdoor activities. Now, not all dogs need a lot of exercise. Perhaps if Bob were a Chihuahua or a Maltese Terrier, he wouldn't have minded his life-style at all. But Bob being a Blue Heeler was bred for high levels of work and mental challenge.

Life-style plays a significant role in the health of your dog. A dog like Bob, who is sedentary all day, is more prone to obesity, to lethargy, to boredom and behavioural problems. Dogs need physical and mental stimulation if they are to achieve optimal health.

Breeding

Most breeders and breed societies take great pains to selectively breed for healthy dogs. But unfortunately some breeds of dogs are more prone to health problems. Most of these are well known, and it is not my intention to go into details here. Suffice it to say that you should always select a breed of dog that suits your life-style first and foremost, even if you have your heart set on a particular breed. You can talk with your veterinarian and breed clubs before deciding, so that any potential breed problems are pointed out to you. Sometimes these health problems can be reduced if you put preventive measures in place. The Internet is another good place to find out more about dog breeds.

Likewise you should make yourself familiar with your puppy's parents, their lifestyle, nutrition and health because these can have a large influence on your dog's health too. It's also important to ensure that your dog becomes a well socialised, well adjusted dog. So make sure you speak to your vet about this and attend puppy preschool or puppy parties to learn more about puppy health and behaviour in order to prevent problems later on.

A Dog's Home Is His Castle

Dogs in the wild live in dens that provide protection from the cold, heat and predators, and provide a sense of security and well-being. Our dogs also have a strong tendency to seek out their own 'den'. This could be under the table, or sofa or a small place to get their backs against so that they can feel safe and secure. In many households it can be difficult for a dog to retreat from the hustle and bustle of family activity and feet, or the introduction of a new puppy that likes nothing more than to dangle off his ear! Providing a kennel or crate or basket of his own, his 'den', will help reduce stress and keep him well adjusted.

Exercise

But dogs also love the outdoors. There are a multitude of fascinating smells and messages from other dogs, think of it like doggy 'email'. There are things to investigate, chase and sniff. Walking your dog provides a mentally stimulating activity that also gets her blood and energy moving. Regular exercise is one of the most important things you can do for your dog's health and vitality (and of course it won't hurt you either!). Just a small word of warning though; don't overdo exercise with young and growing pups, especially if they are large. Normal puppy-play and short walks are all that is needed. Any stressful jumping or exhausting walks can play havoc on growing joints. Take care with old and overweight dogs too, and build up exercise gradually.

Environment

Be conscious of your dog's environment. Carbon monoxide from car exhaust fumes, invisible pollution in the air, ultraviolet light from the sun, low grade radiation which you can't avoid, and toxic chemicals from weedicides, floor cleaners, insecticides and fumes from paint abound. Pollutants that build up in the food chain and when eaten become stored in the body fat. A healthy dog can usually cope well with such insults. The body adapts and works to detoxify foreign substances on a continual basis. However, when your dog is unwell, pollution and free radical damage can further contribute to poor health. There is not a great deal you can do to avoid these in the urban environment. However, it is important to consider the unseen pollutants, because dogs don't wear shoes, have their noses and mouths into everything and they are low to the ground. In some ways they are far more likely to be exposed to these things than we are. Open parks and clean air are great revitalisers for dogs. So take the short cut, and get to an open space with lots of trees.

Joanne and Bob, as part of a holistic approach to restoring Bob's health, spent one hour each day, walking to the beach, resting under a tree, playing ball for 20 minutes and returning. The great benefit was that not only did Bob's weight go down quickly, but Joanne found her own weight and stress level dropping too. She looked forward to the morning walks as much as Bob!

Veterinary Care

Your vet cares very much about you and your dog. That's why they want to see you at least once a year for routine check-ups and health maintenance. They want to prevent disease and detect disease early and will help keep you informed about important health issues. It is essential for your dog's health that he is checked regularly.

Most dogs benefit greatly from conventional veterinary care. Their problems are prevented or fixed, and managed. But there are dogs who simply do not get better or who cannot cope with normal care. They may be dogs that will need a lifetime of treatments to suppress or manage the symptoms of chronic disease. Their bodies are already so overwhelmed and stressed, that additional drugs, or treatments may overload the body, making them sicker, and unable to return to a normal state of health.

Vaccination is a routine procedure that protects dogs from several diseases. Unfortunately there are some circumstances where vaccination may contribute directly to illness. Particularly so, if your dog is already stressed, or has a chronic disease or low vitality. This is discussed in more detail later.

Another area for concern is the use of corticosteroids such as prednisolone. These can be life-saving drugs in veterinary practice, and are certainly used frequently for skin disease and other diseases. However, you need to be aware that they do not remove the cause of the disease, they simply suppress the symptoms, which can be a great relief for you and your dog, short term. On the other hand they may actually contribute to long-term disease if used for an extended period of time. They contribute to obesity, skin weakness and a compromised immune system. So anything that can be done to decrease the dose or remove the cause of the problem is certainly worth doing.

Bob's Restoration

In Bob's case, he had been on corticosteroids for over five years. He had gradually put on weight, and the medication along with his sedentary life-style was a major contributing factor to his poor health. We modified Bob's diet slightly to better balance it, while at the same time reducing the calories so that he could lose some weight. Joanne committed herself to increasing Bob's walks and time in the park. She also changed his collar to a harness as I suspected his neck problems could be due to his constant straining on the lead—he liked to drag Joanne on his walks.

We also treated Bob, with a conventional flea product (which is not absorbed systemically) and decided to keep him on his corticosteroid tablets for three to six more weeks while setting the foundation to improve Bob's health. Unless directed, never stop or reduce medications without talking with your vet first. It is often better to initially continue medication and monitor closely so that medications can be reduced safely as your dog's health improves. We started Bob on some supplements along with his modified diet, and a Bach Flower remedy to assist his level of stress.

Three weeks later we introduced a herbal tonic to support his liver and adrenal glands while he was gradually weaned off his corticosteroid tablets. Six weeks after we had first met, Bob had lost 1.5 kilograms in weight. His eyes were clearer, his skin much better. We still had some work to do, but the results of all Joanne's efforts were showing. Six months later Bob is a different dog; he is calmer, happier and well. Health restoration does take time, and in all but the worst cases, great improvements are nearly always possible.

How Healthy Is Your Dog?

Answer the following questions to your best ability to assess what areas of health you need to investigate further with your vet:

GOOD HEALTH	YES	NO	UNSURE
Does your dog have more than 30 minutes of exercise like walking or running daily?			
Does your dog have abundant energy when exercising or playing?			
Is your dog relaxed with other dogs, strangers, friends and family?			
Does your dog have the company of another dog or family member for at least 6 hours during the day?			
Is your household harmonious amongst its humans?			
Is your household harmonious between its animals and between family members and your dog?			
Is your dog well behaved most of the time?			
Does your dog have a 'den', somewhere inside or outside where he is safe and secure and can retreat to in privacy?			
Does your dog have clean, white teeth without yellow or brown staining or build-up of calculus?			
Is your dog a normal weight for his breed? (Can you see a waistline just behind his last rib and just feel his ribs through his coat?)			
Does your dog visit the vet at least once yearly?			
Is your dog always healthy?			
Does your dog get vaccinated annually?*			
Are your dog's parents and/or siblings free of disease?			
Does your dog's breath smell nice?			
Does your dog have a shiny full coat with minimal shedding except at moult?			
Is your dog itch free and does he have healthy skin all the time?			

Does your dog pass firm consistent bowel movements daily?

Does your dog easily pass urine?

Does your dog move freely without any stiffness or soreness?

Are your dog's eyes bright and clear all of the time?

Are your dog's ears clean and odour free?

Does your dog have a strong healthy appetite?

* Vaccination may not be necessary on annual basis (*see* Vaccination later in this book).

HEALTH ISSUES	YES	NO	UNSURE
Is your dog exposed to cigarette smoke frequently?			
Has your dog been exposed to home renovations such as new carpet and fresh paint in last 6 months?			
Has your dog ever had more than two courses of antibiotics in a 6-month period?			
Has your dog ever had diarrhoea or severe illness as a puppy?			
Has your dog been treated with anti-inflammatory medications for any period more than 3 months?			
Has you dog been vaccinated when not 100 per cent healthy? (e.g. he has arthritis or skin allergies and is also vaccinated)			
Does your dog live in an urban environment with exposure to car exhaust or smog on a regular basis?			
Does your dog suffer anxiety when you leave him?			
Does your dog have chronic arthritis or joint problems?			
Does your dog have chronic skin or flea problems?			
Does your dog have regular wind, or irregular or loose bowel movements?			
Does your dog have eye or ear problems on a regular basis?			
Does your dog require regular medication or veterinary visits for any condition?			
Has your dog ever been diagnosed with cancer?			
Has your dog ever been diagnosed with autoimmune disease?			
Has your dog ever been diagnosed with heart problems?			
Has your dog ever been diagnosed with kidney problems?			
Has your dog ever been diagnosed with liver problems?			
Has your dog ever been diagnosed with gastrointestinal disease?			
Has your dog ever been diagnosed with diabetes, pancreatitis, hypothyroidism or other hormonal problems?			

If your dog has health problems it is important to identify all possible influences that can lead to disease. Only then can you do something about them to remove or reduce the obstacles to your dog getting better.

Once we have recognised the obstacles to good health, we need to address the building blocks of health. The most important foundation is good nutrition. When we supply important nutrients to the body, the body has a better chance of harnessing the immune system and natural healing mechanisms. There is a lot we can do for good health just by paying attention to diet. So let's explore your dog's diet in more detail.

CHAPTER 3

What Do Dogs Eat?

Feeding Your Dog

It's true to say that the way to any dog's heart as well as his health is through his stomach. But it requires care to ensure that what you feed him also prevents disease and promotes health and vitality that lasts a lifetime.

A Natural Diet

If we look at the diet of the wolf, considered a close cousin of dogs, their food is incredibly diverse. Their diet includes deer, goats, pigs, rabbits, mice, squirrels, birds, eggs, reptiles, frogs, beetles, earthworms, fish, and in times of need carcasses and sick members of their own kind, berries, fruit, fungi and melons, all depending on geography and season. When wolves make a kill they eat muscle meat first, followed by fatty tissue, the heart, lungs, liver, stomach and contents and the remaining internal organs. Then with their powerful jaws and teeth they crush large bones. The average wolf eats 2 to 4.5 kilograms of meat each day and also drinks large quantities of water. However, they can also go without food for up to two weeks.[7]

Max and Sherpa

How does this translate to feeding Max, a Chihuahua who has difficulty enough tackling his dry biscuits, let alone a huge beastie, and Sherpa, a Pekingese who would not be caught dead eating anything so vulgar as stomach contents?

While a wolf's diet consists largely of whole animals, the reality is that in our home environment, goats and squirrels are off the menu for most dogs. So if a natural diet is not available what is the next best thing? Some people recommend home-made diets, raw or cooked, diets based around raw meaty bones, diets based on organic meats and vegetables, diets without grains, others suggest 'natural' prepared pet foods, or commercial dog foods and others recommend 'premium' pet foods. The choices can be overwhelming and confusing.

The Correct Way to Feed

What is the right way to feed your dog? The answer is simple: there is more than one right way to feed a dog! The bottom line is that there is no one type of diet that suits all dogs. Each dog is unique. There are biochemical differences, differences in genetic make-up, life stages, environmental factors, levels of activity, exposures to pollutants, toxins, emotional stresses and so on. All these factors can impact upon your dog's health and nutritional requirements. As well, you will have your own feeding preferences and so will your dog.

However, it is important to be aware that the foods you are feeding your dog might actually be contributing to poor health too. This can be quite insidious. Many people buy their dog foods or prepare the foods at home believing they are doing the best they can for their dogs. Poor quality dog foods or home-made diets will not promote good health. If important components in the diet are missing, or are in excess, or the foods include potential toxins, these can contribute poor health.

So what do you feed your dog? Over the course of a week, you might like to jot down a list of the foods you feed your dog, brands and the quantities. Then you can consider ways to improve the diet with some of the suggestions that follow. One of the easiest things you can begin to do immediately, if you don't already, is to incorporate some fresh foods daily into your dog's diet, and fresh, raw, meaty bones once or twice weekly. Even the quantity of food needs evaluating—one of the commonest health and nutrition problems in dogs is obesity, affecting one out of every four dogs.[8]

MY DOG'S DIET

AM

_____

_____

_____

_____

PM

_____

_____

_____

_____

SNACKS

_____

_____

_____

_____

OTHER

_____

_____

_____

_____

Commercial Dog Foods

Many people would agree that the best way to feed a dog is the natural way. Feeding fresh meat and bones, along with vegetables, fruit and grains is often suggested to be a substitute for wild prey. In today's society providing this kind of diet is sometimes difficult. Many people don't have the time to prepare food for themselves, let alone their dogs!

While some commercial pet foods are simply awful (and bad for your dog's health), there are many others that provide excellent nutrition in a safe and convenient form, especially when they are fed along with some fresh foods and raw meaty bones. For many dogs, dry foods provide an excellent form of nutrition, especially when they have extra needs, such as growing puppies, pregnant bitches and performance dogs, where more concentrated foods provide extra benefits.

Selecting a Good Quality Dry Food

Dry foods can be very economical and are more energy-dense than fresh or canned foods so that your dog needs to eat less to get the nutrition he requires. Many people complain that they only feed their little-but-plump dog a small amount of dry food. But for the same calories you can feed three to four times the same volume with fresh or canned foods.

Preservatives and additives are usually necessary and effective in preserving dry foods, but there are some that may contribute to ill health,[9] especially if a dog is already overwhelmed with other insults. However, most preservative and antioxidant systems in dog foods are used in safe concentrations, required to keep the food nutritious and to delay spoilage and there are many very healthy dogs fed entirely upon dry dog foods.

Dogs with chronic or serious disease will, however, benefit from a complete nutritional overhaul. This is best done under the supervision of a veterinarian where the ideal is a veterinary prescribed therapeutic diet (usually dried or canned) specifically indicated for your dog's condition or alternatively a completely 'natural', veterinary prescribed organic diet either alone or in combination with the commercial diet. This will depend upon your preferences in terms of time, cost and your veterinarian's advice.

Key Features to Look for in Dry Foods

One of the most common nutritional disorders seen in dogs besides obesity is dry, itchy skin and coat. Many times these dogs are being fed poor quality dry dog food with borderline fatty acid content. While the food provides energy and basic nutrition and may even be complete and balanced, a change to a higher quality, higher protein and fat product will provide amazing differences in the skin and coat condition in just a couple of weeks.

The bottom line is to look for the best quality you can afford. Generally better quality ingredients cost more, but the results are worth it. Low cost foods often reflect lower cost ingredients and lack of feed trial testing. Also be aware that some 'natural dog foods' are marketed that way but may be no more beneficial than other commercial dog foods.

Your veterinarian can recommend a premium diet or a veterinary clinical diet for a particular condition. Most premium quality products have superior ingredients, consistent formulations, higher energy density and better digestibility than regular products. If you wish to make any changes to the diet you should check with your vet first. Ideally choose premium meat-based dry food, which is complete and balanced, tested through feeding trials with a statement to that effect on the packaging and preferably colour free. If you decide to feed a dry food diet for convenience and economy, consider giving your dog an appropriate raw bone or alternative two to three time weekly for dental hygiene. Also feed 20 per cent of the diet (20 per cent of your dog's energy requirements which are discussed in the next chapter), as fresh meat, some fruits and vegetables for variety. These fresh foods can provide extra antioxidants, variety and health giving properties and will also 'dilute' the calorie content of dry foods, which can help keep your dog slim.

DRY FOOD CHECKLIST

1. Check that there is a statement on the package that the food is complete and balanced according to 'animal feeding tests', there should be reference to AAFCO (American Association of Food Control Officials). If the label says 'formulated to meet AAFCO requirements', the food may not have been tested in feeding trials.
2. Check that the food is appropriate for your dog's life stage.
3. Identify the animal protein source (e.g. chicken).
4. Look for rice or maize as the cereal component.
5. Is the food free of artificial colours and preferably with natural antioxidant preservative systems (such as vitamin C or vitamin E (mixed tocopherols) and rosemary). Note that synthetic preservatives are actually better at preserving the safety and nutritional quality and are usually used in very small, safe concentrations.
6. Check the manufacture date or the expiry date on the packaging. The product should be fresh and no older than 1 month.
7. Check that there is a contact number should you wish to contact the manufacturer for further information.

The real test for your dog will be the product's performance and your dog's health. Is the food suitable for your dog? Is he fit and healthy? Is his coat healthy and shiny? Are his stools regular and firm?

Selecting Canned Foods

Canned foods offer variety and palatability for many dogs. Some dogs won't eat anything else. And while many canned foods offer complete and balanced nutrition in every can, or tray, it is important to balance the convenience with textural variety. Soft foods, whether fresh minced meat, cooked vegetables or canned food, can lead to dental problems. Canned foods can be fed daily, but I recommend including balanced fresh food recipes, bones and good quality dry foods to improve the health of your dog.

As for all things, you get what you pay for. A cheap product will have cheap ingredients, probably be poorly digested and your dog will suffer flatulence and soft voluminous stools. Your dog's stools should be firm and easy to dispose of. If they are not, consider changing the food you are feeding. Good quality products will have better ingredients and will have undergone feeding trials. This ensures that the products are digested and utilised by the dog and that the nutrition is actually available.

If you are feeding canned foods solely, or as a major part of the diet I recommend that you consider a change, firstly by adding some raw, meaty bones for starters (to help keep teeth clean) and some fresh foods. Have a look at the product you are feeding now.

CANNED FOOD CHECKLIST

1. Check that there is a statement on the can that the food is complete and balanced according to 'animal feeding tests' with a reference to AAFCO.
2. What are the ingredients?
3. Check that it is free of artificial colourings. Most canned foods do not contain preservatives.
4. Check that there is a number to contact the manufacturer if you need more information.

Bones

Veterinarians have different views on whether to recommend bones or not. Bones can cause bowel obstructions, constipation and perforated bowel linings as well as fractured and worn teeth. However, gnawing on raw bones provides two main benefits: First, they keep your dog occupied as he gnaws the meat off. An occupation that dogs seem to love. Second, the bones help to keep his jaw exercised (and other muscles too) and his back teeth and gums clean. Ox tail bones have been proven to be beneficial for dental hygiene in dogs.[10] Dental hygiene is really important because low-grade gum disease or gingivitis can undermine your dog's health as his immune system is constantly keeping the infection under control.

However, some dogs cannot tolerate bones well, particularly dogs with digestive problems or constipation. You also need to be really careful with puppies, as it is quite easy for them to break their baby teeth or alter the eruption of their adult teeth. So try lamb ribs or raw chicken wings which are softer than large bones. Talk to your veterinarian about the most appropriate bones or alternatives for your dog. It is also important not to ignore the front teeth, which are not usually used in gnawing bones. These may need to be cleaned regularly with a toothbrush.

Bones from young animals (lamb, veal and chicken) are generally softer, more pliable and digestible than bones from older animals.
- *Large dogs* try large meaty bones such as brisket bones and knuckle bones
- *Medium dogs* try ox tails, lamb ribs and chicken wings
- *Small dogs* try ox tails, chicken wings and necks

A general recommendation is no more than 2 per cent of your dog's body weight in raw meaty bones three times weekly. This means a 20-kg dog would receive 400 grams of raw meaty bones three times weekly. Beware that bones contain large mounts of calcium and phosphorus, which can upset the balance in a growing puppy's diet. Check with your vet first.

If your dog has not had bones before, supervise him the first few times. There is actually an art to gnawing a bone, and by keeping a close watch you will be able to help him if he seems to be in trouble. If you teach him the 'Give' command before introducing bones and then limit his bone munching to five to ten minutes the first few times, you will be able to have more control over the bone. At the same time, be careful that children do not approach your dog while he is busy. Some dogs can be possessive about their treasure. Finally bones can be a bit messy, so consider feeding him outside. Make sure you know where the bone is, because they can cause nasty injuries if you step on them.

Home-made Diets

Home-made diets are very popular with people looking for a more natural approach to dog health. But there is a danger in believing that just because you made it, it's safe. The biggest concern I have about home-made diets is that they are very often unbalanced and incomplete. We can learn how to prevent this from all the research that is available on dog nutrition. Because meat, and vegetables and grains are not the same as whole animal carcasses, dietary supplements are nearly always essential. It is also important to realise that some of the foods that you buy fresh may not be as safe as you think. Fruit and vegetables can be contaminated with pesticides, fish with heavy metals, and grains with moulds and meats with bacteria. Fresh pet meats usually contain sulphur preservatives. However, many people observe improvements in the health of their dogs through changes in the diet, including fresh foods and using particular supplements. There is a whole chapter devoted to the making of complete and balanced homemade diets coming up.

Consider your dog's diet that you described and listed earlier in this chapter. Is there anything you need to do to improve the level of nutrition you are providing? Check the foods you are feeding now. Contact the manufacturers if necessary. Read on.

Let's take a look at what dogs actually require in their diets.

4

What Do
Dogs Need?

So what do dogs need in their diet? Well, in addition to specific nutrients like vitamins and protein, food has to supply energy. Energy, remember, is a fundamental requirement of any living creature because it provides the power for cells in the body to function. Energy from food also determines whether your dog is fat, thin or just right. Excess energy (too many calories) is stored as fat, and if a dog is not fed enough food energy, the body must use its own energy reserves and so loses weight. Energy balance occurs when the dog's energy needs are matched by the energy provided by the diet. In this way the body weight is maintained. Individual nutrients such as protein, vitamins and fats then have to be balanced in the right proportions to the energy.

You can see how much energy your dog needs each day using the following table.

First find your dog's current weight in Table 1. To the right of it, is a figure that is the energy needed each day in calories (kcal). Circle this figure. For example if my dog weighs 22 kg, she needs approximately 1120 calories each day. If you don't know the weight of your dog, most veterinary practices will be happy for you to use their scales. Alternatively you can use your bathroom scales.

Now if your dog is a normal, healthy dog then this figure is your dog's approximate daily energy or calorie requirement. However, if your dog is growing, is very active (working or performance), is pregnant or feeding puppies then you will need to multiply the above figure by one of the following factors:

For example a bitch is seven weeks into her pregnancy; her current weight is 25 kg. From Table 1 her energy need is 1230 kcal. I have to multiple this by the factor by 1.30 for pregnancy. This equates to 1600 kcal. This is her new increased energy requirement that we need to provide for her in her diet. You can make a similar calculation for a growing pup, a working dog and for a lactating bitch.

TABLE 1: ENERGY REQUIREMENT OF THE DOG[11]

Weight (lb.)	Weight (kg)	Energy Needed (kcal)	Weight (lb.)	Weight (kg)	Energy Needed (kcal)	Weight (lb.)	Weight (kg)	Energy Needed (kcal)
2.2	1	110	46.2	21	1080	114.4	52	2130
4.4	2	190	48.4	22	1120	118.8	54	2190
6.6	3	250	50.6	23	1160	123.2	56	2260
8.8	4	310	52.8	24	1190	127.6	58	2310
11.0	5	360	55.0	25	1230	132.0	60	2380
13.2	6	420	57.2	26	1270	136.4	62	2430
15.4	7	470	59.4	27	1300	140.8	64	2490
17.6	8	530	61.6	28	1340	145.2	66	2550
19.8	9	570	63.8	29	1380	149.6	68	2610
22.0	10	620	65.0	30	1410	154.0	70	2660
24.2	11	660	70.4	32	1490	158.4	72	2720
26.4	12	700	74.8	34	1550	162.8	74	2770
28.6	13	750	79.2	36	1620	167.2	76	2830
30.8	14	790	83.6	38	1680	171.6	78	2880
33.0	15	840	88.0	40	1750	176.0	80	2940
35.2	16	880	92.4	42	1820	180.4	82	2990
37.4	17	920	96.8	44	1880	184.8	84	3050
39.6	18	960	101.2	46	1950	189.2	86	3100
41.8	19	1000	105.6	48	2000	193.6	88	3160
44.0	20	1050	110.0	50	2070	198.0	90	3210

(If you need to convert kcal to kJ multiply by 4.184.)

TABLE 2: FACTORS TO ALLOW FOR DIFFERENCES IN LIFE STAGES[12]

Life stage	For:	Multiply by Factor of:
Adult maintenance		1.00
Pregnancy	First five weeks	1.00
	From six weeks	1.15
	From seven weeks	1.30
	From eight weeks	1.45
	From nine weeks	1.60
Lactation	Up to 3–4 weeks	3.00
Growth	Weaning to half grown	2.00
	50%–80% of adult weight	1.50
	80% to near adult weight	1.20
Highly active adult	Depending on how active	2.00
Working dog	Medium work	1.70
	Hard work up to	3.40

How much do you feed?

In order to know how much to feed your dog, you need to know the energy that your dog's food provides. If your dog needs 1000 kcals each day for her energy needs, and there are 350 kcal provided in every 100 grams of dry food for example, then your dog will need to eat (1000/350 x 100) =285 grams of food. 350 kcal is about the average energy supplied by 100 grams of dry dog food.

Often you can find the energy of the food on the label; it may be energy in kcal or kJ per kilogram, pound or 100 grams. If you can't find the information then contact the manufacturer for the details.

Some guidelines:

1 cup of dry dog food holds about 100 grams (3.5oz) of kibble = average 350 kcal (1470 kJ) per cup.

A 400-gram can of canned dog food contains about 330 kcal (1386 kJ)

Each of the recipes in the next chapter provides 1000 kcals.

Changing Dog Foods

If you are currently feeding one type of dog food and want to upgrade to a better product it is important not to assume that you can just feed the same amount, because the energy provided by the new food is probably going to be higher. So if you switch from a regular dog food to a premium or veterinary diet you will need to feed less.

If your dog has been on one particular food for a long time, a gradual change-over will be necessary to avoid tummy upsets. This can be done by decreasing the old food by one quarter each day, and increasing the new food by one quarter each day. Watch for changes in faeces consistency.

Now that you have upgraded your dog's usual diet, you may also wish to add some raw bones and some fresh foods (no more than 20 per cent of the calories to maintain balance). Or you might like to substitute some meals with a home-prepared meal (*see* recipes in the next chapter). If you choose to feed a fresh food diet see the next chapter.

Guidelines for Feeding Puppies:

- The young puppy needs a higher plane of nutrition than an adult dog to provide the fuel for rapid growth and activity. Suitable foods are those that are formulated for puppy growth including commercial diets and carefully balanced home-prepared diets, or combinations.
- Do not supplement a commercial puppy food with calcium or phosphorus, and limit bone feeding to two times weekly.
- Puppies have small stomachs so should be fed three to four times daily until half grown then reduce this to twice daily until fully grown. Avoid leaving food out for puppies through the day as this can lead to overeating.
- Do not overfeed puppies as this can lead to obesity in later life. Mild restriction of energy (calories) during growth may actually extend longevity.[13]
- Provide them with double their maintenance requirements in energy (from Table 1) from weaning to half grown. Decrease this to one and half times their

maintenance requirements (as their body weight changes—keep referring to Table 1) until they are 80 per cent of their expected adult weight, and from then, 1.2 times their energy requirements until fully grown. It is important to weigh your puppy every couple of weeks to monitor growth especially for large breed dogs until at least 6 months of age.

- Large breed and giant dogs are prone to growth problems because of the speed at which they grow. Correct nutrition is CRITICAL for these dogs to avoid both short-term and long-term problems with skeletal development. You can't afford to make mistakes at this vulnerable stage so discuss your puppy's diet with your vet.
- At the same time, limit exercise in growing puppies, especially large breed puppies, to simple play and very short walks of 15 to 20 minutes' duration. Too much exercise and stress from jumping and running can contribute to skeletal problems later on.

I prefer to recommend formulated diets for large breed puppies because the nutritional requirements are so critical. The diet has to provide not only the correct ratios of calcium and phosphorus but also all the essential amino acids at the appropriate levels. In addition to commercial diets for growth, these puppies can also be fed a variety of home-made recipes (approximately 20 per cent of their diet). Keep them lean, and monitor their growth.

The Pregnant Dog

- No change in the amount of food is necessary from week one to week five of pregnancy. Overfeeding early in pregnancy should be avoided since it may predispose the bitch to problems at whelping. Feed a good quality diet which is energy dense and nutrient dense.
- If feeding a commercial diet (and no more than 20 per cent other foods), supplementation of calcium and phosphorus is not recommended.
- Gradually increase the amount fed from about five or six weeks pregnant, by about 10 per cent per week, and divide the food into several smaller meals throughout the day. By the time she is due to whelp she will be having about one and a quarter to one and a half times her normal amount of food depending on size and how many puppies she is carrying.
- A couple of days before she is due to whelp she may begin producing milk. Just before she is due to give birth her appetite may disappear and her temperature will fall 12 to 18 hours beforehand.

Feeding During Lactation

- Once she has had her puppies her energy requirements may be increased by up to four times depending on the size and age of the litter. As a guideline feed one and a half times her requirements in the first week, two times her requirements in the second week, and two and a half times her requirements in the third and fourth weeks.

- There is no need to supplement with additional supplements if her diet is already balanced for calcium, and other nutrients. Her increased feeding will provide proportional and safe increases in nutrients. Over-supplementing with calcium can lead to problems in developing puppies.[14]
- If she is unable to produce enough milk or eat the amount of food needed, then early weaning of the puppies may be necessary.
- Around weeks three to four the puppies can be introduced to solid and moistened foods. You can begin to reduce the bitch's food gradually as the puppies gain their energy from other foods. You should also feed the bitch separately so that the puppies don't steal from her.
- She will need to be fed small meals often, or leave food out for her. Include foods that are more energy dense (consider including good quality dry food) to provide the energy.
- At weaning (approximately seven to eight weeks), reduce her food over the next four to five days to her normal maintenance level.

Adult Dogs

- Feed once or twice daily to help control weight.
- Feed a complete and balanced commercial, home-made or combination diet to healthy dogs, along with raw meaty bones two to three times weekly, and include some fresh foods in the diet.
- Daily exercise will help keep muscles toned, improve metabolism and maintain a lean body mass (less fat).
- Snacks should consist of small amounts of fruit, or foods from the normal daily ration, so those extra calories are avoided.
- Weigh your dog regularly to ensure weight maintenance, especially in older dogs.
- Feed the best diet you can, to promote health and longevity.
- Every dog is individual and the diet and amount fed will vary according to activity, body condition, breed, and weight and health status.

Senior Dogs

- Ageing is both unavoidable and irreversible. As animals get older their muscles decrease in mass and their metabolism changes. However, providing a good diet that takes into account your dog's needs, helps in the care and management of his life-style.
- Older animals generally have lower energy requirements because their level of activity decreases and their metabolism slows down and so thought should be given to providing a lower energy food to avoid obesity. However, the food must still be energy dense because their appetites may also be reduced. Simply feeding less of their normal diet may lead to a common problem of protein and essential fatty acid deficiency. In fact it is more common that elderly dogs are underweight than overweight.

- Older dogs, contrary to popular belief may actually have a higher protein requirement than younger dogs to help maintain their muscle mass and avoid deficiencies. Provided your dog is healthy he can be maintained on a normal adult diet or diet designed for senior dogs.
- About 1 in 5 dogs over the age of 5 have changes in their blood, which indicate early changes to the kidneys.[15] If they have signs of early kidney disease they will benefit from a change to a moderate level of protein and a low phosphorus diet. The diet should be of high quality and good digestibility. You should talk to your veterinarian about the best senior diet for your dog's individual needs.

Protein Requirements

Proteins are made up of amino acids. Essential amino acids have to be provided in the diet, but there are many other non-essential amino acids that the body can make itself. When there is insufficient protein in the diet we see poor growth, rough, dry coats, weight loss, wasting of the muscles, poor appetite and increased susceptibility to infections and other diseases.

Protein comes from two main sources. Meat proteins are much more easily digested and utilised by dogs and will produce smaller stool volume than vegetable proteins.[16] Proteins also vary in quality and the degree to which they can be digested and used by the body.

Fat

Fats and oils are the most concentrated source of energy in the diet. They are also a source of essential fatty acids (EFA) and fat-soluble vitamins A, D, E and K. Deficiencies of fatty acids may manifest as dull, scurfy coats, dandruff, hair loss, anaemia, poor fertility and liver problems.

Too much fat in the diet can lead to vomiting, diarrhoea, and inflammation of the pancreas called pancreatitis. The pancreas takes about one to two weeks to respond to an increase in fat in the diet. So dietary changes of any kind should always be done carefully and slowly to avoid dietary upsets. The other side-effect of a high fat diet and continued fat surpluses is weight gain and eventually obesity.

Carbohydrates

Carbohydrates are a source of energy and excess carbohydrates will be stored as fat. Dogs do not actually require carbohydrates in their diet, because they can make their own sugars from some of the amino acids from proteins. However, they readily digest cooked starches[17] such as rice. Up to 40%–50% of the calories as carbohydrate in the diet is tolerated well and unlikely to be any less beneficial than a total fat and protein diet.[18]

However, with higher carbohydrate diets, generally the food is less efficiently digested and utilised. This is one of the reasons that low quality cereal-based dry foods can lead to poor coat and skin condition and noticeably larger stools. Some dogs such as German Shepherds and Huskies also seem to be less tolerant of high cereal diets and may reprocess the food by eating their stools (coprophagy).[19]

Dietary Fibre

Fibre in the diet is supplied through plant materials. The fibre is not fully digested and most passes on to the large bowel unchanged. The requirement for fibre in dogs has not been determined, but has been demonstrated to help regulate bowel movements and can be used to help treat conditions such as constipation, diarrhea, gastrointestinal tract disorders and other problems. Excess fibre in the diet can lead to diarrhoea, constipation and also reduced absorption of important nutrients.

Water

Water quality is very important. In some areas water is contaminated with parasites or toxins, or very high levels of water additives such as chlorine and other chemicals designed to help kill bacteria. All of these can impact upon health. Because water is essential and required daily, a filtered water source, or spring water is recommended. This is especially important for animals that are very sick or which have chronic problems. All dogs (and their people) will benefit from filtered water supplies to reduce chemical exposure.

Vitamins

Vitamins are organic nutrients that help regulate the processes in the body. These include growth, energy production, metabolism and protection against damage by toxins and waste products. Most vitamins cannot be made in the body so must be supplied in the diet. There are fat-soluble vitamins (vitamins A, D, E and K) and water-soluble vitamins—the main ones are vitamins B and C. Dogs can make their own vitamin C in their bodies; however, supplementation with vitamin C is beneficial in many circumstances, particularly in stress.[20] Vitamins are discussed in more detail soon.

Minerals

Minerals are essential to many processes in the body. All body tissue and fluids contain minerals. There are macro-minerals that are needed in relatively large amounts such as calcium, phosphorus, sodium, magnesium and potassium. Micro-minerals or 'trace elements' are needed in very small amounts and include selenium, manganese, zinc, copper, iron, chromium and iodine. Collectively the minerals are sometimes referred to as ash.

Minerals can be toxic in excess and deficiencies can go unnoticed. They also need to be provided in a balanced way as they can affect the absorption or uptake of other minerals. For example excess zinc can reduce the uptake of calcium and phosphorus from the diet. High cereal diets contain phytates, which can block the uptake of some minerals.

Balance

A balanced diet is one that meets the energy needs of the dog, while providing all the nutrients needed in the right proportions and amounts. If all the nutrients are balanced according to the energy needs, when we feed the right amount of food, it will also contain all the nutrition the dog needs. Nutrient requirements for dogs are an evolving science. Each year new information is brought to light as researchers make new discoveries.

Guidelines set by the American Association of Food Control Officials (AAFCO) have gained acceptance as the standards for quality pet foods. They provide minimum and maximum requirements for dog nutrition, and testing procedures to assess the health of the animals on these diets. Foods that have been fed in feeding trials according to the AAFCO protocols help to ensure that for the majority of dogs, not only is the food complete, providing the right nutrients, the food is also digested well, and the nutrients are available for use by the dog.

Now let's look at making dog foods at home.

Home-made
Diets for Dogs

Home-prepared dog foods can be fun (maybe not for you, but your dog will certainly enjoy cleaning the dishes!), creative and relatively straightforward. You may prefer to make your dog's diet all of the time or just occasionally. Your dog may have special requirements that can't be met by a commercial diet, or you simply want to combine pet foods with home feeding. If your dog is unwell, it will certainly benefit from fresh foods that offer the benefits of wholesome nutrition along with inherent benefits from many of the ingredients including plant (phyto) chemicals. But there are many opportunities to get your dog's diet wrong. So if you choose to feed your dog on home-made diets, then it pays to do it properly.

Food Types

Meat

Meat in general is high in protein and can be high in fat. All meat materials (except bone) are low in calcium and unbalanced for calcium and phosphorus. For example raw, lean beef or lamb contains about 2 per cent of the calcium needed.[21] Lean meat is also deficient in vitamins A, D, E and K but is very high in amino acids, iron, niacin, thiamine and riboflavin.

Muscle meat (such lamb, chicken, turkey, rabbit, beef and pork) should constitute no more than 80 per cent of the diet; however, some dogs cannot tolerate this amount of meat in their diet, and may bring up undigested meat or suffer colic. If you use a diet based largely on meat, it should be lean (more protein) rather than fatty. Ideally you would use organic meats. Human grade meats are the next best option, and you should be cautious about pet meats. Ask your supplier whether additives, preservatives or other substances have been added. Many people are surprised to learn that the pet mince is frequently preserved with sulphur dioxide (which destroys thiamine). Some dogs digest cooked meat far better than raw, and may actually prefer the taste of cooked meat. You will need to experiment.

Meat by-products such as heart, kidneys, tongue, glands and lung are high in protein and very low in fat and are a frequent inclusion in commercial dog foods. A combination of muscle meat and organ meats is good (a ratio of 3 to 1 is suitable). Glandular meats include the liver, pancreas, kidney, thymus and spleen. These meats are very high in purines and pyrimidines (both of which may be a problem for Dalmatians). These types of meats should be restricted to less than 20 per cent of the diet.

Fresh liver (organic is best) is an excellent source of vitamin A and can be chopped into pieces and stored in ice cube trays and frozen. Approximately 25 g or one ounce per square. Check this the first time you do it with a measuring scale. Liver can be fed fresh or cooked, although in some areas it must be cooked because of the danger of hydatid disease. Liver can also be purchased in a dried, dehydrated form and given as a treat or included as part of a home-made diet. Liver powders are also available.

Avoid processed or smoked meats such as smoked ham, bacon, sausages and salamis. These may contain nitrates and other substances that are implicated in contributing to poor health and some forms of cancer.[22]

Fish

Fish is another good source of protein. Fish may be fat or lean. Fat fish include salmon, tuna, mackerel, pilchards, sardines, sprats, trout, eels, herring and whitefish with a fat content of around 5%–18%, therefore resembling medium fat meat. Lean fish store fat largely in the liver. They include white fish such as whiting, sole, cod, plaice, flounder, haddock and bass. The fat content of the flesh is around 0.5%–2%, making them similar to very lean meat.

It is important to consider the source of fish, as some fresh fish supplies may be contaminated with heavy metals such as mercury. Fish are also high in iodine and zinc, and whole fish—including bones—are better-balanced sources of nutrients than most meats.[23] On the other hand filleted fish are seriously deficient in calcium and phosphorus and will need to be supplemented.

Chicken

Chicken is an excellent source of protein; whole fresh chickens probably reflect the closest 'natural' food for dogs. Whole, plucked, eviscerated chicken along with viscera (called 'digest') is a common ingredient in dog foods.

Milk and Dairy Products

Dogs generally love dairy foods because of their high fat content. Cheese is like very fatty meat; it can be used as a meat substitute or grated on the top of food to encourage dogs with poor appetites to eat. Milk and some milk products are a common cause of food allergy in dogs. As well, many dogs do not have sufficient enzymes to digest the milk sugars or lactose. If you wish to add the occasional milk drink then 15–20 ml milk per kilogram body weight is a useful guideline.[24]

Yoghurt (find ones that have Lactobacillus, Bifidobacteria or 'live cultures') and kefir are cultured milk products that contain gut 'friendly' bacteria. Dogs who can't tolerate milk can often take these products without any problems. However, if they are allergic to milk proteins you should avoid these altogether. If your dog needs gut friendly bacteria as part of his treatment he will benefit from a probiotic supplement rather than yoghurt. Probiotics are discussed later.

Cereals

Wheat, corn, barley, oats, rye, maize, sorghums and rice are common additions to dry dog foods and can be an important component of home-made diets, providing a good source of carbohydrate and energy. Cereals should be limited to no more than 40 per cent (on an energy basis) of the diet. Many cereals contain phytates that bind important minerals so that they cannot be absorbed in the digestive tract. Fine grinding, soaking and/or cooking markedly increases the digestibility of all cereals and actually increases the nutrient availability.

Rice and maize are well digested[25] and form the basis for many diets—particularly for those dogs that are sensitive to glutens (which occur in almost every other cereal), or those with digestive problems. Basmati rice is a particular variety that I recommend for its superior palatability. Oatmeal is great for home cooking because it is relatively high in protein and fat and reasonably palatable. It can also be given in the raw state by soaking overnight in water, or water and yoghurt. Wheat germ is also a good cereal to use because it is high in fat and vitamin E. Wheat bran is also useful as a source of fibre.

Vegetables

Vegetables should be as fresh as possible. If necessary you can substitute fresh with frozen occasionally, but try to avoid using canned vegetables because these often have salt and sugar added to them.

Green vegetables such as cabbage, lettuce, cauliflower and broccoli should be lightly steamed, finely chopped or grated (still crunchy); zucchini, sprouts, squashes and mung beans, red peppers (capsicum), corn, bok choy, choy sum and mushrooms provide a varied source of tastes and nutrients for your dog. Uncooked vegetables can be grated, finely chopped or you can put them through a blender or food processor, otherwise steam them. The smaller the pieces the more easily they are digested.

Yam, parsnips and potatoes need to be cooked to make them digestible. Most dogs will eat cooked potatoes and sweet potato readily. Carrots are poorly digested unless cooked, grated or chopped very finely. Pumpkin and sweet potato are excellent sources of fibre and most dogs find them very palatable.

Pulses, lentils, peas and beans provide a rich source of both protein and B vitamins. Tofu and soybean are not well digested by dogs and should be fed sparingly as it ferments in the large bowel causing wind and a bloated tummy. Soaking beans overnight before cooking will improve digestibility and reduce the 'wind effect'. Ideally beans and lentils should be cooked, washed and cooked again to help release and remove many of the indigestible components.

Seeds should be ground to break the husks and improve their digestibility. If you don't grind them (a coffee grinder will do just fine) you will find them coming out your dog the same way they went in! Flax seeds, pumpkin seeds, sunflower seeds and nuts such as pecan and almond are high in fatty acids and can make a good substitute occasionally for oils and fats in the diet.

Fruits

Many dogs enjoy fruits as a snack or as a regular part of the diet. Grated apple is an excellent addition to oatmeal; small chunks of apple can be given as treats. Pears, bananas, avocados, cantaloupe, rockmelon, watermelon, kiwi fruit, strawberries, and other berries can also be given raw on their own or included with other foods.

Eggs

Eggs are an excellent source of protein and fat. Cooked eggs are far more digestible than raw.[26] As raw eggs may be a source of salmonella, boil them for five minutes to help sterilise them. Eggshells are also a good source of calcium, but dogs tend to eat broken shells gingerly (wouldn't you?). If using shells, grind them up finely.

Cooked versus Raw Foods

Most dogs benefit with raw foods like some fresh meat in their diet. And naturopathically speaking, a raw food diet is considered to be beneficial especially if your dog has a serious disease such as cancer or autoimmune disease. Here the properties of raw foods (especially antioxidants and phytochemicals) can really help. Raw meat and vegetables are suitable for many dogs. However, there are many dogs—particularly older dogs and some very sick dogs—that cannot cope with raw foods, and will vomit or have loose stools. So raw foods, while an ideal, may not be all that practical. Root vegetables have to be cooked but other vegetables can be chopped finely or processed to make them easier to digest. Grains (such as oats) should be at least soaked or cooked otherwise they will not be digested in dogs.

There are some benefits to cooking. Cooking destroys bacteria such as E Coli and Salmonella, which cause food poisoning. Cooking kills moulds, eggs and larvae of parasites in meat. It also deactivates several toxins that can be found in raw foods (such as thiaminase in some fish). Cooking improves the digestibility of meat, eggs, cereals, grains and root vegetables.

Cooking can be by way of baking, frying or simmering. Over-cooking should be avoided because it can also reduce the nutrient profile of the foods especially some of the amino acids (lysine and methionine) and vitamins. Thiamine deficiency is also possible with over-cooking.[27] Boiling destroys 40 to 60 per cent of vitamins in cereals, meat and meat-based dishes and vegetables whereas frying and baking destroys about 20 per cent of the vitamins.[28]

Burnt fats and oils can give rise to cancer-inducing carcinogens—one of the important reasons why all burnt or blackened table scraps should be avoided, especially after a barbecue. And it is very important not to use any oil in your dog's diet that has already been used in your cooking. The best oil to cook with is olive oil, a monosaturated oil that is more resistant to the damaging effects of heat than most other common oils. Small amounts can be used if necessary to cook meat, but oils are best added after cooking, when the recipe has cooled. Then health-giving oils such as sunflower oil, fish oil and flaxseed oil or other supplements such as Evening Primrose oil can be added according to need.

If you want to feed raw meat but want to minimise the risk of contamination with food poisoning bacteria, either sear the outside of the meat by either placing in a very hot pan, and turning the meat quickly, or place the meat into boiling water for half a minute. Make sure that you wash your hands after handling meat, and do not use the same chopping board or utensils for other foods without washing them in hot soapy water first.

Organic Foods

Organic foods offer some worthwhile benefits. They are usually (not always) free of pesticide contamination, which can be important for a dog that has a severely over-whelmed system or liver-toxicity. Organically raised animals and vegetables are generally considered to be free of synthetic hormones, toxins and other pollutants. They are also raised on soil which has generally not been leached of vital nutrients, so on the whole their mineral composition is usually higher than normally farmed produce. The downside is that organic foods can be far more expensive and more difficult to obtain so realistically, good quality human grade foods are another option.

Where to Start

Whatever diet you are feeding now may be just fine. You don't necessarily have to change it and you can always combine your current diet with some of the recipes that follow. Ideally your dog will have raw foods in his diet daily, and these can include some vegetables, fruits and raw meaty bones. So you can make up some of the following recipes and give a portion each day to your dog along with a premium quality pet food or feed a home-made diet instead. Each recipe unless otherwise indicated provides 1000 kcals, enough to feed a 15–19 kg dog for one day. This is the equivalent of three cups of good quality dry dog food so you can simply exchange one-fifth of your recipe (200 kcals) for two-thirds of a cup of dog food for example (20 per cent of the daily calories).

Knowing your dog's energy requirement means that you can determine how much to prepare. If a recipe provides 1000 kcals, and your dog requires 2000 kcals, you need to double the recipe. Similarly if your dog only requires 500 kcals, you can either divide the recipe in two, or make it and feed it over two days.

The following recipes are formulated to be complete and balanced, according to AAFCO nutritional requirements. However, these recipes have not undergone AAFCO feeding trials. Because there can be differences in digestion and utilisation of nutrients in foods and the ingredients you choose will vary in their nutritional content, the recipe may not be complete and balanced for your dog. So it is important to provide variety in the ingredients, the sources of meat, grains, vegetables and fruits and to monitor your dog's health closely. Consult with your vet if you are unsure.

Feeding the Recipes

Dogs are best 'meal fed' rather than leaving food out all day for them. The recipes can be broken up into two meals daily, such as a cereal and fruit for breakfast, then a meat dinner. Or the whole lot divided into two or three meals. Supplements can be mixed into a grain and vegetable mix, or crushed, or hidden in a morsel of meat. The recipe can be made into a cooked (grain, root vegetables) and raw (meat and other vegetables) combination; the whole recipe can be cooked, or fruits can be given raw as a treat during the day. You will need to experiment with what suits your dog. You can also combine two recipes or three if you wish. Because they are balanced to the energy of the recipe, the total recipe will also be balanced.

Allow your dog access to the food for ten minutes once or twice a day, at regular times if at all possible. What she doesn't eat, remove and refrigerate and feed at the next meal. This will help your dog to get used to a regular routine; it makes elimination times more regular and avoids weight gain due to nibbling throughout the day.

BASIC COMPLETE AND BALANCED RECIPE[29]

Beef boneless, 50% trimmed of fat, raw	300 g (1.5 cups)
Rice, raw (basmati) white	0.5 cup (1.5 cup cooked)
Vegetable leafy green	0.5 cup
Beef liver, raw	25 g
Sunflower oil	0.5 tbs
Bone-meal	1.5 tsp (6 g)
Pinch of iodised salt	

Method: Cook rice in boiling water (with a little meat for flavour), cool. Grate or finely chop or cook vegetables (bake root vegetables and steam others). Bake or fry meat and add rice and vegetables.

Alternatively you may feed the meat and vegetables raw, cooking the rice. Add bone-meal, oil and a pinch of salt to rice after cooling and mix thoroughly.

Yield 1kg

1000 kcal

Energy from protein, fat and carbohydrate is 32%, 33% and 32%.

1 cup = 240 mls

1 tbs = 15-ml tablespoon

1 tsp = 5-ml teaspoon

25 g =1 oz

Consider replacing any plastic bowels with stainless steel or ceramic bowls to prevent sensitivity to plastics. Some dogs get quite red around the muzzle because they are sensitive to the bowl. Also consider providing wide-based bowls so that food can be spread out over the plate, encouraging a slower eating, than the 'insert your nose and vacuum' approach. Large dogs may benefit from feeding in an elevated position, particularly if they have a tendency to regurgitate or vomit after feeding. This is also a good idea if your dog suffers from any neck or back problems, or is old.

Recommended Supplements

For optimal nutrition, supplement daily with:

A balanced multi-mineral and vitamin supplement including vitamin B complex, vitamin E and vitamin C or a commercial multi-supplement formula designed for dogs.

You can also add kelp 1/4 teaspoon, nutritional yeast 1 teaspoon and lecithin 1 teaspoon to the recipe. Add any garden herbs such as parsley, mint, garlic (no more than 1 small clove per recipe) and ground almond, flaxseed, pumpkin seed, sunflower seed or similar.

Alternatives

The following are some alternatives to the basic recipe. Simply exchange the beef with one of the listed meats or protein sources below, noting any changes to the quantity of oils, vegetables, rice or bone-meal in the recipe changes section. The far right column shows the nutritional analysis for protein, fat and carbohydrate. There are also options for substituting rice for other carbohydrate sources, oils, and suggestions for vegetables and fruits.

Meat Exchanges

You can replace the 300 grams of 50 per cent trimmed raw beef with the following, and the recipe will still be complete and balanced.

These diets are suitable for normal adult dogs. A variety of recipes helps to provide a balance over a period of time and helps prevent boredom. The growth diets are also suitable for adult dogs.

Adult Maintenance Recipes

Replace basic recipe 300 grams lean beef with:	Weight	Volume	Protein%: Fat%: Carbohydrate% contribution to energy needs
Beef mince, regular, raw	300 g	2.5 cup	30:38:32
Beef mince, raw plus	60 g	¼ cup	37:29:32
Beef, heart, raw	350 g	2 cup	
Beef mince, raw plus	125 g	½ cup	32:32:34
Beef, kidney, raw	200 g	½ average	

continued over

Replace basic recipe 300 grams lean beef with:	Weight	Volume	Protein%: Fat%: Carbohydrate% contribution to energy needs
Beef, raw, lean plus	175 g		31:34:33
Beef, ½ tongue, raw	125 g		
Lamb, heart, raw plus	3 average		36:29:32
Lamb, kidney, raw	2 average		
Turkey, raw, lean and skin	300 g		35:37:27
Pork, lean, raw plus	215 g	1 cup	35:31:32
Lamb tongue	2 average		
Cottage cheese, low fat plus	200 g		32:31:35
Cottage cheese, regular	200 g		
Carrot		1/2 cup	

Growth Recipes

These recipes are suitable for puppies and growing dogs (alongside a good quality puppy food) as well as adult dogs. Puppies benefit from a combination of premium quality dry food and home-made food. Because they have little stomachs and because dry food is very energy dense, they can receive their nutrition in smaller quantities. These recipes can help replace some dry food meals, or can be fed with dry food. If using home-made diets solely, vary the meals and include raw meaty bones three times weekly for additional calcium.

Replace basic recipe 300 grams lean beef with:	Weight	Volume	Comments	Protein%: Fat%: Carbohydrate% contribution to energy needs
Beef, 50% trimmed, raw	300 g	1.5 cup		32:33:32
Beef, raw, with fat	260 g	1.25 cup		28:38:32
Beef mince, raw, regular	280 g	1.2 cup		29:37:32
Chicken, lean with skin, raw	250 g		Reduce oil to ¼ tbs	27:39:33
Chicken breast baked, lean with skin		2 average	Reduce oil to ¼ tbs	29:36:33
Chicken breast, lean with skin, raw	280 g	2 average	Reduce oil to ¼ tbs	31:35:32
Turkey, raw, lean and skin	300 g			31:35:32
Lamb, raw, 50% trimmed	140 g	0.75 cup		33:34:32
Lamb kidneys, raw	5 average			
Lamb, lean, raw	215 g	1 cup	Reduce oil to ¼ tbs	33:33:32
Lamb tongues, raw	2 average			

continued over

Replace basic recipe 300 grams lean beef with:	Weight	Volume	Comments	Protein%: Fat%: Carbohydrate% contribution to energy needs
Lamb, 50% trimmed, raw	230 g	1.25 cup	Reduce oil to ¼ tbs	26:39:33
Pork, 50% trimmed, raw	270 g	1.5 cup		26:41:31
Hamburger mince, raw	180 g	0.75 cup		27:38:32
Lamb kidney, raw	2 average			
Tuna canned in oil, drained	250 g		Reduce oil to 1/4 tbs no liver	28:35:34
Grated carrot	1 average			

Low-fat Diets

Low-fat diets can be useful for weight control programs and where fat is not digested well as in pancreatitis or malabsorption syndrome and in chronic diarrhoea. The following recipes should be fed under the supervision of a veterinarian:

Replace basic recipe 300 grams lean beef with:	Weight	Volume	Comments	Protein%: Fat%: Carbohydrate% contribution to energy needs
Beef, raw, lean	350 g	1.75 cup	Increase vegetables to 1 cup	39:23:35
Chicken, baked, lean	260 g		Reduce oil to ¼ tbs	37:28:32
Chicken, boneless, raw, lean	350 g	½ whole average	Increase raw rice to ⅔ cup	38:27:22
Chicken, lean, raw	400 g			39:26:32
Turkey, raw, lean, no skin	400 g			41:24:32
Turkey, raw, lean, no skin	300 g		Increase raw rice to ⅔ cup	34:22:41
Lamb, raw, lean	360 g	1.66 cup	Increase vegetables to 1 cup	40:24:34
Fish, raw	350 g		Increase raw rice to ⅔ cup no liver	34:18:45
Grated carrot	1 average			
Tuna, canned in brine, drained	350 g		Increase raw rice to ⅔ cup	38:17:43
Grated carrot	1 average			
Rabbit, lean, raw	350 g			41:24:33
Cottage cheese, low fat	250 g		Increase raw rice to ⅔ cup	30:22:45
Cottage cheese, regular	125 g		No liver	
Carrot		½ cup		

Low-protein Diets

These diets are low in protein and should only be fed under the supervision of a veterinarian.

Replace basic recipe 300 grams lean beef with:	Weight	Volume	Comments	Protein%: Fat%: Carbohydrate% contribution to energy needs
Lamb, fatty, raw	200 g			19:48:29
Pork, fatty, raw	200 g			20:47:30
Eggs		8 average	Do not add liver	23:43:33

Carbohydrate Exchanges

Rice, raw, white	⅓ cup	½ cup	⅔ cup
Rice, raw, brown	⅓ cup	0.5 cup	⅔ cup
Oats, raw, rolled	⅔ cup	1 cup	1.33 cup
Pasta, egg, dry	1 cup	1.5 cup	1.66 cup
Pasta, spinach, dry	70 g	100 g	130 g
Pasta, white, dry	70 g	100 g	130 g
Pasta, wholemeal, dry	70 g	100 g	130 g
Barley, dry	⅓ cup	⅔ cup	¾ cup
Potato, cooked	3 medium	4 medium	5 medium
Sweet potato, cooked	2 cups	3.5 cups	4.5 cups
Lentil, dry	100 g	140 g	180 g
Bread crumbs	⅔ cup	1 cup	1.33 cup

Vegetable or Fruit Exchanges

For Vegetables	½ cup	
Apple	1 average	Grated or sliced as a snack, good source of soluble fibre
Banana	1 small	Mashed/whole high in potassium
Grapes	0.5 cup	Raw good source procyanthinomids
Carrot	0.5 cup	Grated source vitamin A
Bean sprouts	2 cups	Raw good for weight loss
Lettuce	2 cups	Chopped good for weight loss
Zucchini	0.5 cup	Grated raw
Pumpkin	0.5 cup	Cooked excellent source of fibre
Sweet corn	0.5 cup	Cooked mashed best

continued over

For Vegetables	½ cup	
Chick pea	0.5 cup	Cooked, washed and cooked
Peas	0.5 cup	Cooked
Celery	1.5 cup	Cooked/finely chopped good for fluid retention and arthritis
Broccoli	0.5 cup	Lightly steamed
Cauliflower	0.5	Lightly steamed
Parsnip	1 small	Cooked
Potato	1 medium	Cooked
Sweet Potato	0.5 cup	Cooked
Cabbage	2 cups	Cooked (can cause flatulence)
Avocado	15 g (¹⁄₁₆th)	Raw
Choko	1	Cooked
Artichoke	1	Lightly cooked
Pear	1 small	Chopped

Oil Exchanges

Sunflower oil	0.5 tbs	7.5 mls excellent for skin
Safflower oil	0.5 tbs	7.5 mls
Sesame oil	0.5 tbs	7.5 mls
Flaxseed/Linseed oil	0.5 tbs	7.5 mls excellent source of omega-3 fatty acids
Sunflower seeds	15 g	crushed
Sesame seeds	15 g	crushed
Almonds	15 g	crushed
Coconut	15 g	
Cheese	25 g	
Avocado	45 g	⅓ of half an average size avocado

Liver Exchanges

Beef Liver	25 g	Approx. 3500 micrograms* Vit A
Chicken Liver	25 g	Approx. 1500 micrograms Vit A
Lamb Liver	25 g	Approx. 8000 micrograms Vit A
Veal Liver	25 g	Approx. 3500 micrograms Vit A
Carrot	½ cup (70 g)	Approx. 1150 micrograms Vit A
Carrot	¼ cup (35 g)	Approx. 575 micrograms Vit A

*Micrograms: a smaller measure than milligrams

Recipes

Here are some other recipes for you to consider including in your dog's diet. Where necessary add water to cook rice and mix ingredients.

Chicken Wing Teeth Cleaner

1 chicken wing provides some 180 calories, and you can substitute 1/2 cup of dry dog food or 200 grams of canned dog food for a chicken wing two to three times a week. Otherwise chicken wings should be taken into account as extra calories in the diet.

Chicken Wing Dinner

Rice, white, raw	½ cup	Oil, sunflower	½ tbs
Chicken wings	2 average	Chicken liver	25 g
Vegetables	½ cup	Chicken lean, raw	80 g

Cook chicken meat, liver and rice together and vegetables. Add oil when cooled. Leave wings raw.

Energy from protein 28 per cent, fat 38 per cent, carbohydrate 34 per cent. 1000 calories (complete and balanced but high in calcium and phosphorus so should be given a maximum of three times a week).

Chicken and Rice Recovery

Rice, white, raw	⅔ cup (then cook)
Chicken breast, raw, lean, skinless	400 g (4 halves)
Chicken liver	25 g

Cook chicken liver and rice together, and poach chicken lightly. Mix recipe together and divide into several small meals.

Energy from protein 44 per cent, fat 13 per cent, carbohydrate 40 per cent calories 1000. This diet is for short-term use only because it is not complete or balanced. It is designed for times when a 'bland' diet is required and, because of the very low fat content, it is suitable for short-term use with diarrhoea.

Lamb Crockpot

Rice, white, raw	½ cup	Lamb tongue, raw	2 average
Vegetables	½ cup	Lamb kidney	2 average
Oil, sunflower	¼ tbs	Lamb heart	1 average
Lamb liver	25 g	Bone-meal	1.5 tsp

Cook all but oil in a pot on a slow heat. Alternatively cook rice and leave the rest raw.

Energy from protein 30 per cent, fat 35 per cent and carbohydrate 33 per cent. Calories 1000, complete and balanced.

Beef and Potatoes

Hamburger mince, raw	¾ cup	Liver	25 g
Beef, raw, lean	1 cup	Bone-meal	1.5 tsp
Vegetables	½ cup	Potatoes	3 medium
Oil, sunflower	¼ tbs		

Cook all but oil together, cool then add oil.

Energy from protein 40 per cent, fat 39 per cent, carbohydrate 21 per cent. Calories 1000. Complete and balanced.

Mutley Muesli Breakfast

Apple	1 average, grated	Oats rolled, cooked	1 cup
Sunflower oil	¼ tbs	Natural yoghurt	50 grams
Nutritional yeast	¼ tbs	Egg raw	1 average

Mix all ingredients together and serve (can be divided into 2 or 3 serves).

This recipe provides 360 calories (you can replace 1 cup of dry food, 200 grams of canned food, or 1/3 of any of the home-made recipes). It provides 15 per cent protein, 35 per cent fat and 46 per cent carbohydrate contributions to energy. It is not complete and balanced, but provides a nutritious breakfast two to three times weekly.

Dog Oat Surprise Biscuits

(Your dog will be surprised because there's no meat!)

Best for multi-dog homes. Halve recipe for single-dog homes.

Oats, rolled, raw	1 cup	Raisins	½ cup
Wheat bran or rice bran	1 cup	Yeast	1 tbs
Olive oil	½ cup	Salt	two pinches
Wholemeal flour	1.5 cup	Egg, raw	1 average
Sunflower seed	½ cup	Milk	1 cup
Sesame seed	½ cup		

In a large bowl, combine all ingredients, mixing thoroughly. Sunflower and sesame seeds should be lightly crushed to aid digestion. Form into 40 large balls, or 60 medium balls or 80 small balls, depending on the size of your dog, and flatten them on a baking tray. Bake in a medium oven for 40 to 50 minutes, depending on the size of the biscuits. Energy from protein 12 per cent, fat 62 per cent, carbohydrate 24 per cent.

Large dog: 40 biscuits each have 100 calories.

Medium dog: 60 biscuits each have 70 calories.

Small dog: 80 biscuits each have 50 calories.

These are high fat biscuits designed for travelling purposes, or when you want to provide a quick snack, and they should be fed sparingly. They are not complete and balanced. Store in an airtight container

Dog Dinner Loaf—Chicken, Beef or Fish

Rice (brown or white), raw	1 cup	Pasta (wholemeal or plain), dry	1 cup
Water	1 litre	Oats rolled, raw	1 cup
Eggs, raw	4 average	Flour, wholemeal	½ cup
Calcium carbonate	1.5 tsp		

Vegetables:

Potato, raw chopped	1 average	Carrot, raw grated	¼ cup
Sweet potato, raw chopped	½ cup	Spinach or silver beet, raw	1 cup
Pumpkin, raw chopped	1 cup		

and

Chicken, raw, with skin	400 g plus chicken liver 100 g

or

Beef mince, regular, raw	2 cups plus 100 g liver

or

Fish, raw	400 g plus olive oil 2 tbs

Cook rice in boiling water, add potato, sweet potato and pumpkin and pasta and cook for further fifteen minutes. Add remaining ingredients, choosing the fish, beef or chicken. The mixture should be moist but firm, add more oats if necessary. Place mixture in oiled loaf tin for up to one hour at 180 degrees. Remove loaf from the tin, and place in oven for further ten to fifteen minutes to set.

Divide the loaf into:

6 slices of 500 calories

10 slices of 300 calories

20 slices of 150 calories

Energy from protein 25 per cent, fat 35 per cent, carbohydrate 39 per cent.

Soups for Dogs

Broths are useful for many dogs. They are good when your dog's appetite is poor, in warm weather, or when you need to feed lightly for a couple of days. They are also good meal substitutes for dogs which are overweight, as part of a weight loss program, and can be used for modified fasting too. Here are some recipes for you to try:

Chicken Soup

Chicken breasts, raw, diced	2	Carrot, raw, finely chopped or grated	½ cup
Barley, pearl, raw	½ cup	Egg, raw	1 average
Olive oil	¼ tbs	Water	1 litre
Chicken liver	50 grams		

Lightly fry chicken and liver in oil. Gradually add water to pan, and add barley and carrot. Once the barley is soft and cooked, turn heat down, and whisk in 1 egg. Cool broth. This provides approximately 1000 calories, and is designed to be fed in 1/2 cup-fuls to whole cupfuls every couple of hours. The energy supplied by protein is 33 per cent, fat 39 per cent and carbohydrate 25 per cent. The fluid can be given on day one, offering more liquid than energy, and then on day two the meaty broth mixture can be fed in several small meals.

Chicken Broth

Chicken lean	300 grams	Carrot, raw, grated	½ cup
Water	2 litres	Celery, raw, grated	2 sticks
Salt	1 pinch	Rice, white, raw, dry	¼ cup

Place diced chicken in pan and cover with water, adding vegetables and rice. Cover and bring to boil, and then simmer for two hours, adding more water if necessary. Allow to cool and remove fat if there is any. Strain to remove solids and keep. Provide half cupfuls to whole cupfuls every couple of hours for a dog that has lost his appetite, or is recovering from tummy upsets. When there is improvement divide the meat, rice, vegetable mixture into several very small meals and gradually go onto solid foods again.

This recipe supplies approximately 400 calories; energy from protein is 33 per cent, fat 13 per cent and carbohydrate 50 per cent. Fish or turkey can be substituted for chicken.

Mutton or Lamb Broth

Lamb, raw, lean	700 g	Barley, raw, pearl	¼ cup
Water	2 litres	Parsley, raw	1 tbs
Carrot, raw, grated, diced	1 cup		

Cut up meat (neck bones of mutton or beef fine as a substitute but will be fattier) and place in pan. Cover with water and bring to boil. Simmer for 90 minutes then add barley and carrot and simmer for a further 60 minutes. Add parsley towards the end of cooking. Allow to cool, and remove any excess fat. Divide into several meals over 1 to 2 days.

This recipe provides 1000 calories, energy from protein is 62 per cent, fat 22 per cent and carbohydrate 14 per cent, and is excellent following surgery, where appetite is poor and protein needs are high.

Supplements

Healthy dogs on good quality diets should not, in theory, require any supplements. However, commercial foods and fresh foods can also lose significant nutritional value through cooking and storage. And there can be differences in how well dogs digest their food, how well they utilise the various nutrients it contains, and what their individual requirements are. Dogs that are in poor health or that have additional requirements such as old dogs, working dogs, very active dogs or growing dogs may benefit from the addition of various supplements in their diet. Dogs that are highly stressed, chronically unwell or that are dealing with toxin overload may have higher requirements especially for vitamins and minerals involved in detoxification pathways in the body.

A word of warning: Supplements and other natural products need to be used appropriately. It is a false assumption that just because it's natural, it is safe. Many of the supplements listed below could become potentially toxic if used carelessly. If at all in doubt, check with your vet first.

Starting with Supplements

As a starting point consider supplementing your dog with a quality multi-antioxidant product (with vitamin A, C, E and selenium) which will help reduce free radical damage and help minimise degeneration in the body. You can also include some organic sunflower oil (this can replace all or some of the oil used in homemade foods).

The supplements that follow are from a naturopathic viewpoint, useful for many conditions outlined later in the book. They are not meant to substitute for a good diet or normal veterinary care.

Vitamins

As a general rule the best vitamin products are those that are balanced with others, a multivitamin supplement for example. However, there are certain times when individual vitamins may be beneficial. It is best to use these under the guidance of a veterinarian.

Vitamin A

Vitamin A is essential for normal growth and development, reproduction, a healthy immune system and is a potent antioxidant. On the other hand vitamin A deficiency can lead to skin, cornea, conjunctiva and respiratory tract disorders, and bone formation problems.[30]

It is beneficial:

- when vitamin A deficiency is suspected (dry eyes and various skin problems).[31]
- for cancer and heart disease.[32]
- in the treatment of 'Dry eye' (keratoconjuncitivitis sicca).
- for skin diseases and the immune system and as an antioxidant; may help prevent cancer, retard ageing and protect the body from damage caused by pollutants and chemicals.[33]

Suggested dose
(instead of fresh or cooked liver in the diet for 4–6 weeks only or under veterinary supervision):

Cod liver oil (with food)

Small dog	¼ teaspoon daily
Medium dog	½ teaspoon daily
Large dog	1 teaspoon daily

Vitamin A tablet/capsule daily. Start on the lower dose.

Small dog	500–1000 iu*
Medium dog	1000–3000 iu
Large dog	3000–5000 iu

* iu: international units

Higher doses than these should only be given under the guidance of a veterinarian as large doses can be toxic when used for extended periods.[34]

Vitamin C

Dogs produce their own vitamin C at around 200 mg/kg per day.[35] However, stress can increase requirements considerably. The primary function of vitamin C is in the manufacture of collagen, which is the main protein substance of the body. It is vital for wound repair, healthy gums and the structures that hold the body together such as ligaments, cartilage and tendons. It is also critical to immune function and is a very important antioxidant.

Vitamin C may be beneficial for dogs that are stressed and also in the treatment of allergies,[36] cataracts, cancer, infections (bacterial and viral), heart disease, liver disorders, arthritis, urinary tract infections, hip dysplasia, disc disease and spondylosis of the spine, dental disease and gingivitis, wound healing, diabetes and canine distemper.[37]

Vitamin C supplements come in powders, capsules and tablets. Most commercial vitamin C is sourced from corn. Ascorbic acid is the most commonly used and economical type, but buffered vitamin C (like sodium acorbate) is available and is gentler on the stomach. The addition of bioflavinoids to the product (look for ones where bio-flavinoid content equals or exceeds the vitamin C content) can improve absorption. The powdered form is the easiest to give, and should be mixed in food and fed quickly.

Dose, long-term

Small dog	50–125 mg twice daily
Medium dog	125–250 mg twice daily
Large dog	250–500 mg twice daily

Short-term

Doses can be increased considerably (1 to 10 grams daily) under veterinary supervision. Vitamin C can be given to 'bowel tolerance'. This involves increasing the dose gradually until there is softening of the stools, then the dose is reduced slightly to keep the dog on the highest dose possible for short periods of time. The side-effect of too much vitamin C is stool softening or diarrhea. Much larger doses of vitamin C can be given intravenously and can be very helpful for dogs with trauma, viral infections (if given early), and as an adjunct for cancer treatment.

Vitamin D

Vitamin D is actively involved in the metabolism of calcium and phosphorus. Dogs at risk of a deficiency are those that are kept indoors on an all meat diet or a mainly cereal diet. Deficiency results in rickets with bone deformities. However, vitamin D occurs in relatively large amounts in fish liver oil, eggs, milk and butter and a properly balanced diet will prevent deficiency.

Vitamin E

Vitamin E or tocopherol is an important fat-soluble vitamin and antioxidant, protecting cell membranes against free radical damage. It is necessary for normal immune function and provides a protective effect in many health problems. Vitamin E requirements increase with an increasing fat content of the diet, so if you are supplementing with fatty acids, supplement with vitamin E too. Poorly stored dry foods or poorly prepared home-made diets can also be low in vitamin E. Vitamin E deficiency is associated with digestive (malabsorption) problems, skin disease, skeletal muscle dystrophy, failure of gestation, poor fertility, retinal degeneration and impaired immunity.[38] Moreover, it has also been suggested that a deficiency causes suppression of the immune system that can make a dog more susceptible to demodectic mange.[39]

Vitamin E is a beneficial supplement for any chronic disease, any degenerative disease and cancer to help increase resistance to disease and for dogs with immune depression, infections, inflammation, allergy, heart disease, skin disease including immune-mediated and autoimmune skin disease[40], demodex and ear margin vasculitis,[41][42] cancer,[43] arthritis, periodontal disease, colitis, cataracts, muscle problems,[44] diabetes, epilepsy and liver disease.

Dosage

Natural forms of vitamin E have a prefix d-, while synthetic forms have a prefix dl-. Stable forms of natural vitamin E include d-alpha-tocopherol acetate and d-alpha-tocopherol succinate. Miscellised or water soluble forms of vitamin E are more readily absorbed by the body.

Small dog   25–50 iu daily
Medium dog 50–100 iu daily
Large dog   100–400 iu daily

No adverse effects were noted at ten times the recommended level in dogs[45] but it should not be used with anticoagulant medication.

Vitamin B Complex

B complex can be beneficial for acute stress, allergies and infections and B vitamins are essential for energy production, growth and a healthy immune system.[46] In people some of the earliest signs of deficiencies include irritability, agitation, nervousness and insomnia. Some dogs with similar symptoms may benefit from supplementation. Dogs with kidney disease or increased urination also benefit from vitamin B supplements.

- Thiamine (B1) deficiencies lead to anorexia, nervous system disorders, weakness and heart failure.[47] Thiamine is easily destroyed by cooking and by thiaminase enzymes that occur in some raw fish. Thiamine is also destroyed by sulphur dioxide, a common preservative used in fresh pet meats.[48]
- Riboflavin (B2) deficiencies lead to eye problems, skin disorders, mouth sores and shrinking of the testicles.
- Niacin (B3) or nicotinamide. A deficiency can lead to problems in the mouth including blood-stained saliva and bad breath, as well as weight loss, and loss of appetite. Niacin is a powerful blood vessel dilator, and so can be useful for dogs with degenerative disease or cancer, as it can enhance oxygen flow to the body, as well as delivering other nutrients. It is particularly useful for joint disease and may also be useful in hyperactivity. It is best given in a B vitamin complex rather than on its own.
- B5 Pantothenic acid is another important enzyme-like substance. It plays an important role in the production of corticosteroid hormones in the adrenal gland and can be depleted if your dog is stressed. It aids the immune system generally. Deficiencies can lead to depression, poor growth, fatty liver, hair loss and gastrointestinal disturbances.
- Pyridoxine B6. Deficiencies lead to weight loss and anaemia, slow growth and nervous disorders.
- Folic acid is closely associated with B12 and essential in the workings of the nervous system. Deficiencies lead to anaemia and a drop in white blood cells (lowered immunity).
- Vitamin B12 cobalamine is important for myelin—the sheath-like material that surrounds nerves. Deficiencies can lead to problems with the nervous system and anaemia.

Dose depends on product, choose a B complex product, and dose according to instructions, alternatively 5–30 mg complex daily.

Minerals

Minerals can be beneficial in many situations. In general a balanced mineral formulation is best rather than supplementing with individual minerals, because some minerals can interfere with the absorption of other minerals in the diet. For example, too much calcium can inhibit the uptake of zinc in the digestive tract.

Calcium

Most reputable commercial dog foods and diets that include raw bones or small whole fish do not generally need calcium supplementation. For puppies, supplementing an already balanced diet can actually lead to joint problems as can feeding raw meaty bones every day. However, diets that are largely meat-based will require supplementation of both calcium and phosphorus either with bones, or a commercial supplement. On the other hand, if only small amounts of fresh meat are added to a mainly pet food diet, then supplementation will not be necessary.

TABLE 3 CALCIUM SUPPLEMENTATION[49]

Source	Level teaspoon	Calcium %	Calcium mg	Phosph. %	Phosph. mg	Add to meat at the rate of:
Bone-meal	4 g	29.5	1200	12.5	630	1–1.5 teaspoon per 200 g
Dicalcium phosphorus	5 g	24	1050	18	925	1 teaspoon per 200 g
Eggshell (5g)	From a 60 g egg	32.6	1650	0.12	2	1 eggshell per 200 grams. Grind finely.
Calcium carbonate	5 g	40	2000	0	0	1 teaspoon per 300 g

Chromium

Chromium is a mineral found in meats and whole grains. Its main use in people is to help improve blood sugar control in diabetic patients and to help promote weight loss. It can be a good support for some dogs with diabetes. It must be given under veterinary supervision as chromium helps make the insulin more effective.[50] It may also be a useful supplement during weight control programs.[51]

Dose

Small dog	20–50 micrograms
Medium dog	50–100 micrograms
Large dog	100–300 micrograms

Copper

Copper is essential for dogs. Some breeds such as Bedlington Terriers, West Highland Whites and Dobermann Pinschers are sensitive to copper excess. So mineral supplements containing added copper should be avoided for these dogs. Their diets should also be low in liver, whole grains and legumes (which are good sources of copper). Supplementation with copper should only be in the form of a balanced mineral formula never as a sole supplement.

Salt

Salt is generally needed when the diet is high in cereal grains. Prepared pet foods have adequate salt. Iodised salt contains 50–100 micrograms of iodine per gram and can be used instead of kelp. Supplementing meat with 1/8–1/4 teaspoon per pound or half kilogram of meat or cooked cereal increases palatability and enhances sodium and iodine content. However, salt should not be added in dogs with heart disease.

Selenium

Selenium is a potent antioxidant and works with vitamin E to prolong cell life, thus having a protective role in fighting degenerative diseases such as cancer and arthritis. Selenium also protects the immune system by preventing the formation of free radicals.[52] Deficiencies are rare but can lead to degeneration of heart muscle and skeletal muscle. As well, red blood cell disorders, cataracts, immunosuppression (including cancer), heart disease and thyroid dysfunction have been linked to selenium deficiency.

Uses

Selenium may be beneficial as a supplement for heart disorders, strokes, degenerative disorders such as cataracts and arthritis, skin disease, cancer and general support of the immune system.

Organic selenium forms such as selenomethionine and selenium rich yeast are more bioavailable than sodium selenite.

Dose

Small dog   5–10 micrograms daily
Medium dog 10–20 micrograms daily
Large dog   20–50 micrograms daily

Caution: Selenium is toxic in excess amounts and should only be used under the supervision of a veterinarian.

Zinc

Zinc is very important for skin health. Alaskan Malamutes, Siberian Huskies and Samoyed and some Bull Terriers have a very high requirement due to an inherited form of zinc deficiency. In these dogs zinc supplementation is not only essential for growth but also for normal coat condition and general vitality. Some disorders such as poor digestion, infections, stress or injury may contribute to zinc deficiency too. Zinc deficiency can also occur when the diet is supplemented with minerals (for example too much calcium) or when the diet is high in cereal phytates (including diets high in corn, fibre and soybeans and vegetarian diets) that interfere with the absorption of zinc. Some poor quality dry dog foods with high calcium contents (greater than 2.5 per cent) can also induce zinc deficiency.

Signs of zinc deficiency include poor growth and development, roughening, cracking and thickening of the skin, especially around eyes, nose and anus; reproductive and congenital defects and defects in the skeleton (dwarfism).[53] Deficiency signs first start on pressure points and then the footpads. There can be loss of hair, redness, inflammation and crusting and bacterial skin infections are also common.

Uses

Zinc supplementation should be considered: when zinc deficiency is suspected; to support the immune system, to help fight viral infections; for male infertility, for arthritis, for chronic skin disease and for copper storage diseases (it reduces the absorption of copper).

Dose

Zinc deficiency dose. Between 1 mg to 10 mg per kilogram per day of zinc sulphate or 1.7 mg per kilogram of zinc methionine.[54]

General supplementation of zinc methionine:

Small dog	5–10 mg
Medium dog	10–20 mg
Large dog	20–30 mg

Caution: The only adverse effects of zinc supplementation are digestive tract irritation, mainly vomiting. Eight times the normal minimum requirement will not produce adverse effects.[55]

Essential Fatty Acids

Certain fatty acids assist in preventing inflammation and degeneration; they help regulate the immune system, aid in brain function, are powerful anti-inflammatory agents and help prevent abnormal cell proliferation (such as tumor cells). A deficiency can be difficult to detect and the signs can be very vague. Some disorders that may be associated with fatty acid deficiencies, or benefit from fatty acid supplementation (especially omega-3 fatty acids) include:

- Poor skin and coat with hair loss and eczema;[56] food allergies, flea allergy, allergic skin disease (atopy)[57] and itchy skin disease;[58] dull, dry coat with excess scale and hair loss and secondary bacterial skin infections; peeling skin, moistness between the toes, and ear infections;
- Poor wound healing
- Heart and circulation problems

- Poor immunity and autoimmune disease[59]
- Arthritis, degenerative joint disease, hip dysplasia, pelvic arthritis[60]
- Degeneration of the retina[61]
- Reproductive failure
- Nervous system disorders
- Liver disease
- Weight loss and obesity
- Behavioural disorders, including hyperactivity
- Diabetes mellitus, hyperlipidaemia (high fat in the blood)[62]
- Digestive tract disorders such as inflammatory or irritable bowel syndrome
- Cancer, lymphosarcoma[63]
- Platelet aggregation disorders[64]
- Renal disease[65]

The most relevant families of fatty acids are omega-6 linoleic acids, which are derived from vegetable oils, meat fats and some dairy products and omega-3 alpha-linolenic acid from green leafy vegetables, grains, soy, canola, flax (linseed) oil, cold water (deep sea) and marine fish oil. The absolute amounts and the ratio of omega-6 to omega-3 fatty acids, influences whether they reduce or promote inflammation in the body. Most diets have adequate omega-6 fatty acids, so it is usually more relevant to supplement with omega-3 fatty acids. Most oil sources contain both types but in different ratios and so some oils are better suited for certain conditions than others.

What to use

The quality of commercial oils varies substantially, and the quality will determine whether the oils you purchase will have health promoting benefits, or conversely disease promoting properties. Many commercial oils are highly refined, involving high heat, bleaching, and colouring. Look for oils that are:

1. Certified organic
2. Packaged in opaque (light resistant) containers.
3. In the refrigerated section of the health food shop
4. Not past the use by date (most have a 4–6 month expiry)
5. Preferably made by cold pressing at low temperatures, as opposed to heat treated.
6. In small quantities for freshness and stability.

Only use olive oil in cooking, as it is the most stable at high heat. All other oils should not be heated, but added after food is cooked.

Caution

Supplementation with high doses of fatty acids can be potentially harmful[66] as they are easily oxidised and can actually contribute to inflammation.[67] Long-term supplementation with omega-3 fatty acids may also lead to deficiencies of omega-6 fatty acid.[68] As well, high doses of omega-3 fatty acids such as cod liver oil can also lead to bleeding problems,[69] lethargy, itchiness, diarrhoea and skin reactions.[70]

Dose

Fatty acid supplementation may actually reduce the required dosage of conventional medicines such as prednisolone and antihistamines. If supplementing an already balanced diet with fatty acids, give vitamin E as well. General improvements from supplementation, especially skin and coat should be seen in about two weeks although it can take between six to eight weeks to become apparent. The dosage can then be reduced. Doses for flax seed, fish oil and Evening Primrose oil follow.

Sunflower oil: 5 mls per 240 g of dry food[71] daily for two months.

Topical fatty acids can also be applied to the skin if on a low-fat diet.

Corn oil: 1 tsp per 400 grams raw meat or 1 tsp per 100 grams dry cereal.[72]

Flax seed oil

Flax seed or linseed oil is very high in omega-3 fatty acids (58 per cent) and is also high in lignans that have anti-cancer properties as well as antibacterial, antiviral and antifungal properties[73]. It may be beneficial in a number of disorders including heart disease, stroke, arthritis, eczema, behavioural disorders, allergies, immune problems, kidney disease, obesity and some forms of cancer.

Dose

Flax seed oil should not be the sole fatty acid supplement, but used in rotation with other oils.

Small dog   ½–1 teaspoon daily

Medium dog 1–2 teaspoons daily

Large dog   1 dessertspoon–1 tablespoon daily

Doses can be increased under supervision of a veterinarian.

Fish oil

Herrings, sardines, salmon, mackerel and other cold-water fish contain high levels of omega-3 fatty acids and can help relieve the symptoms of skin allergies[74] but should be used with caution. Quality is very important as fish oils can be contaminated with heavy metals and pesticides and are high in vitamins A and D. It is better to use capsules so that the dose can be regulated carefully. Another option may be to include two to three fish-based meals each week, to increase the amount of omega-3 fatty acids consumed. Fish oil may be especially beneficial for old dogs, skin allergies, heart disorders and arthritis.

Dose

Supplement under the supervision of a veterinarian.

Small dog   100–200 mg daily

Medium dog 200–500 mg daily

Large dog   500–1000 mg daily

Evening Primrose Oil

Evening Primrose oil is an especially rich source of gamma linolenic acid (GLA) an omega-6 fatty acid, which is anti-inflammatory in a range of conditions.[75] Evening

Primrose oil would be the choice source of omega-6 fatty acids in the treatment of allergic dermatitis.[76] However, it may actually be more helpful to supplement with omega-3 oils (e.g. fish and flaxseed oils).

Evening Primrose oil is safe; however, it is important to use this supplement under guidance. The most common side-effect is softening of the stools. Oil capsules should be given with food.

Dose

500 mg per 12 kg

Caution: There is a single report of a reaction to Evening Primrose oil in a person with epilepsy. It should therefore be used with caution in any animal with epilepsy.[77]

Fibre

Fibre is beneficial because it helps remove toxins from the bowel, provides the right environment for gut-friendly bacteria, helps to restore inflamed bowel lining and alters the rate of digestion. Some types of fibre have the ability to help regulate blood glucose (useful in diabetes) and reduce the risk of some types of cancer.

Dietary fibre and fibre supplementation may be of assistance in irritable bowel syndrome, ulcerative colitis, chronic diarrhea, constipation, obstipation, bowel cancer, as a preventive measure against diseases of the bowel, diabetes and high levels of fat in the blood (hyperlipidaemia) and anal gland problems.

However, like most things, too much can cause problems. Fibre increases the size and volume of stools and reduces the digestion and absorption of many nutrients and can cause constipation and even diarrhoea.

There are two major types of fibre. Soluble fibres include oat bran, grains, legumes, nuts, seeds, psyllium seed husks and pectins (found in the outer skins and rinds of fruits and vegetables). These all help to promote regular bowel movements and help nourish intestinal cells. Insoluble fibres include wheat bran, which also helps to regulate bowel movements and increase stool size. Moreover, they also nourish the intestinal wall and support intestinal bacteria.

High fibre containing foods include pumpkin, apples, carrots, beets, bananas, cabbage, lentils, nuts, seeds, beans, peas, grains, potatoes, corn and brown rice.

Supplements include:

- Wheat bran and other insoluble fibre; they increase the size of the stools (which reduces straining and the risk of diverticuli or ballooning in the large bowel). They also decrease the time food takes to go from the mouth to the anus, limiting exposure to possible cancer-causing compounds and toxins that may be present in foods. Even though insoluble fibre reduces the time food stays in the gut, it also reduces the rate that it leaves the stomach, so there is a slower release of food into the small intestine, and a more regulated digestion takes place. This is useful in diabetes as well as other conditions.
- Oat bran, guar and pectins are particularly good at lowering the fats in the blood, which can be useful in the treatment of hyperlipidaemia (fatty blood).

- Pectins and legumes when fermented produce important fatty acids that have potent anti-cancer activity and are therefore useful to protect against cancer and also to treat ulcerative colitis.
- Rice bran is particularly good as a fibre supplement when there are wheat and gluten allergies.
- Psyllium is an excellent intestinal cleanser and stool softener. Constipation and anal gland disease often responds well to psyllium.

Dose

Start out with a low dose and increase gradually as necessary. Too much too soon can lead to bloating and wind. Starting doses of wheat bran, oat bran, rice bran, psyllium:

Small dog   ½–1 teaspoon daily

Medium dog   ½–1 dessert spoon daily

Large dog   ½–1 tablespoon

Caution: Encourage your dog to drink plenty of fluids. Avoid capsules and pills, which can expand in the gut. The easiest way to dose is to add to moist foods, mixing well, with a little water. Fibre supplements can reduce the availability of minerals and other nutrients, and also inhibit the absorption of some drugs, so it is wise to give the fibre supplement a couple of hours away from medications.

Probiotics

Probiotics are 'gut-friendly' living bacteria that are found naturally in a healthy digestive tract. They improve the health of the digestive tract by altering gut acidity, aiding digestion and helping to detoxify harmful materials. Probiotics enhance immunity and actively produce antibiotic substances.[78] They have also been shown to be active against certain tumors.[79] Oral administration of lactobacillus acidophilus improves white blood cell activity and results in improved immune defences.[80]

Poor diet, stress, antibiotics, corticosteroids and some other drugs can destroy these good bacteria allowing unfriendly bacteria to take over. Even antibiotics that target infections can affect the friendly bacteria. When the balance of bacteria is affected it can result in symptoms such as wind, bloating, constipation, loose stools and poor absorption of food and other problems. As well, an overgrowth of bad bacteria can affect the skin, joints and immune system. It is also possible for your dog to develop allergies or sensitivities to food when this happens.

Friendly bacteria can be obtained through soured products such as yoghurt. While they do provide some health benefits they don't really colonise the gut of dogs. While yoghurt can be used daily in the diet, good quality powdered products are more effective for therapy because they are far more concentrated; each teaspoon contains literally millions of good bacteria. Because these products contain living bacteria, they should be stored in the refrigerator.

Main Uses:

- Probiotics may be useful in chronic skin disease, allergies, arthritis, cystitis, candidiasis, colitis and irritable bowel syndrome and some forms of cancer.[81]

- After antibiotics: supplementation is very beneficial to prevent and treat antibiotic-induced diarrhoea and dysbiosis (imbalance of bacteria). While they are not as effective while given during antibiotic therapy, research supports their use both during and after antibiotics, to prevent overgrowth of bad bacteria, and reduction of the good bacteria.[82]
- Diarrhoea: supplementation can help rebalance the population of bacteria that are affected in acute and chronic diarrhoea.
- Cancer therapy: Lactobacillus bulgaricus and Lactobacillus acidophilus have anti-cancer properties.[83] They can also be beneficial in dogs receiving chemotherapy or radiation involving the digestive tract.

Dose:

Powdered acidophilus, bifidus and other organisms (12 million organisms per gram). Follow product directions or:

Small dog ¼–½ teaspoon daily

Medium dog ¼–1 teaspoon daily

Large dog 1–3 teaspoons daily

For during, and ten days following antibiotic therapy.

Live cultured yoghurt as a food supplement not as a therapy:

Small dog 1 dessert spoon daily

Medium dog 1 tablespoon daily

Large dog 2–4 tablespoons daily

Daily as a food supplement.

Probiotics are very safe; however, overdose may cause mild digestive upsets.

Prebiotics

Fructo-oligosaccharides (FOS) are food components that are derived from fruit and vegetable sources such as Jerusalem artichokes, asparagus, leeks and garlic. These sources are called prebiotics because they actually feed the growth of friendly bacteria in the digestive tract. They therefore improve digestion and help keep the gut healthy. They also improve liver function and help with the elimination of toxic compounds. While the food sources do provide some benefit, a dog would have to eat considerable amounts, so supplementation with FOS can help boost the intake and promote gut-friendly bacteria. Many good quality dry foods contain sources of FOS.

Main uses[84] include intestinal dysbiosis, inflammatory bowel disease, chronic colitis, chronic diarrhoea, and food allergies and can be used in detoxification programs.

Dosage FOS

Small dog 200–500 mg

Medium dog 500–1000 mg

Large dog 1000–2000 mg

Antioxidants

Today most pets are exposed to the damaging effects of free radicals. These are formed from the body's exposure to oxygen, sunlight, stress, poor nutrition, heavy metals, pollution, chemicals, some food additives and rancid oils in some foods. Antioxidants protect enzymes, cell membranes and other compounds from damage by free radicals.

Antioxidants include nutrients such as vitamins A, C and E, betacarotene, bioflavinoids, Coenzyme Q, and enzymes such as Glutathione peroxidase, Super Oxide Dismutase and Catalase, Selenium and even green tea. Antioxidant supplementation is recommended as a daily supplement for even the healthiest of dogs for long-term protection and health.

Antioxidants are particularly beneficial for ageing pets, or pets that are suffering the symptoms of any chronic disease. Autoimmune disease, cancer, diabetes, cataracts, dermatitis, gingivitis, infections, hepatitis, infertility, heart disease, arthritis and many other conditions will benefit from antioxidant supplementation.

Carnitine

Carnitine (L-carnitine) is a vitamin-like compound that is essential for converting fat into energy. It occurs naturally in meat and dairy products but grains, fruit and vegetables contain almost no carnitine.

If the level of L-carnitine is deficient, a number of health problems associated with fat metabolism may arise. As well, low carnitine is associated with dogs suffering from dilated cardiomyopathy heart disease.[85] Many other disease states may benefit from carnitine supplementation such as other forms of heart disease (including heartworm disease), hyperlipidaemia, poor physical performance, exercise intolerance, kidney disease, diabetes, and liver disease.

Dose

50 mg–100 mg per kilogram 3 times daily[86]

Alternatively *large breed dogs* 2 grams every 8 to 12 hours

Medium size dogs 1 gram every 8 to 12 hours[87]

Note: L-carnitine (not D-carnitine) is the preferred form. Carnitine and Coenzyme Q work synergistically, and choline (lecithin) supplementation can help conserve carnitine in the body.[88]

Coenzyme Q

Coenzyme Q10, also known as ubiquinone, plays a vital role in energy production in the body. When levels are low cells are unable to obtain all their nutrients and get rid of all their wastes, making them vulnerable to disease. Coenzyme Q also supports the immune system and helps correct age-related decline in immunity[89] and assists the functioning of white blood cells.[90] It is a completely safe substance, and available in most foods. However, stress and over-cooking of foods can lead to deficiencies of this vital nutrient.

Coenzyme Q may be beneficial in the treatment of periodontal and gum disease, immune deficiency, cancer, obesity, diabetes and heart disease. It is also an appropriate supplement for older dogs and performance dogs to improve energy production, provide an antioxidant effect and enhance immunity.

Dosage—tablets or capsules
15 mg per 10 kg body weight daily for four weeks, then half the dosage daily, or the give the full dose every other day for maintenance.
Coenzyme Q can be used with carnitine for heart disease, and may reduce the adverse effects of beta-blockers.[91]

Dimethylglycine

Dimethylglycine (DMG) is a vitamin-like substance found naturally in meat, seeds and grains. It may enhance metabolism and immunity and is considered a useful anti-stress supplement. It has had a long history of use in greyhounds and other performance dogs. It is useful because it aids recovery following heavy exercise or performance, but more importantly it helps boost the immune system. It should be considered as a supplement for dogs with seizures, allergies, immunosuppression, heart disease, respiratory problems and inflammation such as eczema and arthritis.[92] It is extremely safe.

Suggested doses
Small dog   25–50 mg daily
Medium dog 50 mg–100 mg daily
Large dog   100–200 mg daily

Enzymes

Digestion relies heavily upon specific enzymes to break down food so those nutrients can be absorbed; enzymes are produced by the digestive tract, but raw foods are another source.[93] However, if you cook, steam, bake or microwave food, the naturally occurring enzymes may be destroyed. Most animals produce enough enzymes naturally but there are other situations when they may be inadequate. If your dog has excess gas, bloats easily, vomits undigested food from the night before, is underweight despite a large appetite, has a voracious appetite, eats strange things or has undigested food in his stools, supplementation with digestive enzymes may help.

Dogs that are ill, very stressed or on antibiotics or non-steroidal anti-inflammatory medications can experience poor digestion. Dogs with diseases of the liver, stomach or pancreas also have difficulty producing enough enzymes. Supplementing these dogs with enzymes can improve the digestion process and uptake of nutrients, helping the body to recover more quickly.

Digestive enzymes may help in other instances too, such as following injury or exercise where certain enzymes act as analgesics or pain reducers. Enzymes can also assist the immune system and have been used in the treatment of cancer and inflammatory disorders.[94] Proteases may have the ability to remove or digest immune complexes and induce the production of anti-tumor factors. L-Arsparaginase may be beneficial in the treatment of lymphoma and leukaemia in animals. Uses include treatment of auto-immune disease, cancer and other inflammatory disorders.[95]

Digestive enzymes may therefore be useful in the treatment of immune disorders, allergic conditions, inflammatory conditions and degenerative disease such as arthritis. Although research into the use of these enzymes in animals is limited, their use under veterinary supervision should not cause any harm and may indeed provide a benefit.

Older pets may also benefit from supplementation. As animals age, the production of many enzymes often slows down. If your old dog or cat has excessive wind, loose stools or other health problems consider adding digestive enzymes to your pet's diet.

Digestive enzyme supplements come in powder, capsule and tablet forms. Powdered forms are easier to add to the diet and usually come in combinations rather than as single enzymes. Enzymes are usually given with meals, but occasionally they can be more effective given between meals to help cleanse and detoxify the gastro-intestinal system. All forms of digestive enzymes should be kept in a cool, dry place.

Dosage
According to label directions.
Caution: Avoid using if your dog has gastritis or ulcer conditions.

Honey

Organic honey is an excellent source of fructose and glucose, vitamins, minerals, anti-oxidant bioflavinoids, enzymes and amino acids (from pollen). It can be combined with water, milk, oats, yoghurt and other foods for a quick energy source if an animal hasn't eaten for a day or two. It has been used as a folk remedy in people for coughs and throat inflammation. It can be especially useful in promoting the healing of super-ficial wounds. It makes a soothing balm for anal gland problems, can be used under dressings for slowly healing wounds, and organic, strained honey can be used as an eye soother (one drop) for sore eyes. It should be avoided in dogs with diabetes and in very young dogs. Honey should be stored in glass, in a dry cool place. Medical honeys are available now with proven wound healing benefits.

Caution: Some dogs can be allergic to bee products including honey.

Bee Propolis

Propolis is a resin-like material used by the bees in the construction of their hive and it acts like the immune system of the hive. It is considered an excellent antibacterial substance and may also enhance the immune system. However, evidence is lacking for many of the claims made on propolis products, which vary substantially in quality and sources.

Caution: Be aware of possible reactions if your dog has allergies.

Liver

Liver is an excellent supplement. It is very high in vitamin A (220–290 mg/kg) as well as many minerals[96] and can be beneficial for dogs with liver problems, anaemia and to improve the palatability of home-made foods. Liver from organically raised animals is preferable and raw liver is of greater nutritional benefit than cooked liver, but some dogs will vomit raw liver or refuse to eat it. Cooking liver reduces the risk of hydatid disease where this is a problem. However, cooking reduces the nutritional value of liver and so cut the liver into small chunks and fry or bake for no more than ten minutes.

Fresh liver can be stored by allocating 1 ounce or 25 grams to each compartment of an ice cube tray and freezing. This makes 'dosage' easy.

Amount

25 grams per 20 kg dog per day on a meat-based diet.

Reduce this amount if feeding a commercial diet to 25 grams per 20 kg of body weight twice a week.

Home-made diets: 25 grams of liver for each 1000 kcals.

Alternatives include dried liver available as dog treats, and liver powders and glandular products.

Bioflavinoids (pycnogenols, proanthocyanidins)

Bioflavinoids are usually associated with vitamin C. Bioflavinoids or flavinoids are pigments that give colour to many fruits and vegetables including parsley, legumes, all berries, apples, pears, peaches, tomatoes, grapes, plums, cabbage and sage.

Flavinoids are considered to be nature's 'biological response modifiers' because they can alter the body's reaction to other compounds such as allergens, viruses and cancer-causing compounds. They have anti-allergy, anti-inflammatory, antiviral and anti-cancer properties and act as powerful anti-oxidants against free radical damage. There are many different types including:

- proanthocyanidins (grape seed and pine bark extracts)
- quercetin
- citrus bioflavinoids
- green tea polyphenols (green and black tea)

Flavinoids in combination with vitamin C can be used to protect the skin against thinning when using corticosteroids such as prednisolone, for diabetic cataracts, allergic reactions, acute and chronic infections and as potent antioxidant supplements.

The toxicity of flavinoids is very low. *See* grape seed, quercetin.

Grape Seed Extract

Grape seeds and pine bark extracts have a high content of flavinoids. The bioflavinoids in grape seed, called 'proanthocyanidins', are unique, because they are the only bioflavinoid that can cross the blood–brain barrier. They are powerful antihistamines and free radical scavengers. They are considered to be more potent than vitamins C and E and selenium in this regard.

They are potentially useful for allergies, inflammation (such as osteoarthritis and other joint and connective tissue disorders), disorders of the retina, and they are also useful to help boost the immune system, during treatment of cancer, following strokes and following brain damage or seizures.

Dose proanthocyanidin complex:

Small dog	10–50 mg
Medium dog	50–100 mg
Large dog	100–200 mg

Garlic

Garlic is one of the most ancient herbs ever used. Garlic oil contains a number of components including fatty acids, B and C vitamins, and is a rich source of organically bound selenium. It is a potent immune system stimulator and natural antibiotic. It was used during World War II to treat wounds and infections[97] and is still used in many countries around the world today for the same purpose.

It can be used for the treatment of diabetes (increases the half-life of insulin), heart and blood disorders (reduces platelet aggregation); it may aid in cancer prevention, it provides immune support, it may be useful for bacterial, fungal, viral and parasitic infections and liver detoxification. Garlic has often been suggested as a treatment for fleas; however, it has failed to show efficacy against fleas and the dose that might be useful, might also be dangerous to dogs. However, there is no harm in providing a small amount of garlic in the diet each day.

Dose

Allicin is the agent in garlic that is responsible for its many beneficial effects. This is also the agent that produces the characteristic smell. Use fresh garlic or look for 'high potency garlic' preparations. Parsley can aid in reducing garlic breath.

Small dog	¼–½ clove daily
Medium dog	½–1 clove daily
Large dog	1–2 cloves daily

Caution: Excessive garlic in the diet can lead to destruction of blood cells (Heinz body anaemia).

Garlic Oil

Garlic oil can be made by peeling a whole bulb of garlic cloves and adding the cloves to 200 mls of olive oil in a clean jar. Allow the cloves to sit for 7–10 days in a cool place. Refrigerate and use in cooking, as flavouring and for the treatment of minor infections.

Glandular Products

Glandular products are animal products usually derived from lamb, beef or pork, used as food supplements or therapy for particular organ and glandular problems. These preparations are usually freeze dried, although fresh glandular meats might also be beneficial. They have traces of hormones and enzymes and other proteins that may be absorbed into the body. For example pancreatic enzymes extracted from pancreas gland have long been used in the treatment of pancreatic insufficiency in dogs, to help replace the enzymes that the dog cannot produce.

Similarly liver extracts and fresh liver may help the functioning of the liver and spleen extracts or fresh spleen may be useful in dogs who have had their spleens surgically removed, in the treatment of low white blood cell counts, bacterial infections, cancer therapy and autoimmune disease. Thymus extracts may be helpful in T cell defects (occurs in some forms of demodectic mange), allergies, immune depression, cancer (radiation and chemotherapy suppress the immune system) and autoimmune disorders. Thyroid extracts may be beneficial in the treatment of hypothyroidism. While the heart and kidneys are not considered to be glands as such, they can be given for heart disease and kidney disease too.

The use of glandular products is quite controversial but their use should certainly do no harm, and may in fact provide long-term benefits by supplementing the body with natural hormones and substances in trace amounts.

Dose

Glandular meats can be added to the diet three to four times weekly in small amounts (50 grams per 1000 kcal). Cooking will reduce their effectiveness. Freeze dried forms are preferred to eliminate the possibility of contracting viral disease.

Extracts will vary according to quality and content and dosage instructions will usually be on the label or in product literature.

Glucosamine

Glucosamine and derivatives stimulate the production of substances for joint repair, the production of the tendons, ligaments, cartilage, skin, heart valves, eyes, and mucous and joint fluid. Glucosamine forms the basic structure of glycosaminoglycans (GAGS), which are incorporated into the body's connective tissues, joints and mucous membranes. Other GAGS include the Green-Lipped Sea Mussel (Perna Mussel), shark cartilage, bovine cartilage and chondroitin sulphates, although these are not in a concentrated form.

As the body ages, natural production of GAGS is reduced and when the body is diseased or injured it needs more. Glucosamine is therefore a useful supplement for conditions such as arthritis and degenerative joint disease, disc degeneration, hip dysplasia and osteochondritis, spondylosis and spondylitis of the back, ligament, tendon and joint injuries. As well it may be useful for bowel disease including inflammatory bowel disease and colitis and when the mucous membranes of the respiratory, genital and urinary tract are inflamed.

Its greatest use is in the treatment of arthritis. Glucosamine helps to protect and nourish connective tissues and cartilage, reducing pain and improving function[98] and it can significantly reduce pain and inflammation, improve mobility and actually regenerate damaged joint cartilage.[99] Glucosamine is available as glucosamine sulphate, glucosamine hydrochloride and N-acetyl glucosamine. Glucosamine sulphate is the preferred form, although glucosamine hydrochloride is also effective. It is a safe and effective alternative to non-steroid anti-inflammatory drugs that may actually inhibit cartilage repair and accelerate cartilage destruction. Although it can take four weeks to see any benefit, glucosamine has been shown to be more effective over longer periods than equivalent non-steroid anti-inflammatory drugs.[100] It is also considered to be very safe and can be used with anti-arthritis medications.

Caution with use in diabetic animals.

Dose

Small dog	250–500 mg daily
Medium dog	500–1000 mg daily
Large dog	1000–1500 mg daily

Glutamine

Glutamine is an important energy source for the cells lining the digestive tract. Whenever the digestive tract is stressed, the need for glutamine increases. Glutamine is especially beneficial for inflammatory bowel disease, and may also be beneficial in the treatment of acute and chronic diarrhoea. Natural sources include pearl barley, wheat bran, oats, grapes and almonds. Commercial supplements are better when using glutamine therapeutically.

Dose

Small dog	250–500 mg
Medium dog	500–1000 mg
Large dog	1000–3000 mg

Green Foods

A number of food supplements are referred to as 'green foods'. These include barley grass, wheat grass, spirulina, alfalfa, chlorella, cracked flower pollen and others. They are excellent sources of beta-carotene (the precursor to vitamin A), minerals, amino acids, fibre and enzymes. They also contain beneficial antioxidants. The fresher the product the more nutritious it is, and some of these can be grown at home. They are useful supplements particularly if your dog does not like vegetables, or is reluctant to take other forms of supplements. Be wary of products with amazing claims that the product will treat all illnesses. They certainly will not hurt and can be added safely each day but probably are not going to solve health problems on their own.

Kelp

Kelp is a general term for seaweed supplements and kelp is a rich source of minerals and vitamins and trace elements, particularly organic iodine. It is a good supplement for all dogs because iodine is needed for the correct functioning of the thyroid gland, which in turn affects health, skin, coat and metabolism.

Caution: The iodine content of kelp is very variable and excessive supplementation is likely to lead to insidious toxicity of iodine (salivation, watery eyes and nose, irritation of the stomach and suppression of the thyroid gland leading to lethargy).[101] So it should be given in measured quantities rather than added liberally. Use under veterinary supervision only in dogs with thyroid disease or autoimmune disease, as it may worsen the condition.

Dose
Small dog ⅛–¼ teaspoon daily
Medium dog ¼–½ teaspoon daily
Large dog ½–1 teaspoon daily
Check directions on packaging.

Lecithin

Lecithin is a form of choline, essential to the manufacture of acetylcholine, which is vital for proper nerve functioning. Choline is also required for the proper metabolism of fats, and without it, fat can build up in the liver. Choline is found in many foods, such as egg yolks, brewers yeast, grains and legumes, liver, cauliflower and lettuce. However, lecithin supplements are a concentrated form.

Lecithin helps the absorption of thiamine by the liver and vitamin A by the intestine. It helps increase the levels of choline in the blood and acetyl choline in the brain and may be of particular use in nervous system disorders, ataxia, degenerative nervous diseases, geriatric dogs and liver problems such as hepatitis, diabetic fatty liver, drug-induced liver damage and toxic liver damage.

Most commercial lecithin contains 10%–20% of the active components. If using lecithin therapeutically, your vet may opt for a preparation containing higher than 80 per cent phosphatidylcholine because less is needed. Lower concentration products may produce side-effects in large quantities. [102]

Dose—Supplemental dose lecithin (1tbs or 7.5g contains 1725mg of lecithin)
Small dog 1 teaspoon daily
Medium dog 1 dessert spoon daily
Large dog 1 tablespoon daily

Dose—Therapeutic (suggested) product containing 80%–90% phosphatidylcholine

Small dog	20–50 mg
Medium dog	50–100 mg
Large dog	100–200 mg

Caution: Side-effects from too much lecithin can include digestive upsets such as bloating and diarrhea.

Perna Mussel

The New Zealand Green-Lipped Mussel is an edible shellfish with a high level of lubricating agents called glycosaminoglycans (GAGS) as well as numerous other minerals, enzymes, amino acids and vitamins. The shellfish acts as a filter converting plankton, kelp and algae into its highly concentrated tissues. GAGS are very important in connective tissue in the body. They can be considered a little like 'glue', that holds everything together. Glucosamine is a concentrated form of the same substances.

Perna Mussel has been shown to be beneficial for arthritis, inflammatory skin conditions, and degenerative disorders in older dogs. It appears to improve the lubrication in joints easing pain and increasing mobility, and helps to inhibit inflammation. Perna Mussel is safe and natural. Dogs generally love the taste, although too much may lead to gastrointestinal upsets.

Dose

Actual dose will depend upon the purity of the product; however, as a guideline the suggested dosage is:

Small dog	100–200 mg twice daily
Medium dog	200–400 mg twice daily
Large dog	400–600 mg twice daily

Double the dose for the first two weeks. It may take four to six weeks before benefits are seen.

Shark and Bovine Cartilage

Studies have shown that bovine cartilage may inhibit some cancers and halt growth of solid tumours. Both shark and bovine cartilage contain glycosaminoglycans (GAGS). GAGS are effective in treating various types of arthritis, cardiovascular disease and immune dysfunction.[103]

Shiitake, Maitake, Cordyceps and Reishi Mushrooms

Extracts of these mushrooms and others have been reported to build resistance to disease by stimulating the immune system, especially against viral infections but also bacteria, fungal infections, and cancer. Shitake is used to treat cancer and Reishi has been shown to regulate immune functions and protect the liver from toxins.[104] They can also be beneficial in inflammatory disorders such as arthritis, kidney inflammation and gastritis. Reishi (also known as Ganoderma) may be beneficial in particular for autoimmune disease, inflammatory disorders and allergies. Extracts are available or the mushrooms can be added dry or fresh to the diet.

Choline

Choline is not a vitamin but is associated with the B complex vitamins as it occurs in foods rich in B vitamins such as egg yolk, liver, brain, wheat germ, soybeans and brewer's yeast. Egg yolk contains the highest concentration of choline and lecithin is another natural source. It is generally readily synthesised in the body; however, deficiencies can occur on poor quality dry dog foods or home-made diets. It is an important component of cell membranes. Deficiencies can lead to an impaired immune system and liver and kidney problems (*see* lecithin).

Wheat Germ

Wheat germ is an excellent source of thiamine (16–21 mg/kg) and wheat bran is an excellent source of manganese.

Yeast

Yeast is actually made up of millions of organisms. Fresh yeast or baker's yeast must be avoided as it is poorly digested. Debittered, dried brewer's yeast (derived from hops) is an excellent supplement as is nutritional yeast. As a powder, it is high in protein and a rich source of vitamin B (pyroxidin 33 mg/kg), chromium and minerals. It is also high in phosphorus so should be avoided in renal disease. Yeast can help in skin disease, heart disorders, nervousness and low energy. It may also boost the immune system.

Dose

Small dog	⅛–¼ teaspoon daily
Medium dog	¼–½ teaspoon daily
Large dog	½–1 teaspoon daily

Caution: Some dogs are sensitive to yeast and can show skin reactions.

CHAPTER 7

Medicinal Herbs

Tasha

Tasha was four when I first met her, a lovely Cocker Spaniel who suffered from long-term moist, itchy skin problems and swollen, painful lymph nodes throughout her body. The problems had been thoroughly investigated by her usual veterinarian, including a referral to a veterinary dermatologist. But despite more than fourteen courses of antibiotics over a sixteen-month period, along with other medications, her problems persisted.

We worked on some dietary changes in order to restore her digestive function and strengthen her immune system. This included increasing the protein content of her diet, improving the balance of her diet and adding some supplements such as anti-oxidants, fatty acids and zinc. The treatment consisted of a glycerin-based mixture of liquorice, astragalus, burdock and St Mary's thistle herbs. Later the treatment was changed to include cleavers. The liquorice was used because it has anti-inflammatory properties not unlike corticosteroids, but without the side-effects, St Mary's thistle because of its liver-protective effects and cleansing properties, astragalus for its immune-enhancing properties, burdock for its skin-supporting effects and then cleavers because it helps to cleanse and stimulate the lymphatic system including the lymph nodes.

After one month, Tasha's skin was already improving, she had one or two minor outbreaks, but she was noticeably less itchy. After two months her lymph nodes were measurably smaller, her appetite had increased and she had put on a little weight. Four months later her skin was normal, and her coat had begun to shine, her lymph nodes were just detectable. Six months later and Tasha's skin, coat and general health has improved markedly and no further herbal treatment is needed.

Herbs

Herbal treatments are gentle and effective and Tasha's story illustrates some important points. While some herbs can work very quickly, for chronic disease it may take several weeks before improvements are noticeable. This is because herbs work to improve the body's natural functioning (such as waste elimination), rather than suppressing symptoms in the way that conventional medicines often do. Also herbs need to be used along with attention to the underlying causes of the problem. There is no point using herbs, for example, if the diet is poor to start with, or the dog is infested with fleas.

Use

There are herbs for nearly every disease or symptom known and herbal medicine is currently used by 80 per cent of the world's human population.[105] Which is not surprising considering plants have for many centuries formed the basis of every system of medicine in the world including the Indian Ayuvedic system, Traditional Chinese Medicine, and even our Western system of medicine has its origins in plant medicine. Despite a relative lack of scientific research into the use of herbs in animals, they have a long history of use throughout the world. The earliest record of herbal treatment of animals was in China thousands of years ago when horses and cattle were routinely treated with herbs and acupuncture.[106]

These days, herbs can be used effectively as medicines in their own right, or to assist conventional medicines. Often herbs will allow the body to better detoxify drugs, or protect organs from side-effects, and may even allow the dosages to be reduced, thereby minimising potential side-effects. One of the ways in which herbs work naturopathically is to aid in the elimination of toxins through promoting urination (diuretics) and bowel movements (purgatives) as well as assisting the immune system (adaptogens).

However, there are many instances where Western medicines are in fact more effective and safer than herbal preparations. For example if a dog is infested with worms, it is far quicker and safer to use a safe conventional worming preparation than waiting for herbal preparations to work.

Safety

Herbs are generally mild in their action, enhancing your dog's self-healing ability. Where drugs have a single chemical ingredient and are therefore very potent, all herbs have literally hundreds of natural chemicals. It is the combination of these plant chemicals that tends to make them gentle. They work better together because while some of the chemicals are very powerful, others help cancel out potential toxic effects.

It is important to note that despite this some herbs can be very toxic and even lethal in very small doses. Digitalis is a well-known heart medicine derived originally from the foxglove plant. Too much digitalis can be fatal. Likewise even the safer herbs can be potentially dangerous. There have been many reports of toxicities ranging from allergic reactions to the plants themselves, through to side-effects caused by the actives in the herbs such as vomiting, diarrhoea and liver damage, through to death (although rare). Herbs work best and are safe when prescribed by a veterinary herbalist who can tailor the most appropriate herbs at the most effective doses for your dog.

Guidelines

As a rule you should never treat your own pet, unless the herbal remedy is specifically formulated for dogs. Even then, it is safest to have the guidance or supervision of a veterinarian experienced in the use of herbs or a herbalist who has knowledge and experience of use of herbs in dogs. Herbs can be very powerful and without knowledge or understanding you can do harm. You might also find that you are wasting your money if you are not using the right herb, at the right time, in the right dose. Many over-the-counter herbs have been shown to contain the wrong species of herbs. And dogs poorly digest many products designed for humans. I have seen one dog suffer severe liver damage because a well-meaning owner had overdosed her dog with herbal tablets for several months.

Always seek veterinary attention for any problem you wish to treat, so that you don't miss something more serious or something that can be readily and safely treated with conventional medicine. Herbs can be used in addition to conventional medicine or in some instances as an alternative.

GUIDELINES

1. Like any conventional medicine, the use of medicinal herbs must be monitored carefully.
2. It is vital that herbal products are sourced from companies that have good quality control measures so that contamination or wrongly identified herbs are avoided.
3. Most herbs are available for purchase as teas, tinctures, tablets, capsules, salves and ointments. Good quality products will list the ingredients by genus and species on the label, as well as the parts of the plants used and the potency.
4. Herbs can be combined with conventional medicines but must be monitored by your veterinarian as the dose rate required for medicines can change.
5. Compared to their pharmaceutical counterparts, herbs generally take longer to work.
6. Use up to five herbs at a time, or a commercial blend of several herbs formulated for your dog's problem. Herbs work synergistically.
7. Some strong smelling herbs can antidote homoeopathic preparations.
8. If using herbs for more than ten days, use a five days on two days off, five days on and two days off regime. Alternatively three weeks on, one week off unless otherwise directed.
9. Small doses can be extremely effective. Start off with a small dose then if your dog tolerates the dose well, it may be increased as needed.
10. The best form of the chosen herb is one that is easiest to give to your dog. Products made for dogs are preferable.

Seek advice about doses from your veterinarian or herbalist before commencing any form of herbal supplementation unless you are using a product for dogs that has the dose rate on it. Dose will depend upon the condition, the herbs used and their individual potency in a formula.

Fresh herbs

Many fresh herbs such as parsley, thyme, garlic and rosemary can be added to dog food. Add as much as you would to your own food. Too much can reduce palatability. Avoid using wild herbs unless you trained in identifying plant species. Dry herbs can be used but are not as effective as herbs that have been infused or extracted as tinctures.

Tablet or capsule form

Products designed for dogs will have suggested dosages on the label. They are either powdered dry herbs or extracted, concentrated and powdered so dosage is variable. Always check with your veterinarian before using them. Some of these herbs have a bitter taste and may need to be disguised in a sardine, some mashed sweet potato, or cheese.

Infusion and decoction

Infusions are essentially like black teas made from fresh or dried herbs. Generally 1 cup of boiling water is poured over 1 teaspoon of herb in a glass or china cup. It is covered and stirred occasionally and after 5 to 15 minutes strained through a coffee filter. This method is useful for fresh herbs, leaves and flowers as well as powdered roots and barks. A decoction is made from hard herbal material such as roots, wood and barks. Usually 1 teaspoon is placed with 1 cup of cold water and brought to the boil in a glass or ceramic vessel, and allowed to boil for 5–10 minutes. It is allowed to cool and then strained. The infusion or decoction should be made freshly each day, and refrigerated. They may be added to cool broth or mixed in with food. Alternatively honey can be added to sweeten the herb.

Tinctures

Tinctures are made by extracting the concentrated actives from the herbs using alcohol. The tinctures are then kept in the alcohol form or the alcohol is evaporated and replaced by glycerin. Alcohol tinctures are very stable, and are particularly useful in acute conditions because the alcohol promotes the absorption of the herb across the mucous membranes and also the skin. The major disadvantage is that most dogs hate the taste of alcohol. They are usually only useful for dogs with good appetites when they can be added to food easily. If your dog is picky you may have more difficulty in dosing. They are best given diluted in water, or in food or add some milk, glycerin or honey to them.

Glycerine tinctures have a sweet and warming taste and are readily accepted by dogs. They are suitable to give to diabetic dogs, when used under the supervision of a veterinarian. They are less potent in general than alcohol tinctures, so more is required. They can be given directly or added to food.

Fresh plant cream

Chickweed, calendula, comfrey, echinacea and other herbs can be made into creams by juicing the fresh plant, then filtering the juice through a coffee filter. Combine 10 mls of the juice with 100 grams of vitamin E cream or sorbelene. There are many commercial skin preparations that you can buy. Remember that whatever you apply is likely to be licked off, so check the ingredients and safety before applying.

Dosages

One of the major difficulties in veterinary herbalism has been the lack of research to provide the most appropriate dosage of specific herbs and formulations for dogs. This is important because many herbs are potentially dangerous. There is a whole field of veterinary medicine called toxicology that focuses on plant-based poisons. Depending on when and where herbs are harvested, the active compounds can vary in potency too. Conventional drugs have precise dosages, consistent formulations (usually with a single active compound) and we can predict the effectiveness and side-effects of any drug-based on clinical trials. So it is much easier to administer correct dosages with conventional drugs than with herbs. Also note that herbs are best used in combination to help strengthen their properties while minimising the potential for side-effects.

Size of dog	Alcohol tinctures # 1:2, 1:3	Glycerin tinctures 1:2, 1:3	Infusion/ decoction	Tablets/ Capsules +	Loose herbs teaspoons
Small <7.5kg <15lbs	¼ ml	½ ml	1 teaspoon twice daily	½–1	½–1 ½
Medium 10–20kg 20–40lbs	¼–¾ ml	½ ml–1.5 ml	1 dessert spoon twice daily	1–3	1 ½–2
Large 20–40kg 40–80 lbs	¾–1 ml	1.5–2 ml	2 dessert spoons twice daily	2–4	2–3
Giant >45kg >90lbs	1–3 ml	2–6 ml	2 tablespoons twice daily	4–6	3–4

Your veterinary herbalist will prescribe the most effective dose for the chosen herbs, which can be different from these.

#Note that with tinctures, the dose is for individual herbs with a potency of 1:2 or 1:3. If more herbs are added the total volume given will increase proportionally.

+ The actual dose will depend upon whether the herbs are concentrated extracted forms (Low dose) or dried powder herbs (High dose).

Useful herbs that are suitable for various conditions are highlighted below.

Alfalfa

Alfalfa has anti-cancer properties, but is more commonly used for arthritis and joint problems, and combines well with liquorice and dandelion. It has a high Vitamin K content and may be beneficial for bleeding disorders. Because it is high in saponins, it may cause gastritis or colic in some animals.

Aloe Vera (*Aloe vera*)

The fresh juice is highly effective when applied to burns, especially in early stages. It speeds healing of wounds[107], injuries and irritations to skin and can be used for wound management, burns, constipation and bowel disorders where there is inflammation. Aloe used on deep vertical wounds such as those produced in surgery for speying can actually delay healing.[108]

    Caution: use only the juice—the skin can cause gastric upset and diarrhoea.

    It stimulates uterine contractions so avoid in pregnancy, lactation.

    Avoid using it internally unless under the strict supervision of a veterinarian.

Bladderwrack/Kelp (*Fuscus vesiculosus*)

This is common seaweed rich in algin, mannitol, carotene, iodine and bromine and is useful for arthritis, especially if the dog is obese. It can also be used externally on joints that are inflamed. Kelp may augment the autoimmune response in thyroid disease, so use only under veterinary supervision. It can be taken as a dietary supplement (kelp) or infusion (1 cup on 2–3 teaspoons dried kelp and steep for 10 minutes).

Burdock (*Articum lappa*)

This is an excellent herb for dry and scaly skin, dry eczema, dandruff and allergies, especially when associated with arthritis too. It is considered a blood purifier, liver stimulator, and is also nutritive. It is useful for systemic toxicities.

    It combines well with dandelion, alfalfa or red clover for chronic skin disease and is safe for long-term use. Externally it can be used on wounds and ulcers when combined with yellow dock, red clover or cleavers.

Calendula (*Calendula officinalis*), Marigold

The tincture of flowers of calendula can be made into tea then put into a spray pack or spritzer. The solution is excellent for local skin problems due to either injury or infection, such as slow-healing wounds and minor burns. It is particularly good for hot spots. It combines well with garlic oil, mullein, Oregon grape or St John's wort for topical use.

    For external use pour 1 cup boiling water on 1–2 teaspoons flowers and infuse 15 mins, allow to cool and then use.

Celery (*Apium graveolens*)

Celery's main use is for arthritis associated with depression. It is a good diuretic and urinary antiseptic. As a food it can be added to the diet to help decrease gas, and is good for dogs that are nervous eaters. It can also be combined as a tea with cardamon and fennel for digestive upsets.

Caution: Can potentiate cartrophen, and a lower dose may be required.

It should not be used during pregnancy or if suffering kidney problems.[109]

Chamomile (*Matricaria chamomilla*)

This is also called German chamomile or 'dogs chamomile' because it smells like a dog's kennel. It is an excellent gentle sedative as a tea or tincture for anxiety and insomnia as well as stomach upsets (stomach pain and colic), inflamed gums and eyes (it can be used as an eyewash for conjunctivitis). It is a good tonic for dogs that whine or complain all the time, or dogs that seem to be up all night. Used topically it acts as an anti-inflammatory for soothing dry and cracked skin.

Tea: 1 cup of boiling water on 2 teaspoons of leaves; infuse for 5 mins.

Cleavers (*Galium aparine*)

This is one of the best herbs for the lymphatic system. It is good for swollen glands (lymphadenitis), tonsillitis as well as bladder infections (it is anti-inflammatory and reduces spasm on the bladder wall), chronic cysts, dry skin conditions, old unresolved infections around the head and ears, and may be used in some forms of cancer where the lymphatic system is involved.

Comfrey (*Symphytum officinale*)

This is a traditional herb used in the setting of broken bones. It contains allantoin, which is very good for wound healing, because it stimulates cell growth. It helps seal wounds so you need to be careful that the wound is very clean and not harbouring germs. It helps to reduce scar formation. It is potentially toxic to the liver with long-term use, so internal use should be avoided. It is a great herb for treating cracks in footpads by using the fresh leaves as a poultice. Use a light bandage and a sock to keep the poultice on.

Dandelion (*Taraxacum officinale*)

Dandelion contains glycosides, choline and up to 5 per cent potassium (leaves). It is a very powerful diuretic, and especially useful for water retention due to heart problems. It is similar in effect to furosemide, a common veterinary diuretic, but where this drug causes the body to lose potassium, dandelion spares it because of its own high potassium content.[110] Dandelion root is also a good general tonic and a specific liver tonic as it increases the flow of bile. It can be used for yeast infections (as it inhibits yeast), liver disease, diabetes (it has a mild blood sugar lowering effect), congestive heart failure and high blood pressure. It may be useful for low-grade infections as well. It may also serve as a useful tonic when undergoing treatment for cancer. It is very safe and gentle and can be used for long periods of time. A suggested dose for large dogs is a tincture of 2.5 mls three times daily. If concurrent heart medications are being given, the doses may need to be reduced very carefully under the supervision of a veterinarian.

Echinacea (*Echinacea angustifolia, E. purpurea*)

Purple coneflower is a primary remedy for bacterial and viral infections by stimulating parts of the immune system.[111] It is useful for bladder infections, infections of the upper respiratory tract, as a blood cleanser for skin infections and skin allergies. It is helpful for arthritis and fevers and can be applied externally to wounds, burns, and abscesses and used in infections where antibiotic resistance has been demonstrated. It has anti-fungal and anti allergenic action. It can be used as an adjunctive herb for the treatment of snakebite (inhibits hyaluronidase), wound healing and to offset some of the side-effects of radiation or chemotherapy.[112]

It should be used at the onset of infections, and used medicinally for short periods of time to avoid over stimulating the immune system. It should be avoided in auto-immune diseases unless prescribed. It can be used hourly in acute conditions, or for 4 to 5 days as a normal course. A suggested dose is to dilute the tincture 20 drops in 25 mls (1 oz) water, shake and give 1/2 ml to small dogs, 1ml to medium dogs, and 1.5 mls to large dogs three times daily in acute infections.

It may be given as a long-term preventive in much lower doses, dilute 3 to 9 drops of tincture in 25 mls and give 1/2 ml for small dogs, 1 ml for medium dogs and 1.5 mls for large dogs once daily. For long-term usage use 4 weeks on, 1 week off.

Essiac

Essiac is a Canadian Native American herbal formula revived in the 1920s by Rene M. Caisse. It contains Indian rhubarb (*Rheum palmatum*), slippery elm (*Ulmus fulva*), burdock root (*Articum lappa*), and sheep sorrel (*Rumex acetosella*).

Phytochemical actives in this formula have been shown to have anti-leukaemia action and anti-tumor activity in mice with induced sarcoma, and a third active has been observed to change some liver enzymes.[113] There are other actives that are immune stimulators as well as pain relievers. There is little scientific evidence that it cures cancer, although there is much evidence that supports its cancer fighting effects. In studies on people the main benefit was a side-effect of lessening of pain associated with cancer. In one report, approximately 50 per cent of animals with cancer responded positively to treatment with essiac.[114] It is used mainly as a formula for cancer, but may be used where pain relief is required, detoxification of the liver and in the treatment of chronic constipation.

Essiac is generally supplied as a powder that is made up as a tea (give a 35 kg dog 60 mls of tea four times daily for three weeks then twice daily) following supplier's directions. This can be given by syringe, or mixed with milk or broth an hour before meals. Alternatively essiac can be obtained in a tablet form. A five days on and two days off regime works well. Dogs should be concurrently supplemented with a vitamin B complex while on essiac.

If essiac is unavailable the formula can be made with the following:

150 g (30 oz) burdock root, 80 g (16 oz) sheep sorrel, 5 g (1 oz) rhubarb root, 20 g

(4 oz) slippery elm bark. Herbs should be powdered, mixed together and stored. To prepare an infusion, take 3 teaspoons (9 g) of the formula and add to 600 ml of boiling spring water in a stainless steel pot and boil 10 minutes. Scrape down the residue and let the formula steep for 12 hours. Then simmer again for 20 minutes covering the pot. Strain the liquid through a coffee filter and cool. Store the tea in a 500-ml glass bottle in the fridge for a maximum of 1 week. Do not use it if mould forms.

Mix an equal part of the tea with warm spring water at each dosing: small dog 20 mls of tea (plus 20 mls spring water), medium 30 mls tea (plus 30 mls spring water), large 40 mls (plus 40 mls spring water) and give to dog on an empty stomach.

Garlic (*Allium sativum*)

Daily garlic supplementation is a good idea. This herb supports the body in ways no other herb does. It acts on bacteria, viruses and internal parasites. It can support the development of natural bacteria while killing disease-causing bacteria. It can be used for chronic bronchitis, coughs, in the treatment of ringworm, fevers and skin conditions. It can be used for diabetes (garlic increases the half-life of insulin and improves circulation), for cardiovascular disease (it improves blood viscosity and decreases platelet aggregation), and in the prevention of cancer.[115] It can be used anywhere immune support is required, and as a powerful antioxidant. It combines very well with echinacea for the treatment of infections.

Caution: Care must be taken to not overdose with garlic as it can cause destruction of red blood cells and anaemia.

Ginger (*Zingiber officinale*)

Ginger has many uses. It stimulates peripheral circulation so may be useful as an adjunctive treatment for diabetes, and for slow healing wounds as well as older dogs who are inactive to help stimulate movement of blood and to help warm the body. It eases spasms and can be used for the treatment of flatulence and colic as well as fibrositis and muscle sprains. Ginger has analgesic properties and is beneficial for arthritis. It can be used as a general tonic for the skin as well as the digestive system, respiratory system and circulatory system. It is a powerful antioxidant and it relieves nausea caused by motion sickness so is useful for travelling.

A simple infusion can be made from 1–2 slices of ginger root, pour 1 cup of boiling water over it and allow to steep for 20 minutes. Give 1/2 to1 ml by mouth.

Gingko (*Gingko biloba*)

Gingko has an affinity for blood vessels: it increases the flow of blood to deprived areas and improvement begins immediately. It is also said to be valuable in preventing blood clots. It has an affinity for nervous and glandular tissues as well as increasing blood flow to the brain. It is useful for deafness in old dogs, central nervous system problems, inner ear disease, head tilt, blindness, following stroke-type symptoms and conditions associated with seizures, dementia and ageing. It acts as potent antioxidant and anti-ageing agent.

Use one tablet (60 mg containing 25 per cent flavoglycosides) for a large dog daily for the first week or until improvement then halve the dose.

Caution: Do not use in pregnancy or lactation for long periods of time in high doses. Adverse reactions can include mild digestive upsets, skin rash and allergy.

Hawthorn (*Crataegus oxyacantha*)

Hawthorn is one of the best herbs for the heart and circulation. It may be safely used in conjunction with heart medications provided it is under veterinary supervision. It is synergistic with digitalis medications and combines well with garlic and dandelion for chronic heart disease. It can be used long term.

A suggested dose for a large dog is 5 drops of tincture in 25 mls of water; give 12 drops of this twice daily.

Liquorice (*Glycyrrhiza glabra*)

Liquorice has a marked effect on the endocrine or glandular system of the body. It contains actives that resemble the natural steroids of the body. It increases the half-life of cortisol. Therefore it can be used as an alternative to, or in conjunction with corticosteroids. However, unlike corticosteroids, liquorice spares the adrenal glands and supports the immune system.

It can be used for bronchitis and coughs, chronic skin conditions, Addison's disease, and long-term cystitis. It helps to protect the liver from toxins so can be used in conjunction with liver-toxic drugs. It is also very palatable and most dogs like the taste. De-glycyrrhizinated (DGL) liquorice helps restore damaged intestinal lining. It increases the life span of intestinal cells and improves mucosal blood flow.[116] It is useful for both inflammatory bowel disease and also chronic constipation. It can be used alongside non-steroidal anti-inflammatory drugs but if used long-term liquorice should be combined with dandelion, or supplemented with potassium.

Nettle (*Urtica dioica; Urtica urens*)

Touching the fresh leaves of the nettle plant causes blistering of the skin. The herbal tincture, however, can be used for many conditions including bladder and urinary tract infections, an eye wash, and for skin disorders where the skin is very red, hot and weeping (applied externally). It can also be used for eczema and for long-term use against allergies and for arthritis. It has nutritive value as a source of iron.

Oak Bark (*Quercus robur*)

Oak bark is a good herb for acute diarrhoea and for dogs with chronic diarrhoea. German Shepherds or other breeds with pancreatic insufficiency might benefit from this herb (along with nettles). It is also useful for puppies with loose, pasty stools, It can be given for up to 6 months, 3 drops of tincture in 15 mls of water three times daily for weak individuals, or 0.5 ml of tincture three times daily for stronger animals.

Panex ginseng

Ginseng is traditionally used as a general tonic to promote health and a long life. It is useful in dogs that are particularly stressed or recovering from disease or surgery. It is also considered protective against some of the side-effects of chemotherapy and radiation, so is a useful adjunct in the treatment of cancer. It helps to protect the heart and improves resistance to infection, so is useful for older dogs as a tonic (in lower doses). It may also be helpful in improving fertility (increases mating behaviour, ovulation and sperm activity). Ginseng can be combined with liquorice and used as an anti-inflammatory. It may be a useful herb to use in diabetics (as it can lower blood glucose), cancer (as it has some anti-tumor properties) and as a tonic for sluggish dogs.

Caution: It should not be used where there are acute infections or high blood pressure.

Peppermint (*Mentha piperita*)

Peppermint is a herb with an affinity for the digestive system. It relaxes the abdomen, relieves flatulence, stimulates digestive juices, helps restore appetite, helps relieve colic and has a mild anaesthetic action that helps allay nausea and the desire to vomit. It may be used to help minimise travel sickness, aid in the treatment of ulcerative colitis and may also help ease anxiety in some dogs. A mild infusion of peppermint tea can be used.

Pumpkin (*Cucurbita pepo*)

Pumpkin seeds are a traditional remedy for tapeworm. The effect is a mechanical one. Use ripe fresh seeds about 60 grams, and crush them, add them to oat gruel and honey. Three doses a week apart may help; however, there are very effective worming preparations, which will be much easier and far more effective than pumpkin seeds. Flea control is also vital, as fleas are a source of tapeworm infection.

Red Clover (*Trifolium pratense*)

Red clover has demonstrated some anti-cancer activity in animals, and may be beneficial in the treatment of cancer. It is indicated when there is a single hard swollen gland such as along the mammary chain, in the axilla (armpit), groin or popliteals (the lymph nodes behind the knees). It can also be beneficial in chronic skin conditions.

Caution: Red clover contains cumerin, which is blood thinning.

Red Raspberry (*Rubus idaeus*)

Red raspberry has a long tradition of use in pregnancy as the herb strengthens and tones the uterus during labour. The herb aids in whelping by strengthening contractions and reducing the risk of haemorrhage. Red raspberry can also be used as a skin and eye wash, by making an infusion and then filtering it. This herb is also indicated for chronic diarrhoea.

Caution: Do not use fresh leaves, as they are temporarily toxic when they first wilt. Due to its ability to increase uterine tone it should only be used during labour and after delivery.

Saw Palmetto Berries (*Serenoa repens*)

Saw palmetto is a herb that tones and strengthens the male reproductive system.

It can prevent the growth of prostate cells, which may make it useful in benign prostate enlargement. It is considered to be a general tonic, and is good for debilitated dogs. It may also be useful for infections of the genitourinary tract when combined with hydrangea. It may take 4 to 6 weeks to be effective.

Siberian Ginseng (*Eleutherococcus senticosus*)

Siberian ginseng may be used to increase stamina in the face of stress and abnormal demands such as in agility/obedience, sled or performance events. It may also benefit dogs that are exhausted, depressed or debilitated.

Dose
25-kilogram dog: 0.2 grams three times daily.

Skullcap (*Scutellaria laterifolia*)

Skullcap helps relax nervous tension and has a calming effect on excitable dogs. It may be useful for dogs suffering from epilepsy, seizures, restlessness and spinal problems. It combines well with valerian.

Caution: Do not use in liver disease (note that liver enzymes are often elevated with phenobarbitone treatment for epilepsy).

Slippery Elm (*Ulmus fulva*)

Slippery elm can be used for problems of the digestive system, in particular constipation, diarrhoea and colitis. It can be made into a paste and applied to wounds, abscesses, bites and mild burns. Slippery elm combines well with red clover, burdock and yellow dock.

Slippery elm comes in a powdered form that is easy to use. It can be added to food, or mixed with a little broth.

St John's Wort (*Hypericum perforatum*)

St John's wort is now famous as an antidepressant remedy in people. It is taught as a poisonous plant in veterinary school but has many uses as a herbal remedy. It can be beneficial for serious injuries involving nerves, as well as for pain such as spinal pain or any long-standing pain due to slipped spinal discs or arthritis. It is excellent where there are injuries with a rich supply of nerves such as the toes, tail and dewclaws. It is a good remedy for animal bites, along with appropriate antibiotics if necessary. It may be used externally for minor wounds and burns and for clipper rash as a diluted tincture. It may be used where there are ear problems that are red and sore but there is no discharge, here it combines well with calendula. And as for people, it is a good anti-depressant for dogs.

St Mary's Thistle, Milk Thistle (*Silybum marianum*)

St Mary's thistle or milk thistle is an excellent herb that has many uses. It is an excellent promoter of milk secretion and is safe to use in lactation. One of the actives is silymarin, which has an affinity for the liver. It helps in the regeneration of liver cells where it improves the flow of bile from the liver. However, if excessive doses are used it can cause loose stools due to the increase in bile it produces. It is a useful herb to aid in the regeneration, protection and detoxification of the liver, particularly following poisoning, liver-toxic drug or chemical use. It is useful in the treatment of chronic skin disease especially allergic dermatitis, any liver disease, kidney, and spleen or bladder problems.

It can be used as an adjunct in the treatment of leptospirosis, parvovirus, hepatitis, jaundice, pancreatitis, and recovery from drug use or following anaesthesia.

Caution: St Mary's thistle may increase liver enzymes if there is no ongoing stress to liver and it may slow liver functions if used excessively.

Thyme (*Thymus vulgaris*)

Thyme is a good herb for dry coughs and kennel cough and combines well with rosemary. The tincture can also be used as a disinfectant for the mouth and gums by using the diluted tincture on a swab.

Valerian (*Valeriana officinalis*)

Valerian has actives which act as temporary nerve and muscle relaxants so is quite sedative in its effect. It is useful therefore for calming nervous and excitable dogs. It also promotes sleep and may reduce pain. It may be beneficial for dogs with epilepsy, or dogs with muscle tremors, and to help curb aggression (in conjunction with behaviour modification). The sedative effect can be variable but as a guide give 0.25 to 1 ml diluted with equal parts of water 30 minutes before the sedative effect is observed. It combines well with skullcap.

Caution: Too much valerian may have the opposite effect and be stimulating in large doses. It is very bitter and dogs may drool after dosing. Be careful if the dog has liver disease. Valerian should not be given in large doses for a long period of time as it may cause lethargy.

Yellow Dock (*Rumex crispus*)

Yellow dock is considered a 'blood cleanser' and combines well with dandelion, burdock for chronic skin disease, and cleavers. It is a traditional treatment for heavy metal toxicity such as lead poisoning. It is also useful in the treatment of anaemia and constipation.

Caution: Yellow dock may cause digestive upsets if used too long and may also deplete vitamin B1.

Acupuncture

Acupuncture is a technique of using very fine needles that pierce the skin at special points in order to treat or prevent disease. It is perhaps one of the oldest forms of medicine in the world, and along with herbal medicine probably one of the oldest forms of veterinary medicine in the world. Although dogs have only recently been treated with acupuncture, in China, horses, cows and pigs have been treated for well over 3000 years.[117]

Acupuncture is part of a whole system of Traditional Chinese Medicine (TCM), which involves diet, Chinese herbs, massage, breathing and other techniques. TCM is used to diagnose, prevent and treat disease, and depends on the principle that the body always tries to balance and regulate itself. TCM therefore acts to support the body to overcome any imbalances that cause disease. Acupuncture helps stimulate energy flow through the body and also reduces pain and inflammation to help balance bodily functioning.

Jake

Jake is a 14-year-old Collie, who has suffered from arthritis for more than four years. Over time he became a lot worse, despite regular treatment with anti-inflammatory medication. From a conventional viewpoint, Jake's arthritis was diagnosed from his history, clinical symptoms and radiographs. These are also important tools for the veterinary acupuncturist. A veterinary acupuncturist will also check his smell, listen to his bark or growl, examine the tongue colour and coating, his pulse and specific acupuncture points. All these give clues to the underlying imbalances in the body.

Disease in TCM is believed to have external and internal causes. There are the external damaging causes such as wind, cold, fire, summer heat and dampness. These conditions can influence the body's resistance to disease, for example heat causes fever, dampness causes fluid swelling. There are internal causes that recognise the role that emotional well-being has to play on health. These include joy, anger, anxiety, sadness, fear and fright and these become important if they are strongly or frequently expressed. And there are other causes including dietary irregularities, fatigue (over-exertion or inactivity), trauma and parasites.[118]

In Jake's case his arthritis was due to chronic changes to the bone and cartilage of the joints and 'invasion of cold', he had what TCM calls 'Bi Syndrome'. For Jake, the winter months were the hardest, when he would become very stiff and sore. Based on this Eastern diagnosis and the information gleaned using regular veterinary techniques, specific acupuncture points were selected and fine needles inserted. These points helped to reduce pain and improve mobility by removing some of the 'cold' from his body. After a series of five acupuncture treatments Jake was clearly improved, regaining mobility, more normal flexion and extension of joints and more importantly he was active and seemed happier.

One of the most common concerns that people have about acupuncture is the 'ouch' factor. However, the needles used for acupuncture are very different from regular needles used for injections. They are incredibly fine and they have a round tip so it separates the skin rather than cutting through it. Most people experience a simple pricking sensation only, and some people even enjoy the sensation. What about dogs? Dogs can be a little apprehensive at first but they very quickly relax, becoming calm and even falling asleep. Most dogs come back the next time, quite content to stand and be treated.

So how does acupuncture work?

Interestingly the acupuncture points on the body are quite different from the skin surrounding them. On the microscopic level there is an increase in the nerve endings, tiny blood and lymph vessels, and specialised cells associated with inflammation.[119] These points also have a lowered electrical resistance, which is measurable, and this resistance actually changes with time of day, illness, body temperature and pressure. So these acupuncture points are not random spots on the body, but specialised points. They are linked in channels or lines across and through the body. The points on the skin are also linked to structures and organs inside the body. Acupuncture can therefore affect all the major processes in the body.

For example there is a point called Stomach 36, located just below the stifle (knee) in the dog. This point relieves nausea and vomiting, and has been shown in research to increase the number of circulating white blood cells in the body,[120] thereby improving immunity. Acupuncture has also been shown to stimulate the release of endorphins[121] (these are the same hormones that produce a 'high' or sense of well-being) as well as other pain relieving, anti-inflammatory hormones.

From an energy perspective it is likely (though not proven) that acupuncture also works by changing the electrical resistance of the acupuncture points, facilitating the flow of electromagnetic energy through the body. TCM views disease as a stagnation or blockage of the vital life force called Qi (pronounced chee), and so acupuncture serves to regulate the flow of Qi and remove blockages from the body.

Precautions for Acupuncture

Acupuncture is a very safe form of therapy if practised correctly and by a trained veterinary acupuncturist. The International Veterinary Acupuncture Society (IVAS) certifies trained veterinarians. You can contact a veterinary acupuncturist through your own vet, the Veterinary Acupuncture Association or Veterinary Association in your area.

- It is very important that a full veterinary check-up and correct diagnosis is completed before acupuncture referral or treatment. Because acupuncture relieves pain and can alter the symptoms, a diagnosis has to be made in the first place otherwise acupuncture may simply mask a more serious problem.
- It is important that your acupuncturist is also a veterinarian, or if not, fully trained in animal anatomy so that vital organs are not accidentally punctured or other structures damaged.
- Acupuncture diminishes pain, and your dog will feel better; it is important to follow your veterinarian's advice concerning rest and activity, as pain is 'nature's' way of slowing a dog down so that he may rest and heal. Your dog may do more damage if he is running around afterwards.
- Your dog should be treated on an empty stomach or light meal only.
- Acupuncture should be avoided if your dog is pregnant.
- Do not plan to bath your dog, immediately before or after acupuncture treatment.
- It is best not to treat a dog that is extremely anxious, aggressive or frightened. Your veterinary acupuncturist may need to sedate your dog first.
- Your veterinary acupuncturist will need to know whether your dog has been given any injections or is being treated with atropine, narcotics or corticosteroids such as prednisolone, as these can affect the acupuncture treatment.
- Your dog should not be treated if he has a clotting or bleeding disorder.
- Your veterinary acupuncturist may not treat your dog if there is a nasty skin infection or local skin tumours where the needles may carry the infection or growth deeper.
- If needle acupuncture cannot be performed, laser acupuncture is another (less potent) alternative.

What can acupuncture be used for?

Traditional Chinese Medicine and Acupuncture are a complete medical system in their own right. Theoretically TCM can be used to both diagnose and treat most conditions that Western medicine treats. However, like many forms of medicine, acupuncture is best suited to some conditions more than others. In addition acupuncture can be used on its own, or in combination with conventional medicine and surgery. It might also be used where medications are not effectively helping or when the dog is suffering side-effects from treatment.

Some of the Major Indications

Some of the major indications[122] include the following:

Muscle and Bone Problems

Acupuncture is perhaps best known for its use in pain relief. It can be used as primary treatment, or in conjunction with conventional treatment. It may be used where conventional treatment is not effective, or the side-effects are too great, or where the dog is at too great a risk for surgery or anaesthetic. Acupuncture helps to relieve pain, reduce muscular spasms, improve circulation, reduce swelling and improve healing. Acupuncture can be used to treat:

- hip dysplasia
- Osteochondritis dissecans (OCD)
- arthritis in the stifle, hock, carpus (wrist), shoulders, hips and elbows
- lameness due to pain or injury
- chronic lameness due to trigger points,[123] which are small muscle spasms, which can resemble the symptoms of arthritis
- muscle and ligament injuries

Nervous System and Spinal Problems

Dogs with disease that affects their spinal cord such as disc protrusions causing paralysis, partial paralysis or severe pain may benefit from acupuncture. Depending on the type of problem, acupuncture may offer a viable alternative to surgery, depending on how long the problem has been there. Other conditions that acupuncture may benefit include:

- degenerative myelopathy
- spondylitis
- *Cauda equina* syndrome
- spinal instabilities
- nerve injuries
- epilepsy
- vestibular syndrome
- deafness (particularly in old dogs)

Skin Disorders

Skin disorders that are poorly responsive to conventional treatment such as some allergies, chronic itching, lick granulomas on dogs' legs, and skin disease due to disorders of the immune system or endocrine system may benefit from acupuncture. Acupuncture can also be used in conjunction with other therapies for skin disorders.

Digestive Tract Disorders

Scientific studies have shown that acupuncture has some distinct effects on the digestive tract.[124] Besides pain relief, acupuncture normalises the movement in the gut and the secretions of digestive juices as well as improving blood flow. Sudden diarrhoea and vomiting can be assisted with acupuncture. Chronic diarrhoea, chronic vomiting, constipation, poor appetite and problems of the oesophagus (food pipe) including megaoesphagus can be improved with acupuncture.

Heart Disorders

Acupuncture has one of its greatest benefits in the treatment of shock, unconsciousness, or cardiac arrest. In an emergency you can stimulate a special point midway along the groove between the nose and the upper lip of the dog. This is Governing Vessel 26, a very powerful point that can be used to revive puppies, or dogs of any age. The point can be stimulated with the nail, a pen tip or sharp needle, depending on what you have in the emergency situation, until you can reach a vet.

Heart failure can be improved with acupuncture along with conventional drugs such as diuretics and beta-blocker medications. The condition needs to be monitored very carefully when acupuncture is used, as the dosages of normal drugs usually need to be reduced as the condition responds. Heart rhythm problems may also benefit from acupuncture as acupuncture can have a direct effect on regulating the heartbeat.

Behavioural Problems

One of the less known areas where acupuncture can help is in the treatment of behavioural disorders. In Chinese medicine, behavioural problems are associated with excessive emotion and what are called 'Shen disturbances'. By treating specific points and harmonising the body, acupuncture can assist in the treatment of fear, aggression, grief, shyness, show ring nervousness, phobias, anxiety and depression.

Immune Disorders

Acupuncture has proven anti-inflammatory and immune stimulating effects.[125] Certain points will also reduce allergy and stimulate different parts of the immune system. This is one of the reasons why dogs, particularly older dogs, benefit from regular 'tune-ups' of acupuncture to help keep them healthy. Any animal with an infection will benefit from acupuncture, by reducing the time it takes to recover. Any dog that is prone to infections can also receive preventive treatments to reduce the severity and number of times the dog gets sick.

Cancer

Acupuncture is a good adjunctive treatment for dogs undergoing chemotherapy or other treatments for cancer. It helps reduce nausea, improves the sense of well-being, and regulates the immune system (especially when it is impaired with certain drugs used in cancer treatment). It may also be used to treat small growths, or where surgery and chemotherapy are not viable options due to age, poor prognosis, expense or other reasons.

Reproduction

Acupuncture can be used in female dogs to help lack of cycling, irregular heat cycles, cystic ovaries and false pregnancies. It can also be used during labour and to help stimulate lactation. In male dogs acupuncture can help increase sperm counts, and reduce any inflammation of the testicles or prostate gland.

Respiratory Disorders

Acupuncture is helpful in the treatment of a number of respiratory problems. Chronic sinusitis, coughing, bronchitis, inflammation of the throat and nose, and pneumonia can all be improved, either in conjunction with other forms of treatment or as a primary therapy.

Urinary Tract Problems

Incontinence of bitches and older dogs can be helped with acupuncture, as can the problem that some puppies have when they pee when they are excited or fearful. Other bladder problems such as difficulty urinating, cystitis and bladder stones can also be assisted with acupuncture. Acupuncture is an excellent adjunct for dogs with kidney failure because it improves the appetite, reduces nausea, reduces pain and helps regulate kidney function.

Eyes and Ears

Acupuncture can be used for a number of eye conditions including dry eye and chronic conjunctivitis. It can also be useful to alleviate age-related deafness in older dogs.

What are the acupuncture treatments like?

There are several different ways to stimulate acupuncture points. Usually needles are inserted and left for 10 minutes up to half an hour. Sometimes veterinarians will inject solutions into the acupuncture points or use a Chinese herb called moxa to bring warmth into the area by heating the acupuncture point. Sometimes lasers are used to stimulate the points. If the problem is an acute, treatments may be required every couple of days until the desired result is seen.

For more chronic conditions there are usually a couple of treatments 1 to 2 times a week, or weekly for a few weeks, followed by regular 'top ups' which might be monthly or six monthly or as needed.

What can you expect?

If the problem is a recent one, a single acupuncture treatment should stimulate a quick response, although follow up treatments may be necessary to restore health fully. If the problem has been a long-standing one, sometimes there is no apparent change initially. A second treatment may show an improvement for three or four days, then the effect seems to wane, but follow up treatments seem to extend the effect more and more each time until the condition resolves. Occasionally the symptoms may actually appear to be worse for 12 to 24 hours, or alternatively your dog may simply sleep restfully for 12 to 24 hours. There is often a change in the dog's temperament; they can seem brighter and more relaxed. Your veterinarian might also show you some points on your dog's body that you can gently massage at home to help enhance the acupuncture treatment. Whatever happens, you should keep your veterinarian informed of your dog's response. It is also important not to give up too early with treatments. Remember acupuncture is stimulating the body's own internal healing mechanisms, sometimes it takes a while for it to wake up and start working!

How successful is acupuncture?

In the hands of a qualified acupuncturist, treatment will usually bring about a marked improvement if not recovery for many complaints. But expectations of how successful a course of treatments will be should be discussed with your veterinary acupuncturist before beginning. This will depend upon your dog's condition, concurrent treatments, the number and frequency of treatments and your dog's innate ability to respond. By discussing the likely outcomes with your veterinarian you should plan a course of treatments, and a point at which you may choose not to continue, or the type of result that you want. For example this may be simply pain relief in an older dog, or full recovery in a younger dog. Importantly acupuncture is a safe alternative or adjunctive therapy to drugs and surgery. However, it does not cure everything. More and more veterinarians are becoming qualified to use this time-tested therapy, and more and more dogs will benefit from pain free lives.

Acupressure

Your veterinary acupuncturist can show you some major points to treat at home between acupuncture treatments. Acupressure is the application of finger or thumb pressure to the acupuncture points. While the stimulation is not as direct as needle acupuncture it can be a gentle and beneficial adjunct to therapy.

To stimulate an acupuncture point you need to find a quiet space, where you and your dog can relax. Start by gently stroking him and talking in a low, calm voice to him. Locate the point you wish to work on. Keep one hand flat on your dog, use the thumb of the other to apply firm pressure to the point. Keep the thumb there for five seconds; you can gradually increase the pressure if your dog is relaxed with it. Alternatively you can make slow, small circles with your thumb over the point. Remember to breathe slowly and keep relaxed during the treatment.

Acupressure can be done daily or as directed by your vet. It should be not be used if your dog is pregnant, has just been fed, is very tired, is very anxious or resents touch. It should only be used under the guidance of a veterinary acupuncturist.

The following points are good ones to practise on, on healthy dogs once weekly to maintain health. Remember to stimulate for only a short time, as over stimulation can be draining for some dogs.

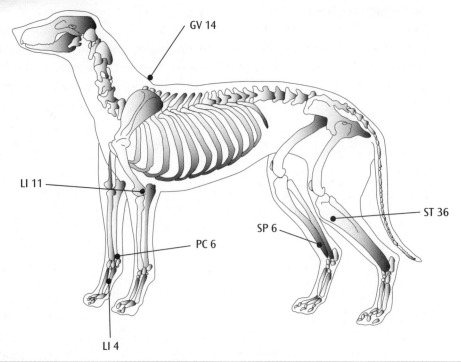

Figure 1. Some important dog acupuncture points

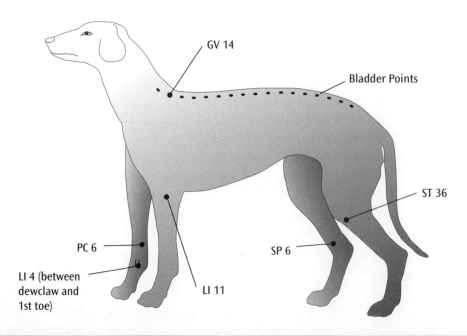

Figure 2. Acupressure points to use between acupuncture treatments

LI 4 Large Intestine 4

This point is located between the dewclaw of the front leg and the first toe. If your dog is missing a dewclaw it will be at the top of the first toe on the side of the toe facing the other front leg. This is an excellent point for stimulating the immune system, for pain relief anywhere in the body, for skin problems, reducing fever and is a major point on the body for conditions affecting the head, neck and mouth.

LI 11 Large Intestine 11

If you bend your arm you will find this point at the end of the elbow crease fold. You may need to bend your dog's front leg to find this point. When you bend his elbow you will find the point at the end of his elbow crease too. Once you have found it, you can keep your thumb on it, and allow the leg to relax. This is a major point for regulating the immune system, for removing heat from the body, it is a good point for pain in the front leg, and is useful for relieving pain and discomfort associated with conditions of the abdomen including the large intestine. It can be used for allergies, skin problems and glandular problems.

PC 6 Pericardium 6

This point is located in people on the underside of your wrist, about an inch and a half from the crease on your wrist, right in the midline. Your other thumb will seem to fall naturally into a depression here. In your dog it can be found on the inside of his front leg, above the crease where his paw begins, above and almost in line with his dewclaw. This point is very good for calming dogs with behavioural problems and is a major point for the chest and abdomen so is also beneficial in heart problems, nausea and upset stomachs.

ST 36 Stomach 36

In dogs this point is located below the knee (stifle) in the top one-fifth of the lower leg, in a depression just beside the shin bone (tibia) towards the outside of the leg. It is a major point of the body and can be useful in digestive tract problems, for stimulating the immune system, for pain control and as a regulator of the hormonal system.

Bladder points

Gentle pressure with both thumbs either side of the spine, running down the back will gently stimulate the Bladder meridian and help tone the major organs of the body. If there are sensitive areas or your dog experiences discomfort you should seek advice as this could indicate early problems with some organ of the body or the spine.

SP 6 Spleen 6

This point is located at the top of the bottom one-fifth of the dog's inside back leg, above the ankle and behind the tibia or leg bone. It is a major point for the digestive tract, urinary and reproductive tract, and is important for skin disorders, allergies, liver, kidney, pancreas problems as well as a good point for older animals.

GV 14 Governing Vessel 14

This point is found on the back, on the midline, in front of and between the shoulder blades. You should not be able to feel the spine under your thumb here, as there is a space between the cervical (neck) spine and the back (thoracic) spine. This is a very good point for enhancing the immune system, for chest conditions, and fever.

These are just a few of the hundreds of points on the body that can help maintain your dog's health.

Bach Flower Remedies

The Bach Flower Remedies are based on the research and findings of an English doctor, Dr Edward Bach. Dr Bach was a medical pioneer in the early 1900s, who became aware of the link between stress, emotions and illness. He was also a specialist in the study of bacteria, and in particular the role of bacteria and chronic disease. Dr Bach sought to find a simple, safe way to restore harmony in the diseased body through emotional wellness. In his search, he discovered properties of flowers, trees and bushes that provided him with the remedies he was looking for.

Since his discovery many more flower essences have been discovered around the world, including FES (in California) and Australian Bush Flower Essences. Other essences have also been developed from gems, shells and other materials. Flower essences, while derived from plants, are not herbal remedies because they do not contain enough plant material. They are prepared by infusing the flowers in spring water and then the liquid is filtered and a small amount of brandy is added as a preservative.

So how do they work? Essences are thought to work through the body's energy system and may work in a similar way to homeopathy and acupuncture. Dr Bach proposed that the remedies work by the transfer of 'life force energy' from the plant to the patient's 'vital force'. They are usually considered a form of 'energy' medicine acting on the emotional and spiritual levels of the body. Use of the essences alters the emotional or mental state in a subtle way. They can also help healing due to the connection between emotional and physical well-being.

This connection is based on Dr Bach's idea that negative emotional states can suppress the healing process. This is interesting because in the last decade there has been a great deal of interest in 'psychoneuroimmunology' or the study of the connection of the mind and its influence on disease. Connections between the immune, nervous system and endocrine (hormonal) system seem to support this concept.

So do dogs have emotional states that can influence their health? Well you can probably answer that yourself. We know many dogs have behavioural problems and we can even describe the personalities of our dogs. Many dogs suffer from stress either because of their temperament, because they haven't been socialised appropriately as puppies, or because their environment is stressful, especially when their owners are stressed too. We know that stress can reduce our immunity, so it is not unreasonable to accept that stress and emotional stress can influence the health of our dogs.

Even though Dr Bach developed his flower essences for people, they have been used in dogs for over fifty years. There are currently no scientific studies to support their use, but many owners observe positive changes in their dogs with use of these non-toxic, gentle remedies. Each Bach Flower Remedy helps deal with specific states of mind. These states include fear, terror, mental torture or worry, indecision, indifference or boredom, doubt or discouragement, over-concern, weakness, self-distrust, impatience, over-enthusiasm and pride or aloofness.

The difficulty with using Bach Flower Essences or other flower essences in dogs is that we can't ask how the dog is feeling. We have to rely on our judgment and observations and sometimes intuition to find the appropriate remedies.

The Bach Flowers are gentle and non-toxic. They can be used alone or to enhance any form of medicine without interference. They can work surprisingly quickly, sometimes with a single use. The more common observation though, is a gradual change-over two to four weeks of use, and sometimes longer. It is important to note that Bach Flower essences should not replace veterinary care, instead they should be considered in the total approach to the health and well-being of your dog.

Guidelines

One of the exciting aspects of Bach Flowers is that they are readily available and safe to use. The remedies are purchased as a stock bottle, which contains the concentrated essence.

Essences are generally diluted before use although they can be given straight from the bottle in emergencies. Stock strength essences contain about $\frac{2}{3}$ brandy, which most dogs hate. So usually 2-6 drops of the stock is diluted in spring water, with about $\frac{1}{4}$ brandy as a natural preservative. If the remedy is to be used in one week, it does not need added brandy.

Preparation

Preparation of Bach Flower Remedies for your dog:
- The remedies are selected and prepared either singularly or in combination (up to six remedies can be mixed together).
- 2–6 drops are taken directly from each stock bottle.
- When preparing and giving the remedies it is important not to touch the tip of the dropper to avoid contamination.

- Protect the remedies from computers, microwaves and electrical power points. The remedies are 'energy' or 'vibrational' medicines and may be affected by other forms of energy.
- To prepare a Bach Flower Remedy place 2–6 drops of each selected essence (or 4 drops of Rescue Remedy) into a 1-oz or 25-ml bottle. Fill the bottle ¾ of the way with spring water and then add brandy, vodka or organic vinegar to fill (so that water to alcohol is 3 parts to 1 part). This dilution bottle should be thumped against the palm of one hand to thoroughly mix the remedies.
- The dilution bottle should be shaken before each dose.
- The remedy is then given by mouth or applied to the ears or head area. It can also be diluted into a spray bottle and sprayed into a room.

Caution: While the remedies are safe and non-toxic, if symptoms worsen, stop using the remedy. Some animals may be affected by the alcohol or preservative. When your dog has settled, you can repeat the dosage by applying the remedy to the top of the head or between the shoulders rather than by mouth.

Dosage

Dosage depends on the pet's individual response. Try 3–4 drops every 10 to 15 minutes in emergency situations and 3–4drops one to four times daily depending on how severe the problem is. Importantly there is no wrong way to give the remedies, and it is not necessary to be accurate with counting the drops. If you choose the wrong remedy there are no side-effects or toxicities and pets cannot be overdosed. The only error is not selecting the right remedy and it not working at all.

Dogs can be given drops directly into mouth either at the corner of the lips or on the tongue. Wash the dropper if it touches the mouth. The drops can be added to drinking water (6 to 8 drops) each day. Drops can also be applied to the skin and ears with equal success, and if necessary mixed in with the food (although this is not preferable). A dropperful can be added to the bath water, as soaking in an essence can be beneficial. A dropperful can also be added to a mister or spray pack so that a kennel, room, cage or dog can be sprayed with the remedy.

Choosing the Remedies

Perhaps the easiest way to choose remedies is to firstly familarise yourself with the different essences that are available and see how closely they fit the description of your dog. The following descriptions are derived from human behaviours and emotions that are matched to remedies and are therefore highly anthropomorphic. You should select the most appropriate remedy, but there may be more than one that matches your dog's circumstances or behaviour. You can select up to six remedies, although the fewer the better. You can count 'Rescue Remedy' as one essence, even though it consists of five separate flower essences.

Remember Bach Flower essences work best in conjunction with appropriate behavioural modification advice from your veterinarian or behavioural advisor.

Rescue Remedy

Rescue Remedy is perhaps the most well known Bach Flower Remedy, consisting of five flower essences: cherry plum, clematis, impatiens, rock rose and star of Bethlehem. It is one of the most useful remedies as it can be used in any first aid situation, emergency, trauma or stressful situation. It can be given every five to ten minutes as necessary.

Agrimony

An agrimony dog appears to be brave, but is in fact highly sensitive and deeply affected by what is going on around him. This is especially so if there is conflict or hostility between his humans. He will try to intervene, wagging his tail but really unsure of himself. He may be restless, and prefers company rather than being alone. He may be the type of dog that doesn't show pain, even though he is injured. He may be susceptible to developing vomiting or diarrhoea if upset, or urinary incontinence if older. He may also be prone to skin problems, parasites, arthritis or heart disease. This remedy is also useful during recuperation following surgery or wound healing.

Aspen

Aspen is a remedy for fear, where the cause is unknown or vague. This dog may be afraid of new things and unfamiliar experiences. She may be anxious and apprehensive or become nervous for no particular reason. This remedy is useful before trips to the vet, or when a storm and thunder is expected. Dogs that suffer separation anxiety when left alone may benefit from this remedy, as may dogs with kidney and bladder problems.

Beech

Beech is for the dog that is critical, fussy and intolerant. He may be fine with his own person, but may show tension or aggression towards other people or other dogs. He is the dog who patrols the front yard, keeping an eye on all who pass by, giving them a snarl and a bark 'keep away'. He might be the sort of dog that really resents the introduction of a new pup into the household. Territorial aggression may benefit from Beech. Dogs who suffer allergies (intolerance) to pollens, grasses, insects and foods or who are intolerant to cold (arthritis worsens) or environmental change may also benefit from Beech. Dogs that are particularly fussy or picky eaters may also benefit.

Centaury

The centaury dog is the one who rolls over at your feet, wanting to please. She is generally quiet, shy, and even timid at times. She is the type of dog who will show her submission to other dogs she meets, by rolling over and crouching before them. She might also be the dog who urinates when she is afraid of other dogs. If she is a puppy she is the type who is easily pushed out of the way, unwilling to defend her position. This remedy is also useful for dogs when fighting an illness or injury.

Cerato

This remedy is useful for the dog that is difficult to train because he is easily distracted and/or he learns very slowly. When you go walking with him, he is likely to dawdle and run towards you, then perhaps change his mind as he is distracted by something else he smells. He may be the dog who is restless, underfoot and who vocalises for attention, but then is distracted. This remedy may also be useful for the dog that barks constantly for no apparent reason.

Cherry Plum

Cherry plum is one of the five flowers used in Rescue Remedy. This remedy is for dogs that lose control. The dog who hates been restrained and struggles furiously to be let go, or the dog who becomes aggressive or hysterical when he is scared, lifting his lips and snarling to warn you, even though he may be a nice dog normally. Fear aggression may benefit from this remedy. Dogs that are very aggressive and difficult to control may benefit from cherry plum but professional advice is absolutely essential for safety. Some dogs who chew their feet constantly, or that have lick granulomas may also benefit, as can dogs that have incontinence.

Chestnut Bud

Chestnut bud is a great remedy for training, obedience and breaking bad habits. The dog that is slow to learn from experience or keeps making the same mistakes or who repeats the same bad habit over and over again may benefit from Chestnut bud. It is a useful remedy to add to any blend for modifying behaviour in conjunction with conventional behavioural modification techniques.

Chicory

Chicory is for the possessive and jealous dog, the dog that is constantly underfoot or demanding attention. She wants to be either sitting in your lap, under your chair, or may have her head always touching you whenever she is able. She is likely to be over-protective towards family members, an excellent watchdog. She may try to dominate other pets in the family, and even family members if she is allowed. She is the sort of dog that will growl at other pets in the household and may even attack other pets.

Clematis

Clematis is one of the five flowers used in Rescue Remedy. It is especially useful when dogs are ungrounded or lethargic such as after surgery, following a shock or trauma, exhaustion, long whelping or period of illness. The remedy can help recovery from unconsciousness. The dog may be absent minded, or dreamy. Many old dogs benefit from this remedy. It is also useful for those dogs that have a very short attention span during training, similar to the effect of cerato. In this case though the dog is almost preoccupied in its own world and even indifferent. Dogs that have central nervous system disorders, poor balance (such as vestibular disease) or that may be senile may benefit from Clematis.

Crab-apple

Crab-apple is an excellent cleansing remedy. Dogs that have smelly skin, discharging wounds or incontinence, and dogs after poisoning, general anaesthetics, infections or rubbish eating, will benefit from this remedy. It can be used externally as well in baths, by simply adding a few drops to the water. It can also be used as a detoxifying remedy at the start of any program for the treatment of long-term chronic disease. This dog may seem to be ashamed (poor self-image), slinking around with her head held low, her tail between her legs, particularly if she has been reprimanded for something she has done, such as leaving a pool of urine on the floor if she is incontinent.

Elm

Elm is a remedy that might be useful when a dog is feeling overwhelmed. He may be attending a dog show, obedience trial or agility trial or grooming salon, where his preference is to sit under the table or behind you. He may also be ill at ease, but not afraid, when travelling, or visiting the vet. This is also useful for dogs that have seen their people in need of help, but they have been unable to assist. There is perhaps a feeling of inadequacy.

Gentian

Gentian is a good remedy for dogs that seem depressed or easily discouraged. Depression can arise from debilitation, following recovery from major surgery or trauma, if your dog loses his friend or is grieving either because of a death in the household, or somebody leaving the household. Sometimes dogs can also become depressed if left alone all day. Some older dogs may also be depressed especially if suffering from obesity or pain such as with chronic arthritis, bad teeth or back pain. Any setback may benefit from this remedy.

Gorse

Gorse is the remedy for despair and hopelessness. This may be a dog that is refusing to eat following sickness or surgery or loss of her person. She prefers to isolate herself or hide away from everything. She may be a dog that is taking much longer than normal to recover from an illness or surgery. She may be a dog that has lost her way and seems to have given up. Gorse will help to give added motivation and encouragement.

Heather

Heather is a useful remedy for separation anxiety, for the dog that constantly vocalises to gain your attention, and the dog that is constantly nudging you for attention. This is the dog that loves to be the center of attention. His behaviour may border on obsessive.

He may whine and cry when left alone or bark for attention. This dog is usually very friendly and is lonely by himself.

Holly

Holly is an appropriate remedy for aggression, particularly where the dog is suspicious, unsure of itself, appears angry or vengeful towards other dogs. This dog will attack to bite, but under different circumstances may be quite a pleasant dog. Holly can be given for most forms of aggression along with appropriate professional advice and behaviour modifying techniques.

Honeysuckle

Honeysuckle is useful when there are changed circumstances, when the dog is re-housed, its owner has left, the dog is kennelled or he is staying at the veterinary hospital. It is a remedy for homesickness. It helps calm anxiety and helps the dog to settle down.

Hornbeam

This is a remedy for tiredness and exhaustion. It may be after a competition or show, or a strenuous weekend walking and running. It is also useful for dogs that seem to be disinterested in playing with other dogs.

Impatiens

As the name implies, this remedy is for dogs that are impatient, irritable, constantly on the go. It is another of the five flowers used in Rescue Remedy, as it may help to alleviate discomfort and pain (caution, do not rely on this remedy as a cure for pain—seek veterinary attention). This dog is typically anxious, she will be fidgety around feeding time, or when trying to work with her. Dogs with nervous symptoms such as tremors, shaking, twitches or seizures may benefit from this remedy.

Larch

This is the remedy for any dog lacking in confidence. It may be unsure of itself in the show ring and competition or the type of dog that is very submissive; rolling over in front of people and other dogs or cowering if approached. Dogs which have been in shelters or that have been abused may benefit from this remedy.

Mimulus

Mimulus is suitable for dogs that are afraid of certain things. It may be another dog, a type of person, black socks, perhaps thunder or loud noises. This dog may urinate if frightened, or hide under the bed. Mimulus can be used with Aspen for the fearful dog. Sometimes when dogs are very afraid they may show aggression or signs of extreme timidity. Dogs that have been abused in the past and show fear aggression may also benefit from this remedy.

Mustard

Mustard is an appropriate remedy for a melancholy dog or a dog that is depressed on and off. It may be because of a chronic illness, or perhaps grief over a lost loved one. This dog prefers to be on his own. Mustard may also be useful where the dog is suffering hormone imbalances as an adjunct to treatment.

Oak

Oak is a remedy for struggling, where a dog might be injured or debilitated but still keeps on trying. She may be a dog that has lost the use of one leg for example, but she struggles to keep up all the same. She may be a dog who has suffered from malnutrition and is weak. Also dogs that compete in endurance trials or long competitions might benefit from this remedy. Oak may be used where there is physical exertion or stress.

Olive

Olive is one step further than oak; it is for complete and utter exhaustion. Like oak it can be used in endurance activities, extra long walks and runs, and for dogs that are lethargic and tired following trauma or physical stress. Where there has been a lot of stress the adrenal glands can become depleted, these dogs sometimes suffer from allergies. Olive may also be useful where a dog has lost some particular function such as the use of its bladder, or paralysis of the legs.

Pine

Pine is for the dog that assumes guilt—although guilt is hard to define in dogs. Often what is taken for guilt is submission because the dog has been reprimanded when his owner has been upset. This remedy may be appropriate where the dog tries to please even though he may be mistreated or rejected by someone in the house. He would be the type of dog that would be submissive and try very hard to please, only to be knocked back because he is all over someone.

Red Chestnut

This remedy is for dogs that show too much concern for others, either their people, their pups or other pets. They are often quite apprehensive about their owners, and while not overly protective, they will worry. This dog is the type to fret after her owner, perhaps suffering from mild separation anxiety. She might also wait at the door for her owner's return or if tied up outside a shop, pull on her lead to be nearer her owner.

Rock Rose

Rock rose is another essence in Rescue Remedy. It is a remedy for extreme terror, fright, panic or shock. Dogs that tremble and shake when they are frightened or that damage furniture or knock things over in a panic should be given this essence. It is useful in storms, thunder, lightning, or when loud noises are expected such as fireworks.

Rock Water

This remedy is the only one not derived from flowers. Nevertheless it is a remedy for stiffness, rigidity and inflexibility. Dogs that are very stubborn, that refuse to cooperate or who reject newcomers may benefit from this remedy. Dogs that have a very fixed pattern of behaviour, always taking the same path, or doing the same things at the same time might benefit from this. It might also be useful for dogs with arthritis and muscular stiffness.

Scleranthus

Scleranthus is the remedy for imbalance, and one-sided problems, be they mood changes, hormonal imbalances, neurological problems such as strokes, hind limb incoordination, head tilt or vestibular disease. It might also be used for travel sickness.

Star of Bethlehem

This remedy is another of the flowers used in Rescue Remedy, a comforter, used to aid in recovery from traumas experienced in the past that still influence behaviour and health now. This dog is quiet, perhaps withdrawn, resigned. Rescue dogs and adopted dogs may benefit, particularly if the past history is unknown. Dogs that suffer separation anxiety may also benefit from remedy.

Sweet Chestnut

Sweet chestnut is for extreme anguish, a dog that has reached its limits of endurance. It can be used in conjunction with conventional drugs used for pain control following particular surgery, or in conjunction with medicines, when the condition is known to be painful. Dogs that are absolutely exhausted physically and mentally may benefit from this remedy.

Vervain

Vervain dogs are highly-strung dogs. They tend to be hyperactive and exhausting for their people to be around. Constantly panting, moving, jumping, barking, on the go. This remedy may assist to calm these dogs. It may also be a useful remedy for dogs that have a tendency to escape or roam when given the opportunity.

Vine

Vine dogs can be very dominant. They may be very stubborn and strong-willed. They may even try to dominate their people. This remedy can be used along with appropriate behaviour management.

Walnut

Walnut is the remedy for change. It helps dogs to let go of one set of circumstances and more readily accept another. This might be when there is a new dog in the family, or family member, a move to a new home, travel, a new owner and following surgery. It can also be used in training to help the dog learn new things. Walnut helps protect from outside influences and may also be useful where there are allergies or skin irritations.

Water Violet

Water violet is an essence for aloof dogs. This is the type of dog who prefers to be alone, avoiding contact with strangers and other dogs. It is also an appropriate remedy for grief.

White Chestnut

White chestnut is a useful remedy for dogs which are always restless, that never seem to settle but they are not hyperactive. Older dogs that have disturbed sleep, getting up in the middle of the night to wake their people, or dogs that seem restless before competition or showing may benefit. This remedy helps settle them and encourages calm and better rest.

Wild Oat

Wild oat is a remedy to assist boredom. This dog might chew on things or destroy things from boredom. He may also be a dog that suffers separation anxiety by focusing on a particular piece of furniture or one door, chewing or scratching away.

Wild Rose

Wild rose is appropriate for dogs that are apathetic, such as dogs confined to small spaces; they have gone beyond boredom and have no zest. This remedy helps pep them up.

Willow

Willow is the remedy for resentment. While it is difficult to know if a dog is resentful it might be a useful remedy for dogs which seem to urinate or deposit a stool in an inappropriate place, or that may be destructive and seemingly willful.

Homeopathy

Homeopathy uses substances to treat a disease when the same substance, in a more concentrated form, could cause symptoms similar to those seen in the patient.[126] For example Apis mel is a homoeopathic remedy derived from the stinger of a bee. It is used to antidote bee stings or symptoms of localised pain, swelling and redness. Dr Samuel Hahnemann (a doctor and chemist) began the medical system of homeopathy in Germany in the early 1800s. Since then it has been used extensively by doctors and homoeopaths in many countries such as Germany, France, the UK and India,[127] it is only now becoming available for pets as more veterinarians are becoming qualified in the practice of homeopathy.

Dr Hahnemann came upon the idea that a substance that can produce symptoms in a normal person can cure them in a sick person. He used dilutions of plants, minerals and body substances and tested them on healthy volunteers to conduct what he termed 'provings'. These provings were the reactions to these substances, which were observed and recorded, including emotional responses, physical symptoms and even mental symptoms.[128] A compilation of the symptoms produced by these substances is a book called the *Materia Medica*.[129] More than 2000 such homeopathic remedies exist and are recorded in such books. Each homoeopathic remedy imitates the signs and symptoms of various illnesses. Just as these 'provings' provide a list of all the symptoms produced by each remedy, the best remedy to treat an illness is the one which exactly or most closely matches the whole range of symptoms that an individual shows. This is the homeopathic principle of 'like cures like'.[130]

The Principles of Homeopathy

Even though homeopathy is a medical system in its own right, it is based on several principles that are true for holistic medicine in general. It is based on the understanding that the body has the ability to heal itself, to regenerate cells and restore health. The body also has inherent weaknesses, genetic deficiencies, and constitutional characteristics and is vulnerable to factors such as inappropriate nutrition, the environment, medications, stress and ageing.

While the body constantly tries to maintain a state of balance, it may do so by expressing symptoms. Symptoms are a signal that the body is not at ease. It is trying to adapt to those factors that affect its vital force. Symptoms are also important defence mechanisms. For example diarrhoea is an attempt by the body to eliminate infectious, offending, toxic or parasitic agents. If we simply aim to remove the symptom but not the underlying imbalance, we may in fact drive the problem deeper because we are not addressing the true cause of the symptom. Homeopathy attempts to alter and strengthen the vital force so that the body's ability to fight the disease is stimulated and enhanced.

Likewise disease is seen as a progression from an imbalance. When a dog becomes ill, the first thing you notice is that he is quieter, his energy is reduced. He may then show some symptoms like sneezing, or perhaps diarrhoea. If he quickly recovers then his health is restored. However, if the imbalance continues, changes in the body tissues can occur. There may be chronic inflammation, or growths or degeneration. Because homeopathy works at the energetic level, the best responses to homoeopathic treatment occur early on, before the imbalance becomes disease. The deeper the disease, the longer it will take for the remedies to work.

Homeopathy depends upon a detailed look at the history of the dog's symptoms, throughout life, especially if the symptoms are chronic. It also depends upon careful observation and because dogs obviously cannot talk, a veterinarian is probably the best person to uncover subtle symptoms by palpating the body, listening to the heart and chest, and using other tests as necessary to get the whole picture. This is one reason why it is always a good idea to work in with your veterinarian if choosing to use homeopathy.

A dog's individual characteristics, temperament, behaviour, preferences and symptoms all help to define the most appropriate single remedy that will alter the total imbalance in the body. This remedy is then used at the smallest dose, at the correct frequency to change the body's energy or vital force. It does this by facilitating the innate healing mechanism.

After giving the remedy we look for the changes in symptoms over time. We know the remedy is working when we see a positive change in symptoms (and sometimes a short-term 'aggravation' or worsening symptoms, which usually stop in 24 hours). Healing and recovery occurs in a pattern, from above downwards, or from the head down to the feet. We see recovery from inside to outside. Healing occurs in the most important organs before the less important ones, from the internal organs to the less essential external structures. And finally we see healing occur from the most recent disorders to the oldest ones. So when treating a long-term problem, it is not uncommon to see symptoms that were apparent many years previously.

The remedies are made by taking a standard amount of the substance, and prepared according to specific instructions. This is then made into a tincture (similar to the preparation of herbal remedies) although these substances can include substances other than plants. One drop of the tincture is diluted in 99 drops of diluent (water or alcohol) and succussed (shaken vigorously). This becomes 1c potency. One drop of this dilution is then diluted with another 99 drops of diluent and succussed producing 2c potency. By the time the remedy is diluted like this 12 times, there is literally no more of the original substance in the remedy. Likewise, less potent remedies are made by taking 1 drop of tincture and diluting it with 9 drops of diluent and succussed (shaken vigorously), this becomes a 1x potency. One drop of this dilution is diluted with another 9 drops of diluent, succussed to produce 2x potency. There are other potency ranges, but the c and x ranges are the most common.

The more dilute the remedy is, the more potent it becomes. So a 12c remedy is more potent than a 6c remedy for example. And a 6c remedy is more potent than a 6x remedy. How can a remedy be potent when there is such a minute amount of a substance in it, or indeed none at the higher potencies? Hahnemann discovered in a series of experiments that the remedies were effective in these dilutions even though the substances could not be detected chemically. The mechanical action of shaking or succussion is thought to liberate energy from chemical bonds in the substances, releasing them into solution. Recent developments in quantum physics have led some scientists to theorise that electromagnetic energy is stored in the remedy and then interacts with the body's electromagnetic energy field.[131] Evidence is also accumulating that homeopathy deals with the transfer of frequency-specific energetic patterns and not with direct molecular effects.[132] While no one has satisfactorily explained exactly how these remedies work, recent developments in laser spectroscopy and bioassay technology that can detect minute dilutions, may provide the answers to how homeopathy works.

Despite how difficult it may be to understand how small doses of substances can have a healing effect, there is a considerable body of literature, scientific and clinical evidence that homoeopathic remedies do have biologic activity and can be effective. It has proved useful in veterinary medicine; however, further research is necessary before it becomes more widely accepted.[133]

Nosodes

Nosodes are often referred to as alternatives to vaccination for distemper, hepatitis, parvovirus and kennel cough or to prevent heartworm and other diseases. Nosodes are homoeopathic remedies made from infected tissue, disease discharges, vaccines or the actual organisms that cause the disease. Nosodes have not been fully evaluated, and as such cannot be recommended to replace vaccination for protection against infectious diseases. However, they are an alternative if vaccination is not appropriate (if the dog is immunosupressed or has concurrent disease or has previously reacted to vaccination). They can also be used in puppies before their first vaccination, and can be used at the same time as vaccination. Nosodes may also be used as part of the treatment when a dog contracts one of these diseases. They may also be useful to reduce a reaction to the regular vaccination.[134]

Dosage

A common program of nosode use is:[135]

> Dose twice daily for three days then
> Twice weekly for three weeks then
> Monthly for six months then
> A dose morning and night each six months

Schüssler Biochemic Salts

These are cell salts that the body naturally contains; however, they are manufactured in homeopathic concentrations. They are very safe and can be useful in many conditions outlined later to supplement the body's naturally occurring salts. They are usually provided in the 6x potency.

Why Use Homeopathy?

Homeopathy is on the whole safe, economical, simple to administer and gentle in action. There are very few serious or prolonged side-effects. That being said, it is an exacting form of medicine. Even after years of study a homoeopath may need to try several remedies before any results are seen.

When *Not* to Use Homeopathy

Do NOT use homeopathy (unless under the supervision of a veterinarian):

- When your dog is very ill, not eating, has collapsed or is very lethargic or suffering from a major problem such as heart or kidney disease. Veterinary attention must be sought, and homeopathy may be used alongside conventional therapy.
- When your dog is injured, bleeding, or in acute pain. Again seek veterinary attention, and homoeopathic remedies may be given at the same time, or on the way to the hospital.
- When your dog has a life threatening condition such as tick poisoning, other poisoning, or has suffered a spider or snakebite, or has cancer. Seek veterinary attention and use homoeopathic remedies along side therapy.

Unless you are working with a homeopathic veterinarian or veterinarian who can help to distinguish serious from non-serious disease, you may risk your dog's life, or your dog may suffer unduly where conventional treatment may save his life or ease pain. Homoeopathic remedies can be used at the same time and may assist recovery and return to health in these situations.

When to Use Homeopathy

Homoeopathic remedies are worth considering in a number of situations:

- As part of first aid treatment while you are on your way to see the vet.
- After you have seen your regular veterinarian, and you know what is wrong with your dog and how serious the condition is, as well as being informed about the conventional treatment options and likely outcomes.

- Conditions where your veterinarian cannot make a diagnosis (either because of the nature of the disease, or tests are unable to be performed), or where conventional treatment is not an option (due to age, side-effects, costs, availability, etc.).
- Conditions affecting pregnant bitches where conventional treatment may be potentially damaging to the foetal puppies.
- Conditions where conventional treatment is not particularly effective, such as many viral diseases. Kennel cough responds well to homoeopathic nosode use.[136]
- Conditions that require long-term use of drugs such as allergies, recurring infections, arthritis, long-term digestive and skin problems.
- Conditions which have not responded to conventional treatment or where the patient suffers serious side-effects, or where administration is difficult.

Guidelines for Use

Potencies

The potency of the remedy is very important, and it is advisable that if you wish to explore using homeopathy with readily available over the counter remedies, you only use low potency remedies such as 3x, 6x, 12x, 30x, 6c, 12c and 30c. These remedies can be used for short-term or mild problems in an otherwise healthy dog. For any serious condition your best chance of success with homeopathy is to consult with a veterinary homeopath.

1. *Warning*: Any potency, even low potencies can cause reactions in over-sensitive patients, and you are advised to contact a veterinary homoeopath immediately if this happens. If this isn't possible and your dog's condition worsens contact your regular veterinarian straight away.
2. If using acupuncture and homeopathy, treat first with acupuncture and wait at least 24 hours before commencing the use of homoeopathic remedies. Because both medicines work on the energy of the body, they may work better when given apart.
3. Remedies should be stored in a dark dry place.
4. Pilules (tiny round tablets) can be placed or crushed on a piece of paper, the papers folded to act like a funnel and the powder or pilules are then poured into the mouth.
5. Liquid remedies can be given by dropper into the mouth, either on the tongue or in the corner of the mouth. Avoid contamination. If the dropper touches the mouth or hands it should be washed before replacing into the bottle.
6. Tablets can be given by mouth provided your hands are clean and not strong smelling (liniments, hand creams, etc.).
7. If it is difficult to give the remedy then it can be given in water, milk, a little chicken broth or melted ice cream. It is probably best to avoid giving the remedies with food.
8. Coffee and strong odours can inactivate the remedies, so avoid using pungent foods and strong smelling solutions when treating with homoeopathic remedies.
9. The actual dose (number of pilules or drops) of the remedy is not critical. These

remedies do not work like normal medicines and it is more important to have the correct remedy at the right potency.

10. The frequency of dosing is important, follow directions carefully.

11. It is important to keep a record of your dog's symptoms if you decide to treat your dog. The reason for this is that if the problem becomes complicated and you wish to keep using homoeopathic remedies, you will need to seek advice from a homeopathic veterinarian. They will need to know what remedies you have used and the responses, to try and work out what is going on and in order to prescribe an appropriate remedy.

Dosing

Acute symptoms

As a guideline give one dose every fifteen minutes until you reach a veterinarian.

Chronic symptoms

For chronic disease, seek the expertise of a veterinary homoeopath who will recommend a dose schedule. If this is not possible, three doses are given twelve hours apart, then wait three weeks and reassess.

Choosing the Remedy

The best remedy is the one that exactly matches the dog's symptoms as described in the *Materia Medica*. However, there are a number of readily available low potency single remedies and also combination products (that contain several related remedies). These are generally safe to use, but only in dogs that are basically healthy or who have very minor problems. The worst thing that can happen is that they do nothing, the best thing they can do is to resolve the minor problem. It is always best to have your dog checked out by a veterinarian if you are at all concerned about your dog's health.

Responses to Homeopathy

Generally if your dog is better 'in himself' that is, if his energy level is better, and he is more normal to you (interest level, appetite, normal behaviour) then it is best to stop treatment.

If there is no improvement in 48 hours in mild conditions, the remedy is probably not correct. If the dog is worse then you should seek immediate veterinary attention.

The treatment of chronic disorders in dogs should only be undertaken by a homeopathic veterinarian. When correct remedies are chosen, the improvement in health can be quite astounding but can take time. Homeopathy is not a cure all, but because it can be very effective, with few side-effects it is worthwhile exploring.

Remember homeopathy will not work if the contributing factors are not addressed. Nutrition, vaccination, environmental and emotional factors need to be considered and addressed too and your regular veterinarian is well qualified to offer you advice.

Aromatherapy

Aromatherapy is the use of pure, essential oils to create a sense of well-being, balance and health. Although these essential oils are widely used in people, the knowledge of the use, toxicity and effectiveness in dogs is more limited.

Essential oils are derived from plants and each essential oil has a number of chemical components that contribute to its healing properties.

How do they work?

Essential oils are readily absorbed through the skin, and through inhalation.[137] They contain plant hormones and chemicals that act like chemical messengers in our bodies. These chemical messengers can influence the immune, endocrine, reproductive, digestive and respiratory systems. Some essential oils can have antibacterial effects, as well as antiviral, immune-stimulating, and mood modifying effects.[138]

Guidelines for Use of Essential Oils

1. Essential oils, though natural, should be used with extreme caution. There have been a number of reports of animals poisoned through inappropriate use. **Never give essential oils by mouth, or in food!**
2. Because pets lick their coats, it is best to avoid using them directly on the skin, unless advised by your veterinarian. Even if using them on the skin they must always be diluted in carrier oil, never applied directly onto the skin.
3. Essential oils are safest when diffused in the air. By selecting the appropriate oils, and placing a couple of drops of each into water and then vaporising, or diffusing them, the heat will evaporate the oils and aroma into the air. You will need either an electrical diffuser or oil burner, which can be purchased from health food shops.

4. Try to diffuse the aroma for about thirty minutes twice a day. And remember that your dog's nose is ultra sensitive. If she really slinks away and doesn't like the smell, then avoid using it. A consultation with a holistic veterinarian, who uses essential oils, will assist in determining exactly the right oils to help your pet.

5. If using oils on the skin in the diluted form, such as lavender, always apply a small amount to a patch of skin, and check that there is no reaction before applying it to a larger area.

6. Do not apply essential oils to pregnant dogs. Diffusion or vaporisers can still be used. Do not use aniseed, basil, clary sage, cedar wood, cyprus, fennel, jasmine, juniper, sweet marjoram, myrrh, nutmeg, peppermint, rose or rosemary at all during pregnancy.[139]

7. Use only essential oils that state the species of plant from which they are derived on the bottle. Do not use oil blends that can contain synthetic oils and aromas.

Caution: Potential side-effects of essential oils include toxicity to the nervous system, causing abortion, skin irritation, photosensitivity, allergic reactions, liver sensitivity and potential internal problems.[140]

Hazardous essential oils include camphor, pennyroyal (even though it repels insects it can produce acute liver and lung damage), wintergreen (often in liniments and ointments for muscular skeletal problems it can induce fatal poisoning if ingested)[141] and tea tree oil (several dogs have been poisoned with very small quantities of this oil, absorbed through the skin).[142] Other oils can be poisonous if used inappropriately.

Some Suggested Uses

Vaporising eucalyptus or peppermint oil can help respiratory infections, and help reduce spread of infection. Cardamon in a vaporiser can help reduce nausea and gastroenteritis. Chamomile (Roman) can help reduce anxiety and nervousness, as can lavender. Neroli is an essential oil which when vaporised is very useful for excessive stress, shock, exhaustion and fear, in a similar way to the Bach Flower Rescue Remedy.

A couple of drops of citronella, lavender and lemongrass on cotton wool balls, placed near bedding (out of reach of curious mouths), will help repel insects. When travelling, try ginger drops on a cotton wool ball placed near the air vent. This may help to reduce travel sickness.

Essential oils for flea control should be diluted in water and then sprayed onto the coat (total essential oils about 15 drops in 500 mls of water). The only oils I would recommend for home use and which are safe are lavender, citronella and cedar. They repel, but don't kill fleas, so may not be effective in a flea infestation. Your holistic veterinarian may recommend other essential oils for your dog.

Lavender (*Lavender angustifolia*) has antimicrobial, antifungal and anti-inflammatory properties and promotes healing[143] and can be applied (1 part pure lavender oil to 9 parts almond oil) to small areas of rashes or mild infections. Use this blend sparingly, and if the symptoms don't improve after two days of treatment, a veterinary check-up is in order. Always try a small patch first, to ensure your dog does not have an allergic reaction to it. Lavender oil can also be added to the final rinse at bath time, by adding 20 drops to 1 litre of water. This will leave a nice smell and help to repel insects. Lavender can also be diffused in a vaporiser for its sedative effect. It can be used to help calm anxious or agitated dogs, as well as calming the two-legged folk as well. It is important to use the right species of lavender, as other species of lavender are potentially harmful if used in excess or for too long.

Chiropractic, Physical Therapy and Massage

Chiropractic care is a holistic therapy which focuses on the health and proper functioning of the spinal column. The spinal column is integral to the health of the whole body. It not only provides the framework for the body but also protects the central nervous system. Many of the major nerves of the body exit and enter the spinal cord, so any problems in the spine can translate into problems elsewhere in the body.

Subluxation

Chiropractors use the term subluxation to describe a vertebra (one of the bones of the spinal column), which is out of its normal position. This may or may not be detected on radiographs, and can include very subtle changes in the spine. If the vertebrae are not normally aligned, they restrict proper movement leading to stiffness and pain. Subluxations can also cause pinching of nerves that can lead to pain or symptoms elsewhere in the body. Subluxation may underlie such problems as back pain, aggression, skin problems such as lick granulomas, itchy skin in a localised area, tail biting, incontinence, chronic digestive problems and joint pain not due to arthritis.[144]

Cervical subluxation (around the neck) can contribute to hyperactivity, dogs with short attention spans, fear biting, recurrent ear infections and some types of seizure disorders. Mid and lower cervical subluxation can relate to anxiety, lick granulomas on the fore legs, hypothyroidism, heart and liver disorders. Thoraco–lumbar subluxation (the spinal area around the last ribs) can be related to chronic cystitis and diarrhoea problems, and lumbar subluxation can relate to the sudden onset of incontinence and constipation[145] as well as tail biting.

How do these subluxations occur?

Agile and athletic (obedience and agility) dogs that jump and leap are prone to subluxation as their spines twist and jolt on landing. Dogs that strain repeatedly on their leashes, the types that take their owners for a walk, are also susceptible. Dogs that have been in a motor vehicle accident or have fallen or those that have been hit by a car can also sustain subluxation. Some dogs can have subluxation following a general anaesthetic for surgery, radiographs or dental procedures where the relaxed muscles make the spine more vulnerable to subluxation. Any dog that has lameness after playing may end up with subluxation because of the altered gait and favouring of one side of the body, and subluxation can manifest as lameness too.

How are subluxations corrected?

A veterinary chiropractor first examines the dog, and may use diagnostic techniques such as palpation, orthopedic and neurological examination and radiographs to rule out other problems which can look like subluxation. This is important because without a diagnosis, chiropractic may cause more harm than good. The chiropractor uses his hands or other devices to adjust the vertebrae and applies a short and rapid thrust on the localised area of the spine in a specific direction to return it to a normal position. He may also adjust the neck and the jaw.

The purpose of the chiropractic adjustment is not just to return the vertebrae to a specific position or to realign the spine. The goal is to initiate or activate the innate restorative mechanisms in vertebral joints of the body.[146] Any chronic problem may take several adjustments before the problem is resolved. This is because vertebrae that are 'out of alignment', over time, cause alterations in various muscles and ligaments, and these need time to readjust too. If the problem is recent, only one or a few adjustments may be needed.

Guidelines

1. Chiropractic requires good diagnosis. Chiropractic is usually contraindicated in acute intervertebral disc disease ('slipped discs'), following trauma, spinal compression, fractures, bone infections, acute myelopathy, acute cauda equina syndrome, and cancer of the spine.
2. Veterinary chiropractic is an addition to, not a replacement for conventional veterinary care. Your dog should be examined by your regular veterinarian before referral. This is important to avoid missing a more serious condition.
3. Ask your vet to help you locate a qualified veterinary chiropractor or ask your vet to work in with a chiropractor who is experienced with working with dogs.
4. Chiropractic and acupuncture work very well together for subluxation and have a longer lasting effect.[147]
5. As a guide it takes about two to three chiropractic sessions for a dog to regain 85%–90% of its normal function.[148]

Chiropractic is not a panacea, but offers an alternative approach to disease where conventional medicine needs additional help. It can be useful as an adjunctive therapy for chronic disease and following accidents and certainly where there is lameness that is not responding to conventional treatment. It can be used preventively in athletic dogs on a regular basis to help keep the spine strong and healthy. Old dogs with spondylosis or back pain also benefit from regular chiropractic adjustments.

Physical Therapy and Massage

Physical therapy and massage are therapies that can be applied to help promote healing, relieve pain and aid recovery. Physical therapies include the use of electrical currents, ultrasound, lasers, heat and cold, and stretching. The latter three are most easily applied in the home setting.

Heat as a therapy

Heating skin and parts of the body helps to increase the circulation to the area and provide some pain relief. Wheat or barley bags, heated in the microwave or oven are very useful for applying to areas of discomfort in dogs, especially those with sore backs or joints. The increased circulation helps to nourish the underlying tissues and aids in healing. Many elderly dogs, especially in cold weather, and thin dogs or those recovering from serious disease appreciate heating pads. Wait at least 72 hours after any injury before using heat as a therapy, once any bleeding or swelling has stopped.

Cold as a therapy

Sudden injuries such as sprains to the limbs, or bruises due to minor accidents can be treated immediately with an icepack. Place ice in a plastic bag, (or use a packet of frozen peas or similar) and then wrap it in a pillowcase or smaller cloth bag. This allows the ice pack to be flexible over and around the place of injury. For smaller dogs, simply apply the ice wrapped in a tea towel directly to the area, moving it gently over the skin. It should be applied as soon after the injury as possible, and held in place for 10 to 15 minutes, while taking the dog to the veterinarian. Icepacks can also be used after surgery if there is swelling, within 48 to 72 hours.

Stretching

Stretching exercises for your dog can greatly aid recovery from injury or following surgery to a limb. Any acute injury or sprain should not be stretched until the swelling goes down. Your veterinarian can show you the stretches to help your dog. Stretching improves circulation, helps to prevent stiffness and speeds up normal functioning of the leg. Older dogs can also benefit from gentle stretching, while they are lying down, to improve mobility of all the joints in the body. Simply extend and flex the joints of the legs gently backwards or forwards to the degree that your dog is comfortable and hold the position for 15 seconds, release and repeat three to four times, twice daily. Canine physiotherapists can be contacted through your veterinarian.

Massage

Massage therapy is particularly good to improve circulation, aid muscle function, reduce pain and relax dogs. There are a number of different kinds of massage including acupressure massage, massage of trigger points and remedial massage.

Massage should not be attempted if the skin is infected, or bruised or if there are muscle tears as this could make the condition worse. It's best to avoid massage in sick dogs, or dogs that are pregnant. And avoid massaging within two hours after your dog has eaten or exercised.

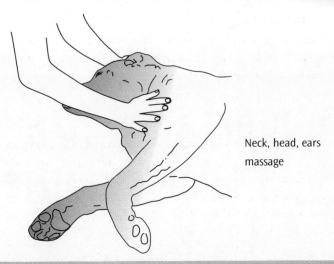

Neck, head, ears
massage

Figure 3. Massage therapy stimulates circulation, increases lymph flow, and helps release tense muscles.

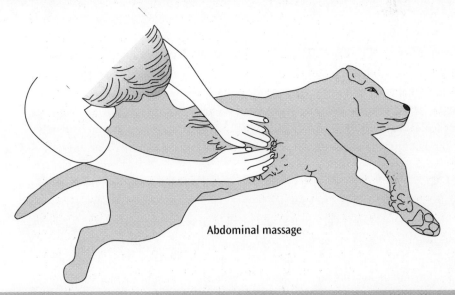

Abdominal massage

Figure 4. Make circular movements in the abdominal area; most dogs will roll on their backs for this.

Trained dog massage therapists can be contacted through your veterinarian or holistic practitioner. They can also show you some basic techniques to apply at home. One of the simplest and easiest forms of massage you can do is simple stroking, which will produce a very relaxed dog (and owner). This is also called TLC or tender loving care and the power of touch cannot be underestimated as a form of therapy. If you would like to begin massaging your dog, apply a steady firm pressure with your finger-tips. Breathe deeply and use circular movements. Always massage towards the heart, so start at the paws and work your way towards the chest area.

CHAPTER 13

Tellington Touch and Hands-on Healing

Tellington Touch/ TTouch/ T TEAM (Tellington-Jones Every Animal Method) was developed by Linda Tellington-Jones as a means of increasing awareness between handler or owner and animals. It was based on her experiences with Feldenkrais—a technique for people to become more aware of themselves through movement and as an aid in learning. This method uses rhythmic breathing and circular touch, which induces relaxation in both dog and owner and can be used to enhance learning as well as aid many other problems.

This is something you can try at home, and can learn more about through seminars and courses. You do not need to have any knowledge of anatomy or physiology, energy work or meridians—this is very simple and involves the connection or bond between you and your dog. It is a very easy way to your communication with your dog.

The TTouch is a very specific form of bodywork, which uses the hand and fingers to move skin and underlying muscle in a clockwise circle. Just like a clock face, the circle begins at 6 o'clock, clockwise up and around, past 6 o'clock again, to 8 o'clock with a pause and a slow release.

How does it work?

Tellington touch works on the understanding that the body's tissues store memories of pain, disease or fear. The circular movement and connection helps release these, by facilitating healing and relaxation. Studies, using biofeedback have also shown that by closing the TTouch circle, animals stay in beta EEG (the thinking and reasoning part of the brain). This level of focus and awareness in both person and animal increases and facilitates the training process as well as communication.[149]

There are four components to TTouch:

Mental Attitude

It is important to be open-minded, simply focus on what you are doing, you do not need to try hard to connect. You do not have to believe in anything for it to work. You do not need to have taken a course or be a therapist.

How to Use Your Hands

The foundation of TTouch is the circular movement described above. Tellington-Jones calls this movement the Clouded Leopard. Begin by visualising a clock on your dog's body. With one hand resting on the dog, take your other hand (right if right handed) and place your fingers at 6 o'clock. Rest your wrist, thumb and little finger lightly against the body to support and steady your hand. Hold your other three fingers relaxed and slightly cupped, like a paw and push the skin around the clock, past 6 to 8 o'clock. Maintain an even, constant pressure. At 8 o'clock pause for a second, then bring your fingers away softly and begin at another random spot on the body. You can press slightly at 8 o'clock and allow your fingers to come off in a gradual release. By placing the circles randomly over the body, your dog will stay alert, but relaxed, wondering where the next circle will be.

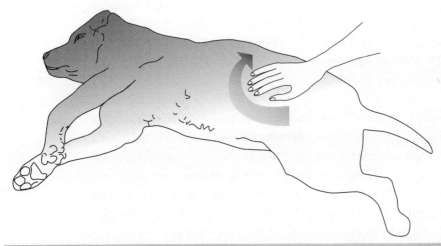

Figure 5. The simplest touch is the Clouded Leopard. Using a gentle pressure, move your fingers in a clockwise direction.

It is important to do one full circle at a time, and move on in different places over the body. There is a tendency at first to massage around and around in the same place, to start with—it is very relaxing for the dog, but is not TTouch. It is important for the circles to be round. The movement should be smooth and flowing. If your dog is apprehensive to start with, make the circles quite fast, taking a second or so to complete the circle. This helps to awaken the body. Once she settles down to enter a state of 'listening' you can slow the movements down to one each two seconds. This helps to relieve muscular tension, deepens breathing and opens the door to deeper communication.

How to Breathe

When we concentrate we often take short shallow breaths or stop! As you do the circles, make sure you breathe regularly, evenly and easily until you become aware of a rhythm. This will help you to become still and focused in your mind, and relaxed in your shoulders, arms and hands. Often you will find your dog breathing at a similar rate with you, as you become attuned to each other.

Pressure

Your touch does not need to be heavy. You are not massaging. Use the lightest pressure and practise on yourself to start with.

Be guided by your intuition, try to trust and let go of controlled thought. Direct contact with your dog will help you know how, where and when to use the TTouch. You will become focused and grounded and highly attuned with your dog. This is different from simply stroking your dog or patting, as you become more relaxed and your breathing slows down, and you will make a deeper connection with your dog.

Be aware that you may not see an immediate response to TTouch. A session should last about ten minutes and can be repeated daily, or several times over one or two days. This is a great tool to build up the communication between you and your dog. Make circles on your dog whenever you can.

There are many conditions that respond positively to TTouch. These include:

Behavioural problems such as obsessive licking and chewing, fear of thunder or loud noises, aggression, abuse issues, hyperactivity, shyness/timidity, biting, barking and it can also be useful to help deal with death and dying, and adapting to new situations such as a new home. TTouch can also be used to assist when dogs are reluctant to undergo teeth cleaning, deworming, grooming and nail trimming, and it may also be useful to reduce anxiety-related travel sickness. TTouch can assist with giving injections, acupuncture, IV therapy, during recovery from surgery, in cases of paralysis and brain injury, injuries and bruising, in seizures, hip dysplasia, arthritis and others.

The Ear TTouch

This is another great way to interact with your dog and only takes a few minutes.

The base of the ear has many acupuncture points connecting up with other parts of the body. This form of TTouch is very useful in situations of shock and trauma. It relieves stress, improves digestion and can help with travel sickness. The Ear TTouch starts by holding the base of the ear, and then sliding your hand to the tip of the ear, gently pulling as you go.

The Tail TTouch

Tail TTouch and TTouches around the hindquarters are useful for dogs with hip dysplasia or arthritis. It also benefits dogs that are aggressive or timid, as well as dogs that are fearful of loud noises or thunder. The Tail TTouch is performed by gently lifting the tail in a straight line from the body and stroking down the tail several times. Keep one hand near the base of the tail and the other further out on the tail to slowly and gently bend the tail into a small arch. Gently move the tail in a circle, rotating in both directions. Slide your hands down the tail in a pattern of gentle pull then hold, gentle pull then hold, each lasting 5 seconds.

The Mouth TTouch

The mouth TTouch improves the ability to focus and learn by affecting the emotional and physical responses of your dog. It is helpful for barking, obsessive licking, biting as well as helping to maintain well-being. Dogs respond well to this in times of anxiety or fear. Simply do the TTouch in small circles on the lips and gums. If the mouth is dry, first wet your fingers with water.

The Belly Lift

This is another gentle touch that aids digestive problems, pain in the abdomen or gas. As well it helps relieve sore backs and arthritis. Like the other touches it also helps dogs that are nervous or timid, or dogs that have other negative behaviours. Either use a towel folded lengthwise under your dog's belly, or cross your hands under the belly from behind the front legs. Lift the abdomen gently and hold for 10 to 15 seconds, followed by a slow release. You can repeat this three or four times.

TTouch is especially helpful during dying. The TTouch deepens the connection between you and your dog and helps to release fear or sadness for both of you.

Hands-on Healing

Healing with hands is perhaps the most 'out there' therapy. And I must admit I was one of the sceptics. Surely hands-on healing must have something to do with belief systems, the placebo effect and mind over matter (I mean that applies to anything that isn't conventional Western medicine!). It wasn't until I had some interesting experiences with animals that I found that there was certainly more to it.

Hands-on healing is described in most cultures throughout the world and has a history dating back at least 5000 years. When you think about it, it is the most natural thing in the world to do to touch the place that hurts. Healing with hands is based on the understanding that the body is made of energy as much as it is made of matter. There is an electromagnetic energy field, sometimes called an aura, that surrounds and interpenetrates the body. It contains an energetic blueprint for all the organs and systems of the body.[150] Disturbances in the mental or emotional aspects of people or for that matter dogs, manifest as disturbances and imbalances in the energy field. These disturbances and imbalances affect the energetic blueprint for bodily organs and systems and are manifested as disease.[151]

Hands-on healing exists in many different forms in the West including Therapeutic Touch, Reiki, Healing Touch, Touch for Health, Reflexology, Shiatsu, Polarity, Craniosacral therapy, Acupressure and many others. Many of these are becoming widely available in hospitals and hospices for people as evidence for their benefits has been researched and validated.[152] These therapies all have several things in common. They employ a pair of hands, they are very gentle, they elicit a profound state of relaxation, and they facilitate healing.

While anyone can place their hands on their dog and benefit each other through the contact, there are certain techniques that can allow perception of the energy fields and movement of energy. These can be learnt in seminars and courses, but the best you can do is experience any of these therapies for yourself first. You do not have to believe them to experience them for yourself. The benefits include relief of pain, relaxation and research has demonstrated improvements in healing time for skin wounds.[153]

Reiki is my personal favourite healing method. The basic level is learnt in a two- to three-day course that then allows a flow of energy to be perceived and experienced. Thereafter it is a very simple matter of placing your hands on or near the body, be it human or dog.

The most important thing to remember with any of these therapies is that you are a facilitator for the dog's own healing. You need to have only the intention to help your friend, and the energy will flow. Each of the hands-on healing techniques have different systems but ultimately they aid the energy fields of the body and therefore the whole body, including physical, emotional and mental states.

As you become more familiar or attuned to energy, you can use your perception to not only facilitate healing but also to help keep check on your dog's health. Often there are changes in the energy fields before changes are observed in the physical body. There is a technique called scanning in which you run the palm of your hand one to two inches away from the body and parallel to it. If you do this in a slow and focused way, you may detect differences in heat coming off your dog's body. I have learnt to use my left hand, because when I used my right hand, I didn't feel anything, I was thinking too hard, and not allowing my brain to merely perceive! Hands-on healing involves leaving your hands near or on the body to facilitate a flow of energy into the patient's body where it is needed, at the same time you are not draining your own energy. This is quite a difficult concept to understand. However, it is easier to experience than to understand.

There are major energy centres around the body of a dog. One can be detected at the level of the throat; one in front of the chest (near the heart); one between the shoulder blades; one on the head between the ears; one on the abdomen where the umbilical or belly button is; one over the lumbar area of the spine, and there is a small energy centre at the tip of the tail. Now all this might sound completely bizarre, and you can dismiss it entirely if you choose. However, if you experiment and learn more about energy you will find a gentle healing gift at your fingertips.

The general philosophy is that hands-on healing can be used as a complement to any other therapy. Your hands do not even need to directly touch your dog (for example if it is too painful to touch or where there is infection or there are burns), since the energy field exists several inches to feet away from the physical body. It causes absolutely no harm, and there are no contraindications. In some cases hands-on healing provides some incredible results. I have found it extremely useful to stimulate the appetite, to ease discomfort or pain and as an aid for all other therapies.

I recommend that if you have this skill and your dog is in need, that you apply it at least once daily for 10 to 20 minutes. No hands-on healing is wasted. It is also a time for you to bond and communicate with your dog, for you to relax, and for both of you to benefit from the energy that flows through.

Reiki is a beautiful energy to share during the dying process or euthanasia, and definitely provides a calming and nurturing influence on all concerned. Personally it has brought a completely different quality to euthanasia, where I no longer find it emotionally draining. The whole process is transformed into a spiritual experience without necessarily engaging in any belief system or religious process. Many millions of people in Australia, the USA and the UK, and other countries have this skill, and it should never be underestimated as a powerful tool to aid in health recovery and well-being of dogs.

P A R T ②

RECOMMENDATIONS FOR HEALTH CONDITIONS AFFECTING YOUR DOG

This section deals with specific health conditions. With natural therapies there are often many different approaches, and your veterinarian may have a completely different approach that is equally valid and effective. The idea is to give you a place to start when working with your veterinarian, especially if you cannot locate a holistic practitioner and you want to begin using complementary therapies.

With your veterinarian, you can begin to research the suggestions and together you can plan an approach that is suitable for your dog. Ideally a holistic veterinarian will speed up this process and offer their experience and clinical insights into your dog's particular problem, taking into account not just the 'diagnosis' but also the pattern of disease, and your dog's individuality. When this happens, there is a greater chance of successfully restoring health.

Guidelines

But before we go on there are some important guidelines:

1. It is important not to diagnose your dog's problem yourself. Your veterinarian (either conventional or holistic) should examine your animal before implementing any therapy. It is important to consider the diagnosis but to also consider the pattern of health problems and any other problems that exist. We are looking at the whole health of your dog, not just the name of his condition.

2. While this next section is focused on conditions, where your dog has more than one problem, approach the main one first, but then read the other relevant sections on chronic disease, other problems your dog might have and also worming and vaccination. Many of the key principles apply to all—good nutrition and removing obstacles to health. A holistic veterinarian takes all problems into account when

planning an approach. Knowing the complete picture helps decide what particular herbs or acupuncture points or nutraceuticals are going to be the most appropriate for the whole dog.

3. Work with your veterinarian. If your dog is currently on medication it may be dangerous to withdraw them or stop them suddenly. Your veterinarian may be completely new to complementary therapies and even resistant to their use. Ideally your veterinarian will be sympathetic to your preferences for your dog's health and refer you to a holistic veterinarian, or a practitioner who is willing to work in with you and your vet as a team.

4. Locating a holistic veterinarian isn't always easy but 'Useful contacts', the resource guide at the back of the book should assist you.

5. If you choose to work alone and use complementary therapies, be warned that if you are mistaken, and treating inappropriately, your dog may suffer unduly and the disease can worsen. Natural therapies and remedies are safe when used appropriately, but may also be harmful if a more serious condition is missed or complications occur.

6. The therapies suggested are guidelines only. Specific therapy will depend upon the diagnosis, your dog's individual symptoms and underlying factors. Many mild problems can develop into more serious problems without proper care. So make sure you keep your regular vet involved in the process.

Treatment Options

Treatment options include:

Diet

In general dogs that are not 100 per cent healthy benefit from upgrading their diet. This may mean changing products, incorporating fresh foods and/or making your dog's meals. Guidance on feeding your dog and upgrading the diet is found in Chapters 3, 4 and 5.

Nutraceuticals and Supplements

There are several options here. The first ones listed are generally the most important. Choose two or three to begin with. Add in others over time if improvement in health is slow or not observed. Guidance for use, dose and precautions for supplements are found in Chapter 6.

Herbs

There are many herbs to choose from. Herbs listed are most appropriate for the various conditions, but actual ones selected are usually based on the individual dog rather than the diagnosis. While there may be five herbs that can be effective for a particular condition, the most appropriate ones will be those that also address the whole health of your dog. Again the guidance of a herbalist or holistic veterinarian will be important.

Often one, two or a combination of herbs will achieve a good result. Guidance for dosages, cautions and usage are found in Chapter 7.

Acupuncture

Several acupuncture points are mentioned for most conditions. An International Veterinary Association certified acupuncturist will be able to tailor points specifically for your dog's needs and may vary them at each treatment. Some veterinarians are trained in point location but are not certified, so can use these points as a guide. Advice and information on acupuncture is found in Chapter 8.

Bach Flower Remedies

You can choose Bach Flower remedies based on the guidelines found in Chapter 9. Better still it is useful to consult a veterinarian or practitioner experienced in the use of these remedies to tailor a remedy for your dog's specific needs. Bach Flower remedies can be used in almost any situation, as they are safe and easy to use and can help the underlying emotional and mental state. Refer to Chapter 9 for more information.

Homeopathy

Some remedies are suggested, but the best response to homeopathy will only happen if the remedy is matched to your dog's specific symptoms rather than the diagnosis. The suggestions are some to begin exploring and should not be used just because they are there. On the other hand Schüssler Biochemic Salts can be used safely and easily without causing more problems. Advice on homeopathy and biochemic salts can be found in Chapter 10.

Aromatherapy and Other Therapies

Aromatherapy, chiropractic, TTouch, Reiki and other therapies can have a place in assisting your dog's return to health. Suggestions for using these remedies are made where they are strongly indicated, although they can be used in most cases. Hands-on work and touch NEVER go astray when it comes to supporting your dog! Guidelines and suggestions can be found in Chapters 11, 12 and 13.

When treating animals holistically, it is always important to address all the factors that may be influencing the course of the disease, as there is usually more than one factor involved in disease. Understanding why your dog is ill in the first place can help you to remove the obstacles to health.

Remember that complementary and alternative therapies are not miracle cures, they take time to work, and success depends upon knowing what you are dealing with, working with your veterinarian as a team and being prepared to put in effort and time. Research your choices, ask for referrals if necessary, and make informed decisions about the treatment of your dog.

CHAPTER

(14)

Chronic
Disease

A naturopathic approach to treating disease recognises the existence of a vital curative force within the body. Many critics of complementary medicine believe that natural therapies are a placebo; that the animal would get better on its own anyway without treatment. In one way natural therapies do harness the body's innate ability to heal, which is not dissimilar to placebo. What we do know is that animals that have chronic disease do not get better by themselves. Some intervention is needed to relieve suffering. Conventional medicine or natural therapies can be used. While a natural approach may be like a placebo, the aim is to give the body the best chance to heal itself through good nutrition, removing obstacles to good health and supporting the various body systems so that the body works better. Sometimes this is all that is needed to see an improvement in well-being.

There are many obstacles to good health and many factors that contribute to chronic disease. These include poor genetics, inappropriate diet, parasites, allergies, hormonal (endocrine) disorders, environmental factors and others. Long-term debility can also involve the immune system, setting up a cycle of poor health. However, there are some other factors that should be considered from a naturopathic perspective.

Toxins

Toxins include any substance that creates harmful effects in the body, undermining health and stressing biochemical or organ functions. Sources include over-cooked foods, contaminated raw foods, medications (including inappropriate use of natural remedies), plants, water, furniture, carpets, exhaust fumes, paint fumes, industrial waste and pesticides. There are also toxins produced by normal metabolic processes that the body is usually well equipped to detoxify and stay healthy. However, if the detoxification organs are not functioning properly, or they are simply overwhelmed then toxins can cause and contribute to ill health.

Naturopaths suggested a century ago that chronic disease such as skin disease is a symptom of internal toxicity that the body has failed to eliminate fully. In 'toxaemia', normal elimination of wastes through the liver, gut and kidneys is impaired, allowing the accumulation of toxins that lead to inflammation in the body. For example, in the case of chronic skin disease, the eliminative process most frequently impaired is the digestive system.[154] The aim of naturopathic therapy therefore is to remove toxins by enhancing and supporting the eliminatory functions of the body.

Diet

Food allergies (involving an immune reaction) are not considered common in veterinary medicine (less than 10 per cent of itchy dogs without parasites are considered to have food allergy) and when present are due to proteins like milk and beef.[155] However, food intolerance or adverse reactions to food may be more difficult to detect. In one study of allergic dogs with skin disease (not due to fleas) and considered not to have food allergy, almost half of the dogs improved on a commercial chicken and rice elimination diet.[156] The reason for this response was unknown, but it demonstrates the importance of considering dietary manipulation in the treatment of chronic skin disease. Underlying food sensitivities have also been associated with arthritis and chronic fatigue in humans. (*See* Elimination Diets)

Leaky Gut Syndrome

Associated with chronic disease is the theory of 'leaky gut syndrome'. The normal gut lining (like the skin) is the main barrier between the environment and the immune system. Leaky Gut Syndrome (LGS) means just what it sounds like. The lining of the intestinal tract is permeable to substances that would not normally enter the body in the digestive tract.

LGS results from inflammation of the gut lining thought to be caused by:
- Antibiotics (they can lead to an imbalance of bacteria in the gut, especially with prolonged or repeated antibiotic use)
- Parasites such as round worms, tapeworms, hookworms, giardia, coccidiosis and cryptosporidium
- Bacteria such as helicobacter pylori, salmonella, campylobacter, E Coli
- Fungi such as candida after prolonged use of antibiotics or glucocorticoids or immune suppression or diabetes melitis; also mould and fungal toxins from stored grains, improperly stored pet foods, improperly stored fresh foods
- Irritant chemicals found in fermented and some processed foods such as preservatives in dried pigs' ears, sulphur dioxide in fresh pet meats, peroxidised fats in some poorly stored dried foods, some dyes
- Enzyme deficiencies such as lactase deficiency
- Non steroidal anti-inflammatory drugs
- Corticosteroids such as prednisone

Symptoms may be very subtle and include irregular faeces, intermittent constipation or loose stools, flatulence, occasional vomiting, or occasional blood or mucous in the stools. An inflamed gut is more 'leaky'. This leakiness allows the passing of imperfectly digested proteins and other substances such as bacteria and toxins through an inflamed or damaged gut lining. This then leads to inflammation in other parts of the body and increases the toxic insult to the liver. LGS is thought to contribute to environmental sensitivities and many chronic and degenerative diseases in people. Unlike veterinary medicine, there are readily available tests for diagnosing this syndrome in people.

Stress

Chronic stress can also be an underlying cause of LGS. The cells lining the gut are constantly being replaced as they are digested or sloughed off. The first organ system to lose its blood supply during stress is the intestinal tract. If a dog has been stressed for a long time, the intestinal tract may therefore be chronically undernourished and begin to function poorly and may even become leaky. This makes the gut much more susceptible to the growth of disease-causing organisms, which then damage the lining even further.

Correcting a suspected 'leaky gut' can help improve overall health, reduce allergies, and help restore the bowel to normal functioning.

Dysbiosis

Related to Leaky Gut Syndrome is a condition called 'dysbiosis'. This is an imbalance in the normal population of bacteria and other organisms in the bowel, thought to be a major contributing factor to chronic disease including skin disorders and food allergies.[157] Dysbiosis follows the repeated use of antibiotics or poor diet or other drugs that alter the normal flora in the gut. Other contributing factors include those listed for LGS as well as a depressed immunity due to chronic stress, liver-toxicity, pancreatic disease or chronic debility.

Dysbiosis leads to poor gut health, poor digestion and leaky gut syndrome. The symptoms include bloating and flatulence and mild diarrhoea or mild constipation and mild abdominal pain. A poorly functioning gut allows food allergens, chemicals or bacterial toxins to enter the blood stream where they can cause further problems such as overloading the liver, food sensitivities, lowered immunity, allergy, malnutrition, and a downward spiral of poor health. Dysbiosis can underlie chronic diarrhoea, immune deficiency, skin disorders, food allergies and may account for 50 per cent of chronic problems.[158] This condition is not usually diagnosed in conventional veterinary medicine; however, treating naturopathically on the assumption or suspicion of dysbiosis, usually results in positive improvements in digestion and overall health.

Vaccination

Vaccination is very important in disease prevention but may in some cases contribute to disease. This is because chronic disease is usually associated with an inappropriately functioning immune system. Vaccinating any dog with chronic disease is therefore not recommended (unless required by law or the risk of infection is very high). Vaccination can actually cause disease in some instances and this is discussed in more detail under the heading of vaccination.

A Naturopathic Approach to Chronic Disease

One strategy for starting to treat chronic disease (and also many types of acute disease) relies on three processes: detoxification, repair and tonification.

Detoxification

Detoxification is the process of clearing toxins from the body. Toxin build-up may not seem obvious externally and is not usually a recognised problem in animals unless obvious poisoning has occurred (plant and spider toxins for example). However, supporting the body to detoxify can make a big difference to how well your dog is able to heal itself with the help of conventional or complementary medicines. As the body starts to function more normally and if your vet agrees, then reducing or withdrawing drugs is often possible. During detoxification try to avoid giving any additional medications or chemical treatments. Improving the diet (whether a premium quality dog food and/or balanced home-made diet) and increasing fluid consumption is nearly always beneficial. Consider a modified fast based on broths (another form of detoxification) for the first one or two days. (*See* Basic Detoxification Program.)

The detoxification organs in the body include those that belong to the respiratory, gastrointestinal, urinary, skin and lymphatic systems. Anything that supports elimination helps to detoxify. In naturopathic medicine, herbs that act as laxatives and diuretics, called 'alteratives', support natural detoxification processes.

Alteratives

Traditionally these herbs have been used to detoxify and help the elimination organs rid the body of waste products. Long-term therapy is usually safe and helpful. A veterinary herbalist can select the most appropriate herbs for your dog's condition and they will usually include some of the following:
- Burdock root (*Articum lappa*), skin and blood cleanser, diuretic, improves liver, antibacterial and antifungal properties.
- Cleavers (*Gallium aparine*), lymphatic system detoxifier (along with echinacea) and useful for skin
- Yellow dock root (*Rumex crispus*), skin, blood and liver cleanser
- Red clover flowers (*Trifolium pratense*), blood cleanser, good during convalesence and healing
- Nettle (*Urtica dioica*), good for detoxing where skin and arthritis occur
- Dandelion (*Taraxacum officinale*), liver and blood cleanser, diuretic and tonic
- Liquorice root one of the best detoxifiers, mild laxative
- Parsley leaf diuretic and urinary tract detoxifier

• Consideration must be given to supporting other systems and organs if needed. For example if your dog is on corticosteroids, support the liver with St Mary's thistle (*Silybum marianum*).

Dysbiosis/Leaky Gut Syndrome Treatment

If dysbiosis or a leaky gut is suspected, the approach will depend on the degree of symptoms and your veterinarian's preferred type of treatment. The approach may include all or some of these:

• A single-protein source diet, good digestibility, low-fat, high-protein
• Remove detrimental microbes (various methods and may include conventional antibiotics and antifungal agents or herbs)
• Liver detoxification—St Mary's thistle
• Lymphatic support—cleavers

Following these eliminatory measures, the next stage of treatment is more sustaining and directed at moving the gut towards health.

• Support beneficial gut bacteria with probiotics and prebiotics
• Intestinal inflammation and leakiness: for healing the gut lining provide glutamine, glucosamine and slippery elm
• Adrenal support if on corticosteroids—liquorice
• Immune enhancement or modulation—echinacea

Repair

In conventional veterinary medicine we are often conditioned to a fast response to treatment. A steroid like prednisolone can diminish chronic itching almost overnight. But an important part of healing is convalescence. The body needs time to repair and heal and in order to facilitate repair we need a number of other supports:

• A healthy diet. This can make the most difference to your dog's long-term health.
• Rest and minimal stress. Very important during and after detoxification
• Mild to moderate exercise and normalisation of body weight (especially if over-weight)
• Regular grooming to stimulate skin and circulation

Tonification

An animal with chronic disease will not always fully recover to robust health and may certainly need further treatment after this initial strategy. This may include regular acupuncture treatment and the use of tonics that include adaptogen herbs (that assist the body in being better able to adapt under stress) such as astragalus and ginseng (*Panex ginseng*). Your dog may need regular check-ups to monitor progress.

Corticosteroid Use

If your dog is being treated with corticosteroids or has finished a course of cortico-steroids recently, consider herbs outlined in 'corticosteroid use'.

Basic Detoxification Program

Most dogs with either a short-term illness or chronic disease such as bowel disease, skin problems and arthritis can benefit from a detoxification program. This can range from a broth diet for one to two days as a quick help, to a longer-term program that restores the health of the organs normally involved in detoxifying the body.

Warning: If your dog is severely ill, this must only be carried out under the supervision of a veterinarian.

Avoid strictly fasting your dog (unless your vet advises so) because it causes body tissues to be used in place of food, for energy. In addition, fasting may accelerate the toxin production with the breakdown of protein from muscles and release of toxins from body fat.[159]

Occasionally detoxification can make your dog feel worse. If your dog has any adverse effects seek veterinary attention and in the meantime use a combination of Bach Flower essences of mustard, gentian, walnut and crab-apple. These can also be used at any stage through the process to assist and support your dog.

The Program

The best approach to detoxification is a gradual one and a long-term one, involving diet and life-style changes. However, a short-term program can be extremely beneficial if your dog has a flare-up of an existing condition, or when he seems off colour or unwell.

Short-term Modified Fast 1–3 Days

The bowel is the most important place to start detoxification. When the bowel wall is not healthy it acts like a very poor filter so that chemicals, toxins and food molecules can leak into the bloodstream from the bowel. These substances can cause inflammation and dysfunction of many organ systems including the liver. The liver is designed to filter and remove these substances from the blood; however, if it is overwhelmed then the toxins accumulate in the bloodstream where they can compromise the immune system resulting in allergies, lethargy, poor health and disease.

We need to start by giving the digestive tract a short break. The simplest way to do this is by providing a broth-based diet for one to two days. This reduces the calories and the amount of food your dog has to normally process and digest, which allows the liver to focus on detoxifying excess toxins already in the bowel and body. Increasing the liquids also assists with hydrating the body, supporting the kidneys and assisting elimination of toxins.

Bowel Detoxification

If your dog has any form of chronic disease, maldigestion, malabsorption, colitis, food allergy, eczema, arthritis, acute poisoning or intestinal infections then a bowel detoxification program is worthwhile starting.

Bowel detoxification means correcting the underlying dysbiosis by removing parasites, bad bacteria and other organisms, and then focusing on helping the digestive tract to repair. We do this by providing it with the right nutrients (glutamine), reinstating the good bacteria (probiotics) and providing a diet (including fibre and prebiotics) that supports good gut health. The successful treatment of chronic dysbiosis requires an appropriate diet, supplements and persistence. Your holistic veterinarian might offer you other options including homeopathic detoxification, or the use of specific products that facilitate detoxification.

Liver Detoxification

The primary detoxification organ of the body is the liver. In a longer detoxification program the liver needs to be supported. Normal detoxification occurs in the liver with a two-phase process. We need to help protect the liver while facilitating these processes to work in a balanced way. We want to decrease the toxins that need to be processed (such as those from food and drugs) and maximise the processing of internal toxins generated by normal metabolism.

Liver detoxification is best carried out through long-term dietary change (to a better diet), herbal support and supplements, although your holistic veterinarian may offer other equally viable options.

PLAN

Stage 1 Short-term modified fast (1–2 days)

- Begin this process the evening before a weekend so that you can keep a close watch on your dog. Start by giving half the dinner your dog usually has.
- A good option is to also start with a generous brushing, grooming and bath.
- Provide a broth-based diet for 1 to 2 days in small and frequent meals during the day.
- Provide a pure source of water such as spring or filtered water.
- Limit exercise to light walks once or twice daily.
- Allow your dog to rest.
- Be aware that bowel movements may be different as the body eliminates these materials.
- On completion of the modified fast, gradually introduce your dog to his diet over the next two to three days. This should include some fresh vegetables, and raw bones (two to three times weekly), and either a balanced home-made diet, or in combination with a natural or premium quality veterinary diet, depending on your dog's condition.

Stage 2 Correction of dysbiosis (1–3 weeks)

- Begin with the modified fast above.
- Preferably begin a balanced, home-prepared diet or some fresh foods in combination with high quality commercial dry food. Consider 'low allergy' diets by using foods your dog has not had exposure to before, such as chicken or fish and rice.

Avoid dairy products and glutens (wheat-based cereal foods). It is useful at this stage to reduce the calorie intake by 20 per cent if your dog is overweight.

- Worm your dog with a conventional all-wormer product, black walnut herbal preparation or homeopathic worming preparation. Conventional wormers are generally safe and very effective. If you don't want to use these, have a worm test done first by taking in a fresh stool sample to the vet. If it is negative you may not need to worm your dog.
- We can help control 'bad' intestinal bugs by using a two-week course of echinacea, garlic or pau d'arco or an anti-candida product or homeopathic bowel nosode to reduce any fungi and bad bacteria in the bowel.
- Optional: Immunoglobulins in milk whey (colostrum) may assist in severe dysbiosis by mopping up left-over bad organisms and toxins while assisting good organisms.
- Add digestive enzyme supplement daily.

Stage 3 Correct nutritional deficiencies and reintroduce friendly bacteria (1–6 weeks)

- If your dog is overweight, maintain reduced calorie intake for further 4-6 weeks.
- Ensure diet includes liver (or vitamin A alternative) and flax seed oil daily
- Include lecithin as a daily supplement
- Include vitamin C twice daily
- Include vitamin E daily
- Include zinc daily (zinc has a critical role in repair of the digestive tract, detoxification and immune function)
- Add fructo-oligosaccaride (FOS) as a fibre source to enhance the gut environment for good bacteria daily. Another alternative is psyllium.
- Add probiotics daily.
- For severely compromised bowel (loose stools and flatulence) add glutamine and slippery elm daily.
- Herbs such as liquorice or boswellia may be useful for the inflamed gut.

Stage 4 Liver detoxification (4–8 weeks)

- Begin at stage 3 when you are ready.
- Maintain supplements.
- Add St Mary's thistle herbal tincture or similar twice daily.
- Burdock is considered a blood detoxifier for systemic toxicity.
- Red clover and burdock are beneficial for detoxification in cancer.

Your dog should show improved vitality, wellness and reduction in symptoms on this program. It is best done under the supervision of a holistic veterinarian who can tailor a program for your dog's specific needs. Their approach may differ considerably from this one but the principles are the same. Remove the toxins, help repair the digestive tract and liver and provide a healthy and nutritious diet.

Skin and Coat

Keeping Skin Healthy

How do you keep your dog's coat and skin healthy? A good diet is the foundation of a healthy skin and coat, and parasite control and regular grooming helps keep it in top shape. A dog's skin is different to human skin (the acidity of dogs' skin is 7.5 and human skin is 5.5). So it is best to use shampoos and conditioners formulated for dogs. Avoid using soap and fabric and wool washes, although they smell nice and are inexpensive they strip the skin of its natural oils. Preferably wash your dog's coat with a natural or oatmeal-based dog shampoo when necessary. Follow the directions on the product for best results. Your vet may provide you with a medicated shampoo, ensure you follow the directions and also rinse very thoroughly, as many shampoos can be drying to the skin.

Shampoo Your Dog

Shampoo on an 'as needs basis' rather than routinely. A healthy skin and coat will not ordinarily smell. Overwashing can dry the skin and predispose it to irritations. Oatmeal is a wonderful skin cleanser. Take one handful of oats and place inside a sock or stocking, swish this in the water and use the milky water left behind to soak your dog in. You can add a couple of drops of lavender oil to this. Rinse your dog with fresh water.

Rinses

- Light coated dogs: use chamomile tea 1 bag to 1 cup boiling water, leave bag in until cool, strain and add juice of 1 lemon (strained). Pour over dog and leave in.
- Dark coated dogs: use rosemary (1 tablespoon) to 1 cup boiling water; cool, strain and add 1 tablespoon of apple cider vinegar. Pour over dog and leave in.

Aromatherapy Oils

Dilute 2 drops of lavender oil per 1 teaspoon of almond oil. Rub this over your hands then rub through your dog's coat, for skin moistening and coat gloss. It is calming and has a mild anti-bacterial effect and a mild flea repellent action.

Chronic Skin Problems

If you have a dog with a chronic skin problem, you are not alone. Typically dogs with chronic dermatitis have been on repeated courses of antibiotics, antihistamines, corticosteroids and various shampoos and other medications, usually with short-term improvement but frequent relapses. The condition can also worsen over time as a result of the side-effects of common drugs.[160] Corticosteroids have side-effects that include increasing the risk of skin infection, urinary tract infections, adrenal gland problems and predisposing your dog to pancreatitis and mange (demodex).[161] From a holistic viewpoint, skin problems typically manifest from deeper causes. However, it is important to rule out the most common contributing factors and to have a conventional diagnosis.

A referral to a veterinary dermatologist is very worthwhile. Most skin investigations require a check for fleas and a skin scraping to rule out mites. For very itchy dogs that don't respond to medication, it is also worthwhile treating for mites (sarcoptes) anyway, even if mites cannot be found on skin scrapes.

There are tests for bacterial, yeast and fungal infections and a skin biopsy can often give valuable information about the problem. Blood tests can help rule out underlying problems such as thyroid disease or other endocrine problems and blood and skin tests are available to help determine allergies. A conventional diagnosis and treatment will usually be the first step in treating your dog holistically. But in order to really resolve the underlying cause and restore health we need to dig even deeper.

General Guidelines

It is important to recognise that several underlying factors can occur at the same time. If we can reduce any of these potential factors we can improve health and reduce symptoms, so an optimal diet with nutrients that improve skin integrity will raise health. Chronic stress (physical, mental, and emotional) or inappropriate vaccination can lower health as will a genetic predisposition for atopy or hypothyroidism. A mild dysbiosis, food intolerance, or toxaemia alone may not be obvious. But when several factors come together, such as poor diet, anxiety, long-term drug use, vaccination and exposure to environmental pollution, the body becomes overloaded and unhealthy or diseased.

As an informal rule, chronic skin disease cannot be corrected quickly. Allow approximately three months' treatment for a condition of one-year standing, plus one month per additional year.

With your vet, consider the following:

Depending on the nature and severity of the skin problem, the goal is to:

- remove barriers to healing (consider underlying factors such as dysbiosis or leaky gut)

- improve the integrity of the skin
- reduce sensitivity
- enhance digestion
- enhance liver function
- restore general health
- minimise or correct effects or side-effects of previous drug treatments
- reduce stress
- use nutritional and herbal supplements which help restore health, reduce sensitivity, modulate the immune system and support the skin

Diet

For a minimum of six weeks try changing your dog's diet to a single source of protein such as chicken, or pork, or turkey. Preferably choose a protein source that your dog has not been exposed to before. If you are not sure, start with turkey or chicken. You can use a veterinary diet prescribed by your vet, specifically designed for food sensitivities or a home-made diet (*see* Elimination Diets). Avoid any other protein sources (such as flavoured snacks). This is most appropriate for dogs with itchy skin, but can also be useful for dogs with chronic skin infections. Even simply improving your dog's nutrition and providing quality food can do wonders.

Supplements

As a basic guide, consider supplementing your dog for 4 to 6 weeks with antioxidants vitamins A, C and E, B complex (especially biotin), a good multimineral supplement that includes zinc, and a fatty acid supplement such as flax seed, safflower or sunflower oil (organic and cold pressed). Many premium quality diets have these nutrients already added. The antioxidants will help with inflammation and immunity, and zinc and fatty acids will help improve the integrity and strength of the skin. Avoid yeast and kelp in this initial period.

Allergic Skin Disease

Allergic diseases include atopy, food allergy, fleabite allergy, insect allergy, contact allergy and drug reactions. Often dogs that chew their feet or that have chronic ear problems have an underlying allergy. Pseudo allergies can occur too, due to adverse food reactions and chemical sensitivities; these resemble allergies but the mechanisms are different.

- Fleas are a very common cause of allergy and a trial flea treatment is worth considering even if you don't think your dog has fleas. (*See* flea control)
- Food allergy is most commonly associated with scratching of the ears, chronic ear problems, chewing the paws and licking the armpit and groin areas. Concurrent digestive problems have been reported in 10%–15% of dogs. Concurrent allergies (atopy and fleas) and skin infection is also common.[162] Food intolerances or sensitivities can also mimic the symptoms of allergies. Diets that help eliminate foods that cause allergies or reactions are worthwhile trying. (*See* 'elimination diets')

- Common contact allergies, chemical sources (of sensitivities) and aeroallergens include:
  - pollens and resins (grasses, trees, weeds), jasmine, wandering Jew (*Tradescantia fluminensis*), dandelion leaves, cedar wood and oleander
  - moulds
  - dust mites
  - medications such as neomycin, soaps, shampoos, petroleum derived products, lanolin, disinfectants, insecticides (shampoos, sprays, dips, and collars)
  - chlorinated water
  - home furnishings, fibres, dyes, polishes, cleansers, rubber and plastics (toys, bowls), dish washing detergents, cat litter, leather and metal collars, fertilisers, carpet deodorisers, cement.[163]

Atopy[164]

Atopy is an inherited tendency to be allergic to various environmental allergens (occurring in up to 15 per cent of dogs). It is the second most common allergic skin disease after flea allergy and once it develops, dogs tend to scratch on and off for the rest of their lives. Eight out of ten atopic dogs are also flea allergic and up to one third are food allergic.[165] Recent studies reveal that 80 per cent of atopic dogs are also allergic to house dust mites or house dust mix (dander, insect parts, moulds and house dust mites). Conventional treatment of allergies includes immunotherapy (hyposensitisation), avoidance of the offending allergens, antihistamines, cyclosporin, glucocorticoids (prednisolone), shampoos and fatty acid supplements.

However, it makes sense to do these first:
- Treat for fleas (whether you can see them or not).
- Put your dog onto an elimination diet.
- Control dust mite (use dust mite covers on bedding, dust mite sprays, vacuuming).

These steps alone can make a big difference!

Immunotherapy

Immunotherapy consists of tailoring an allergy vaccine specifically for your dog. Small skin injections are given daily, then weekly, then up to monthly. The body begins to tolerate the allergic substance so that eventually it no longer reacts to them. The success rate varies. Fifty per cent of dogs will show a good response or cure to this form of treatment, particularly if they are allergic to pollens or dust mite.[166] You will need to discuss this treatment with your vet or veterinary dermatologist.

Recommendations

Severe scratching

Consider using anti-inflammatory doses of vitamins. Very high doses of vitamins C and E and selenium for short periods can be beneficial but must only be given under the guidance of a veterinarian. Washing your dog with water can relieve itching quickly while steps are taken to address underlying problems. For itchy dogs that scratch all night, a 30-minute bout of exercise will assist greatly to reduce restlessness and scratching.

- In the case of severe scratching a bath can help calm and cool the skin. An oatmeal bath has therapeutic properties. Place ½–1 cup oatmeal into a sock or stocking and squeeze into water. The water should go a milky colour. Soak your dog for 10 minutes for skin soothing and calming. Three drops of lavender oil can be added to the bath water. Rinse your dog thoroughly in luke warm water and allow to dry.

Supplements

For improving skin integrity: Sunflower oil (omega-3 and 6) and flax seed oil (omega-3) or fish oil (omega-3). Add sardines to the diet (80 grams of sardines provides 800 mg of essential fatty acids). zinc, biotin, vitamins A, C and E and selenium as antioxidants to help reduce inflammation.

Also consider: quercertin, bioflavinoids, pycogenols, proanthocyanidins, B complex vitamins if stress involved, digestive enzymes and dimethylglycine.

Essential fatty acids

Up to 40 per cent of atopic dogs respond to essential fatty acids alone.[167] Safflower oil (1 teaspoon per 10 kg each day) may be useful where fatty acid deficiency is suspected (if your dog has been on a poor quality dry food diet) but may promote inflammation in some atopic dogs. Therefore concurrent supplementing with omega-3 fatty acids (flax seed, fish oil) is recommended.

Rinses and washes

- Shampoos and washes to remove allergens, should be beneficial. Weekly bathing with oatmeal shampoo may be beneficial.
- Cucumber slices applied to intensely inflamed areas will help to cool the skin and provide lots of antioxidants if your dog eats them!
- Aloe vera gel can be applied to skin directly if very red and hot
- Calendula can be made into an infusion and put into a pump pack and sprayed on irritated areas
- For itchy feet, soak them in Epsom salts in cool water for 5 to 10 minutes to relieve itching. Apply plantain gel or infusion of calendula to the red and inflamed skin between the toes
- Use evening primrose oil cream instead of hydrocortisone[168] or German chamomile (*Matricaria chamomilla*) as a 2 per cent cream to reduce inflammation and reduce the level of topical corticosteroid use.[169] Chamomile can also be used as a fresh infusion for dermatitis. Avoid using in dogs that are sensitive to daisies, ragweed or chrysanthemums.
- Thyme (*Thymus vulgaris*) is antiseptic, antifungal, and antioxidant. Add a couple of drops of essential oil to rinse water after a bath.
- Peppermint (*Mentha piperita*) is analgesic, antipruritic (anti-itch), antifungal and antibacterial. Peppermint is suitable as an infusion when there is intense scratching

or when there are hotspots, which are painful. Either make peppermint tea, cool it and apply as a final rinse or use a couple of essential oil drops in rinse water.

• Witchhazel (*Hamamelis virginiana*) reduces redness, has potent antioxidant activity and applied as a cream twice daily can improve atopic dermatitis; it also has a mild analgesic effect. It is very good where there are moist, sticky eruptions.

• Products containing chickweed gel are useful for hot and itchy skin and nettles for red, hot and weeping skin and eczema.

Herbs for internal use

Consider the alterative herbs for detoxification and support of the skin (burdock, cleavers, nettle, yellow dock, red clover).

• If you are using corticosteroids or after finishing a course of corticosteroids consider liquorice, St Mary's thistle, bupleurum or Rehmannia. (*See* Corticosteroid use.)

Herbs that are particularly useful include:

• Nettle (*Urtica dioica*, *Urtica urens*). Nettle leaf is an anti-inflammatory and has a traditional use as a 'blood purifier' for the treatment of chronic skin eruptions. It can be used to treat eczema and other skin conditions.[170]

• Burdock root (*Articum lappa*). Burdock has a traditional use for dermatitis. Inulin, the main active, modifies the inflammatory process and burdock also has direct antimicrobial activity for staph infections.[171]

Evening primrose oil from evening primrose plant (*Oenothera biennis*) is anti-inflammatory and corrects omega-6 essential fatty acid deficiency. It may be beneficial in atopic dogs[172] and those with autoimmune skin disease. Long-term treatment appears to be safe.

Acupuncture

Acupuncture and Traditional Chinese Medicine can assist skin allergies by regulating the immune system and supporting the body. Acupuncture points are selected based on the individual symptoms, but some good points to consider are: GB 20 to remove 'wind', GV 14 to remove 'heat', SP 6 & 10 to remove 'damp', LI 4 and LI 11, ST 36 to modulate the immune system, HT 7 for calming and LU 7 to disperse 'wind'. Other points to be considered include those associated with the affected meridians. Blood deficiency is a common problem and the herbs in the formula Xang Fen Sao can assist here. Other Chinese herbs that may be useful include Xang Feng San and Liu Wei Di Huang Wan. Choice will depend upon the patterns observed and the TCM diagnosis.

Bach Flowers

Check to see if stress or behavioural problems are also present. If so, choose Bach Flower remedies according to your dog's needs. Crab-apple is a cleansing remedy considered useful in detoxification.

Homeopathy

For skin allergies, a veterinary homeopath should be consulted. Homeopathy combines well with nutrition and supplementation. Some remedies to consider include: Apis mel if rash is red and swollen; Cantharsis if skin is red and angry looking; Graphites for moist, red skin especially in the armpits or groin; Psorinum for hot, itchy skin and dog prefers heat; Pulex for flea allergies; Sulphur for the dog who has hot, itchy skin who prefers cool places; Urticaria if the skin is itchy or worse with cold.

Biochemical salts

Potassium sulphate 6x, Potassium chloride 6x

Chronic or Recurrent Skin Infections

While skin allergies are very common, there are other frustrating skin problems that can be helped along with natural therapies. Once again a diagnosis is essential, and a referral to a dermatologist is very worthwhile.

Bacterial Skin Disease and Hotspots

Chronic bacterial infections (also called pyoderma) usually respond well to systemic antibiotics only to flare up again some time down the track. Other conventional medications used include topical antibiotic preparations, medicated shampoos and other medications. For hot spots (pyotraumatic dermatitis) the conventional combination of corticosteroids and antibiotic products produce the best results and quickest healing. Recurring bacterial dermatitis may be associated with allergy (food, atopy, contact), parasites (demodex, flea, sarcoptes) and dandruff also called seborrhoea (possibly diet, endocrine, keratinisation or environment) or because of compromised immunity. Many dogs have a concurrent superficial yeast infection on their skin and respond to shampoos formulated for the treatment of 'malassezia' or other antifungal agents. If these conditions recur or respond poorly to antibiotic treatment or other conventional treatments, a naturopathic approach can be considered.

Naturopathic Approach to Pyoderma

If there is a history of repeated or long-term antibiotic use, consider dysbiosis or leaky gut as a possible underlying contributing factor to the chronicity of the problem, and possibly a compromised immune system. Also consider the following:

Diet

Raise the plane of nutrition either by using a good quality, fatty acid supplemented diet that includes antioxidants. Consider adding zinc, fatty acids, and vitamins A, C, E as a minimum. A home-made diet may be formulated incorporating these supplements. Take into account possible leaky gut.

Herbs

A veterinary herbalist can tailor the best herbs that suit your dog's condition.

- Consider the herbs that are used for detoxification.
- Consider herbs that support the skin (nettle, alfalfa, cleavers, red clover, burdock, and yellow dock) as well as immune-enhancing herbs such as echinacea and astragalus or withania in combination.
- For animals with poor immunity and or recurrent infections consider:
- Immune-enhancing herbs: Echinacea, astragalus, picrorrhiza, liquorice, andrographis, phytolacca (especially if lymphatic involvement)
- Golden seal (*Hydrastis canadensis*) contains berberine, a well-documented antimicrobial agent. It has also been found to stimulate immunity and decrease inflammatory processes.[173]
- Tonic and adaptogenic herbs: ginseng (*Panex ginseng*), withania (not during an acute infection)

Hydrotherapy

Water is an excellent therapeutic agent, used to remove crusts, scale, debris and dirt, in order to clean wounds and fistulae and to reduce pain and pruritus (itching). The water may be cool or above body temperature. In order to properly hydrate the skin, 10–15 minute bathing must be allowed. If the contact time is too short and baths are given too frequently, then the continual drying actually leads to dehydration of the skin. Take care not to immerse your dog for too long as this may cause injury to the skin with a loss of the protective barrier function.[174]

- Warm water soaks and whirlpools, povidine iodine or lavender oil can be added.
- If using shampoos, rinse for a long time to decrease undesirable irritant effects. (At least 5 minutes.)

Compresses

For localised infections use warm compresses to soak areas e.g. pressure point pyoderma, chin pyoderma, abscesses between the toes. Warm tea bags (green tea) can help dry moist eruptions and are high in antioxidants. Tea is also useful for non-healing ulcers and excellent for hotspots.

Moisturising agents

Use moisturising agents in rinses to decrease skin dryness and irritation caused by anti-bacterial agents. (Look for emollients, emulsifiers and humectants). These agents lubricate, rehydrate and restore the normal skin surface and soften the skin and hair coat.[175] These are commercially available. Otherwise consider a couple of drops of lavender oil in sesame or almond oil. Oatmeal milk may also be soothing and moisturising.

Topical agents

Consider the following:

- Evening primrose oil cream.[176]

- Thyme (*Thymus vulgaris*). Oil of thyme has shown antibacterial properties against staphylococcus species.[177] The active ingredient in thyme is thymol, which possesses some antiallergic and anti-inflammatory properties.[178] It may be useful as an external rinse after shampooing, and as an essential oil, diluted with almond oil or in bath water.
- Echinacea (*Echinacea sp*) has wound healing, immune modulating, and anti-inflammatory and antimicrobial activity when applied externally. It can be applied as an infusion, or diluted ethanol extract in water.
- Tea tree oil, diluted as a rinse (be wary, there have been reported cases of toxicity and deaths with tea tree).

Hotspots

For simple hotspots, trim the hair around the area. If this is painful for your dog or difficult you will need to take him to your veterinarian. The area needs to be cleaned using salty water (1 teaspoon per cup of water). An oatmeal compress can be applied to the area. Stir ½ cup of rolled oats in 1 cup of luke warm water until moisture is absorbed. Drain excess water. Place oats between gauze or muslin so that your dog is not covered in porridge. Not a good look!

Apply the poultice for 10 to 15 minutes. The oatmeal is soothing and healing. Rinse with lukewarm water and pat the area dry.

Alternatively witchhazel can be cooling and soothing, or apply a green tea bag as a poultice.

If the hot spot does not look noticeably better overnight, you will need to seek veterinary attention. Corticosteroids and antibiotics work very quickly to provide relief. Your dog may require flea treatment too.

Acupuncture

Stimulate the immune system with ST 36, LI 11, and LI 4, remove heat with GV 14, SP 6 and SP 10 for damp and to harmonise blood, GB 20 helps to calm and BL 40 can assist if there is pain and heat associated with the pyoderma. Use local points and others depending on the pattern observed and TCM diagnosis. For moist eruptions Lung Tan Xie Gan Pill, Lien Chiao Pai Tu Pien when there is excess heat, itching and scabs.

Bach Flowers

Check to see if stress or behavioural problems are also present. Choose Bach Flower remedies according to your dog's needs.

Homeopathy

Chronic skin disorders can respond well to homeopathy. Success will depend on accurately matching the dog's symptoms to the remedy and may include constitutional remedies.

Psorinum for hot, itchy skin and if the dog prefers warmth; Urticaria for hot, itchy skin and if the dog prefers the cool; Hepar sulphuris if there is a sticky discharge.

Biochemical salts

Silica 6x, Calcium sulphate 6x, Potassium sulphate 6x

Yeast or Malassezia Dermatitis[179]

Malassezia is a normal yeast of dogs commonly found in the ear canal, anal sacs, paws, lip fold, rectum and vagina. It can become a problem when other diseases alter the microenvironment of the skin and disrupt the normal skin barrier thus encouraging overgrowth of this organism. It is often associated with atopy, food allergy, fleabite allergy, contact allergy, hormonal conditions (hyperadrenocorticism, diabetes mellitus, hypothyroidism) and cancer, and also zinc responsive dermatosis. It may be a cause of atopy as well.[180] It is typically very itchy, with red skin, a greasy surface, odour, pigmentation and thickening of the skin, hair loss and scale.

Conventional therapy

This is aimed at removing the yeast using:

- shampoos with miconazole, chlorhexidine, selenium sulphide twice weekly 10–15 minutes, symptoms may worsen initially as dead yeast releases cytotoxins.
- systemic treatment with oral ketaconazole

Naturopathic approach

Depending on the nature and severity of the overgrowth, the following can be used as a complement to conventional therapy or as alternatives:

Diet

Avoid known allergens or suspected allergens since these can weaken the immune system and provide a more hospitable environment for the yeast. Fish, poultry, meat and vegetables are usually suitable. Consider an Elimination diet.

Supplements

Sunflower oil and flax seed oil and fish oil rotated each day, zinc, biotin, vitamins A, C and E as antioxidants to help reduce inflammation. Consider bioflavinoids (inhibit inflammatory process, stabilise cell membranes, increase effectiveness of vitamin C).

Topical agents

- ½ organic vinegar and ½ water as a soak for feet, or douche for ears (⅓ vinegar and ⅔ water), or poultice for focal areas. Or after washing in shampoo apply as a rinse to leave on and dry for residual action. Vinegar can also be given internally 1 teaspoon per 5 kg diluted in drinking water or food.
- Thyme (*Thymus vulgaris*). The liquid extract used internally. An infusion (thyme leaves), essential oil or extract can be used externally. It may be useful as an external rinse after shampooing, and as an essential oil in bath water.
- Avoid olive oil because it enhances growth of Malassezia.

Systemic

Consider herbs that support the skin (nettle, cleavers, red clover, burdock, yellow dock) as well as immune-enhancing herbs such as echinacea and astragalus or withania.

- St Mary's thistle (if treating with ketaconazole to protect the liver) and liquorice and marshmallow for gastrointestinal protection.
- Pau d'arco (taheebo) has anti-yeast properties.
- Garlic has demonstrated antifungal activity against a wide range of fungi.[181]
- Ginger (*Zingiber officinale*), thyme (*Thymus vulgaris*) and rosemary (*Rosmarinus officinalis*) contain anti-yeast compounds and can be used externally as essential oils (diluted in water) or infusions.

Acupuncture

Depending on patterns observed consider these points to remove damp heat GV 14, SP 6, 9, 10. Also LI 11, ST 36 to stimulate immunity. Lung Tan Xie Gan pill may be useful.

Dry Skin and Dandruff

Dry skin and dandruff can be associated with diet (especially poor quality dry foods and unsupplemented home-made diets), flea allergies, food allergies, atopy, skin mites, skin infections, thyroid disease, diabetes, adrenal gland problems, sex hormone abnormalities and other conditions. So it is important to have a diagnosis and if necessary have a referral to a dermatologist.

Recommendations

Provided you have had your dog checked by a veterinarian and the skin is basically dry and the dandruff uncomplicated, start by upgrading the diet. Try a premium veterinary diet, or a low allergy veterinary diet. Alternatively make your dog's own diet following the guidelines and recipes in Chapter 4. Remember to change diets over slowly to avoid digestive upsets.

Supplements

Antioxidants vitamins C, A, E, zinc and chromium, sunflower or flax seed oil or evening primrose oil or fish oil rotated, digestive enzymes, lecithin, kelp.

Vitamin A is a very useful supplement for keratinisation disorders, follicular hyperkeratosis and sebaceous gland abnormalities.

Herbs

Consider:

- Burdock for dry scaly skin and dandruff especially when there is also arthritis
- Dandelion, alfalfa, red clover and burdock for chronic dandruff
- St Mary's thistle especially if long-term medication is also involved

Bach Flowers

Crab-apple is appropriate.

Homeopathy

Consider: Arsenicum album, fluor. acid, sepia, sulphur, thuja

Biochemical salts

Potassium sulphate 6x, Potassium chloride 6x

Other

Shampoos with sulphur and salicylic acid can be useful but very drying. They may be used initially followed by oatmeal shampoo. Rinse thoroughly. Consider applying humectants to moisturise the skin. Ensure sunshine, exercise and play.

Hair Loss and Shedding

Excessive hair loss can be related to genetics, hormonal imbalances (such as thyroid disease, sex hormones or Cushing's disease), a poor diet, parasites and other infections, immune problems, stress, corticosteroid use, allergies and can also be secondary to other problems. So it's important to have your dog checked before using complementary therapies.

Diet

Upgrade your dog's diet to a minimum of a premium veterinary diet, or a low allergy veterinary diet along with fresh foods. Ensure plenty of good quality protein to assist with regrowth of hair. Alternatively make your dog's own diet following the guidelines and recipes in Chapter 4. Remember to change the diet slowly to avoid digestive upsets.

Supplements

Antioxidants vitamins C, A, E, vitamin B complex, magnesium and chromium, zinc, sunflower or flax seed oil or evening primrose oil or fish oil rotated, digestive enzymes, lecithin, kelp

Herbs

Traditional tonics include fenugreek, dandelion, parsley, alfalfa and peppermint

Homeopathy

Consider: Arsenicum album, thallium, selenium, lycopodium, nat. mur.

Biochemical salts

Silica 6x

Anal Glands

Anal gland problems include inflammation (sacculitis), impaction or blocked anal glands and abscesses. These can be triggered by irregular bowel movements, soft stools, recent diarrhoea, poor muscle tone around the rear end, docked tails and excessive glandular secretions, worm infestations, and can be made worse by obesity. If your dog constantly licks his bottom or is irritated, another possibility is a food allergy or sensitivity.

Recommendations
If your dog is overweight, blocked anal glands will be an added incentive to lose the extra pounds. Regular exercise will assist in normal bowel movements, which will help normalise the anal glands.

Diet
Try a medium- to high-fibre diet. Add pumpkin (it's sweet and high in fibre).

Supplements
Consider: Metamucil or psyllium husks to increase the stool bulk. If inflammation is present use Vitamins A and C and B complex, Flax seed oil. If loose stools are a problem consider dysbiosis

Herbs
If inflammation or infection is present consider echinacea and garlic. If chronically blocked try stoneroot, gravelroot and cornsilk.

Externally
Apply calendula tincture diluted.

Homeopathy
Silica 6c for repeated blockages, Hepar sulph. if red and swollen.

Biochemical salts
If infected or inflamed Iron phosphate 6x, Potassium chloride 6x

Other
A compress of Epsom salts and water on cotton wool, or gauze held against the bottom for 10 minutes twice daily will help relieve discomfort. Be prepared to chase your dog!

Honey applied to a red and sore bottom will help heal the skin.

Lick Granulomas
Lick granulomas or acral lick granuloma are chronic skin lesions, usually found on the legs. They can be caused by joint pain, referred pain (from neck or shoulders for example), boredom, obsessive-compulsive behaviour (often worse with stress) and allergy.

Recommendations
A diagnosis is important to rule out underlying problems, especially if referred pain or an allergy. If referred pain is present then consider chiropractic and/or acupuncture.

Diet

Consider a low allergy diet, especially if allergy is suspected. Add raw meaty bones to the diet to provide behavioural enrichment.

Supplements

Vitamins A, E and C, zinc and sunflower oil or flax seed oil

Topical

Vitamin E from a punctured capsule once daily or aloe vera gel applied twice daily or calendula cream applied daily

Bach Flowers

Select the most appropriate Bach Flowers for your dog.

Acupuncture

Acupuncture can be very effective in the treatment of lick granulomas, which are seen in Chinese Medicine as a blockage of Qi. Needles are placed around the lesion 'circling the dragon'. Other points help improve the immune system and calm the dog. Consider PC 6, GB 31, GV 20, GV 19, GV 20, HT7, PC 6, plus master points of leg.

Doggy Odour

Abnormal odour could stem from an ear infection, skin disease, hormonal problems, kidney disease or tooth and gum problems. Also consider dysbiosis as a possibility.

Diet

Upgrade your dog's diet; include fresh vegetables and some fruit if possible.

Supplements

Vitamin B complex, vitamin C, chromium, lecithin, digestive enzymes, kelp

Herbs

Parsley (1–3 teaspoons depending on size) fresh, added daily, alfalfa, St Mary's (or milk) thistle, dandelion

Biochemical salts

Silicea 6x, Kali phos.-Potassium phosphate 6x

Acupuncture

Acupuncture can be considered for chronic body odour, where points are selected on the nature of the smell, tongue colour, pulse and history. Points to enhance the immune system may also help.

Demodectic Mange

Demodex is a mite that lives in the hair follicle. It is quite normal for these mites to be found in healthy dogs. But when they are in abnormally high numbers, they can contribute to hair loss and bacterial infection. A genetic or immune disorder is thought to underlie mange in dogs.

Localised demodectic mange results in patches of hair loss especially around the face and eyes. Most cases heal spontaneously. Most young dogs recover as their immune system matures. If an adult dog succumbs to demodectic mange it is a signal that there is something very wrong. This form of mange may be associated with corticosteroid use, immune suppression, cancer or internal disease, so it is vital that your dog's condition is checked out.

Conventional treatments include injections, chemical washes and some new experimental drugs. Antibiotics are usually necessary because bacterial infections associated with demodex can be life threatening.

Recommendations

It is wise to take up conventional treatment for demodex and to use complementary therapies as well. Consider upgrading the diet to a premium quality diet or home-made or a combination. Include fresh vegetables, liver and if possible (raw, slightly cooked) thymus gland or glandular product containing thymus.

Supplements

Vitamins A, C and E, dimethylglycine, digestive enzymes, kelp, zinc, fatty acids

Herbs

Herbs can be very helpful to support the immune system, where conventional treatment does not have a great deal to offer. A veterinary herbalist must be consulted.

Echinacea, pau d'arco, garlic

Neem can be applied externally and given internally.

St Mary's thistle to assist detoxification especially if conventionally medicated.

Xiao Yao San may be useful.

Bach Flowers

May be useful as a support, particularly if your dog is depressed.

Crabapple, Walnut, Olive, Mustard

Acupuncture

Acupuncture can be a very useful adjunct to enhance the immune system and help control infection.

Consider LI 4, LI 11, ST 36, SP 6, BL 13, GV 14 and if on the face LU 7.

Digestive System

The digestive system can be affected by stress, anxiety, depression and many medications as well as a lack of fibre, by parasites, food allergies and dysbiosis. It is
sometimes difficult to appreciate how the digestive tract can affect general health, but
if food is not digested properly it can lead to a whole cascade of other problems. Many
chronic diseases such as arthritis and skin disease can have digestive disturbances as
an underlying cause.

Digestion can be supported by feeding your dog the best diet you can.

Supplements

Consider Vitamin B complex, digestive enzymes, probiotics, prebiotics
Flax seed oil, glutamine, glucosamine

Herbs

Consider alfalfa, fenugreek, dandelion, peppermint, slippery elm, marshmallow

Acupuncture

Consider:
Acute gastrointestinal signs ST 36, PC 6, ST 25, GV 11, VC 4, CV 6, LI 4, LI 11, treat
once or twice daily for three to six treatments.

Chronic gastrointestinal signs, same points but treat once or twice weekly for
three to six treatments

Vomiting and diarrhoea, chronic diarrhoea, constipation LI 4, LI 11, GV 14, PC 6

Gum Disease and Periondontal Disease

Are your dog's teeth stained with brown material? Is his breath unpleasant? Can you see
any grey, white or yellow material around the base of the teeth where they meet the

gums? If so, your dog probably has gingivitis or periodontal disease. Periodontal disease is the most common disease occurring in dogs, it is insidious and can be easily over-looked. It is estimated that between 60 per cent and 80 per cent of all dogs are affected.

Periodontal disease is initially caused by the accumulation of plaque (and plaque bacteria) on the teeth and surrounding structures, it progresses steadily and may become incurable. Plaque accumulates due to poor oral hygiene, but it can be made worse if the dog has concurrent disease or compromised immunity. There are some 200 different bacteria associated with plaque, some are harmless but others destroy tissue, produce harmful substances and can damage the bone and teeth. There are also reports suggesting an association between the presence of periodontal disease and illnesses affecting the lungs, kidneys and heart. Moderate to severe cases of peri-odontal disease may result in bacteria entering the bloodstream.

Calculus, the hard brown stuff on teeth, forms when plaque is mineralised with calcium salts from saliva. In itself it doesn't cause any harm; however, it provides a rough surface for bacteria to accumulate around. Prevention of periodontal disease requires removing existing plaque and calculus and preventing further accumulation.

Diet

Hard, fibrous foods are more effective than sticky, soft diets (such as fresh meat or canned food) at preventing the accumulation of dental deposits and development of gingivitis. Include raw meaty bones and fresh vegetables and fruit (celery, apples, car-rots, and cauliflower) in the diet to increase the hardness of the diet. Some biscuits and chews are specifically designed to help clean teeth. Not all dry foods are equally effective at reducing the build-up of plaque and not all soft diets have the same effect on plaque accumulation. The following are some other suggestions to prevent dental disease.

Options

- Feeding your dog raw meaty bones early in life and on a regular basis will help towards preventing periodontal disease, but not in all dogs or for all teeth. Raw hide chews, dried pigs' ears, chews, very hard biscuits, special dental diets, dental ropes and other types of chews should be considered. The abrasive effect of gnaw-ing also helps strengthen the periodontal ligaments of the teeth.
- Tooth brushing needs to be done daily to be effective.[182] Small dogs with crowded teeth should begin having their teeth brushed as puppies. They are prone to peri-odontal disease especially in the front teeth, due to hair and food getting caught between the teeth. Dog toothbrushes and toothpastes are available. Baby tooth-brushes might also be useful.
- Oral cleansing gels that contain zinc, vitamin C and sulphur amino acids can be used daily and are easy to apply since they are wiped on the gums instead of brushing.
- A veterinary dental scale and polish can be carried out at most veterinary practices. There are veterinarians who also specialise in veterinary dentistry should you want a referral. Dental scaling requires sedation or anaesthesia to be performed

correctly. Simply cracking off brown calculus is not enough. The space underneath the gum and between the teeth and gums needs to be cleaned too. After teeth have been cleaned they can be kept clean by some of the suggestions above. If your dog has severe periodontal disease, some teeth may need to be removed and more treatments may be necessary to prevent progression of the disease.

Supplements

Antioxidants vitamins C, E (vitamin E can be rubbed directly on inflamed gums), Coenzyme Q10 for periodontal and gum disease

Herbs

If periodontal disease is severe, your veterinarian may recommend antibiotics. In addition to, or instead of, consider echinacea, pau d'arco, golden seal (or Oregon grape root), astragalus

Gum rubs

- One tablespoon of medical honey use with cloth or brush gently.
- Chamomile tincture and tea can be used for inflamed gums.
- 1 teaspoon Slippery elm powder mixed with warm water, use with cloth or brush gently.
- Fennel tincture can be applied to the gums for gingivitis.
- Plantain tincture or fresh crushed herb is good for gum disease and tooth root abscesses.
- Thyme tea and tincture can be used as a disinfectant for the mouth and gums by swabbing.
- Neem toothpaste can be beneficial for mild gingivitis and periodontal disease.
- Myrrh tincture or myrrh powder can be swabbed or brushed gently onto infected gums.
- St John's wort can be used if the gums are very painful.

Homeopathy

Sore gums: Arsenicum album; Bleeding gums: phosphorus; Swollen gums and foul odour: Mercurius solibulis, hypericum, Ferrum phos.

Bad Breath

Bad breath may be due to poor diet, poor digestion, enzyme deficiency, indigestion, poor hygiene, chronic constipation, stress and anxiety, gum disease, food intolerance problems or another problem. The most common reason is bad teeth and gums.

Recommendations

Have your vet check your dog first. If the cause is not obvious (pay particular attention to the teeth) then consider the following:

Diet

Provide a good quality premium pet food or home-made diet.

Cut out scraps, feed raw carrot, bones and oxtails.

Consider raw hide chews to stimulate saliva to help clean the mouth.

Include fresh fruits and green vegetables, parsley and sprouts.

Increase the fluids in the diet with some soupy meals.

Supplements

Chlorophyll, charcoal, digestive enzymes, probiotics, vitamin C, vitamin B complex plus coenzyme Q 10 if periodontal disease is suspected.

Herbs

Fennel, dandelion, parsley, peppermint

Bach Flowers

Crab-apple

Homeopathy

Mercurius solibulis

Biochemical salts

Potassium chloride 6x, Potassium phosphate 6x

Other

Ensure your dog has plenty of exercise to improve elimination of wastes. Clean the teeth and gums with myrrh gum powder or pet toothpaste. Groom your dog daily.

Acute Diarrhoea

Acute diarrhoea is quite common in dogs. Intestinal parasites, food poisoning, too much food, rancid or unripe foods, lactose intolerance, too many antibiotics, undue stress and viruses and bacterial infections are possible causes. Diarrhoea is the body's way of eliminating the offending stuff quickly! Antibiotics may lead to disturbances of normal gut bacteria and can lead to chronic diarrhoea,[183] so are not normally used in treating mild diarrhoea. Most diarrhoea is self-limiting and dogs recover quickly with some general support.

If there is no response to the suggestions below within twelve to twenty-four hours or if there is vomiting, fever, thirst or abdominal pain, veterinary attention must be sought. Dogs can die of severe dehydration. Contact your vet if you are not sure.

Recommendations

Consider a short fast for twenty-four hours.

Your veterinarian can provide you with a commercial fluid replacer with electrolytes and also canned and dried foods suitable for feeding after diarrhoea, they are usually made from a single protein source such as fish or chicken to minimise the risk of developing food allergies.

Alternatively provide chicken broth for twenty-four hours (cool and remove fat then strain liquid, reserve solids), and then feed the solids from the broth, providing small meals four to five times the following day. Feed a bland diet of chicken or fish and rice. Gradually reintroduce normal diet over the next two to three days.

Chicken and Rice recipe

Rice, white, raw	⅔ cup
Chicken breast, raw, lean, skinless	400g (4 halves)
Chicken liver	25g

Cook chicken liver and rice together, and poach chicken lightly. Mix recipe together and divide into several small meals.

Energy from protein 44%, fat 13%, carbohydrate 40% calories 1000. This diet is for short-term use only because it is not complete or balanced. Use when a 'bland' diet is required.

Carrot Soother for Diarrhoea

1 well cooked carrot
½ teaspoon rice flour
¼ cup warm (boiled) water

Combine 2 teaspoons of mashed carrot with flour and water. Mix well and give to dog.

Supplements

Glutamine helps promote recovery and normal activity when the intestine is inflamed,[184] Fructo-oligosaccharides, Fibre such as Metamucil or psyllium, Probiotics powdered acidophilus, bifidus and other organisms, digestive enzymes, vitamin B complex, potassium, activated charcoal

Herbs

Carob powder (1 gram per kilogram per day), diluted in broth. It is safe and high in dietary fibre.
Slippery elm powder (1 gram per kilogram per day)
Golden rod or Oregon grape root for bacterial infections or garbage eating
Marshmallow for inflammation
Oak bark for acute diarrhoea

Bach Flowers

Crab-apple may be useful. Also consider any underlying stress factors that could be contributing to, or triggering episodes. Try walnut, crab-apple, star of Bethlehem, Rescue Remedy and olive.

Acupuncture

Consider: ST 36, BL 21, BL 20, BL 25, LI 4, LIV 13, LI 11, CV 12.

Homeopathy

Pulsatilla when stools are sloppy, then normal, then sloppy; sulphur for diarrhoea worse in the morning and in hot weather; nux vomica after eating too much food or rich food; Arsenicum album when there are traces of blood in diarrhoea

Biochemical salts

Iron phosphate 6x

Other

Avoid exercise except for a gentle walk, because your dog may be weak.

Chronic Diarrhoea

Chronic or long-term diarrhoea may have several underlying causes. Veterinary attention must be sought. Chronic diarrhoea can be due to bacteria, malabsorption of food, inflammation of the large bowel, food allergy or sensitivities, pancreatic disease, anxiety, stress and many other problems. Sensitivity to particular foods can be difficult to prove, but the most common problem foods are milk proteins, soy proteins (including tofu), wheat, beef, egg, horse, chicken and pork.[185] Food additives, artificial colourings and preservatives are also possible.[186]

Often a combination of conventional drug therapy, diet and alternative therapies offers the best chance of success. Complementary therapy will depend on the individual dog's inherent health and severity of the problem, and whether there are other problems besides the diarrhoea. Many dogs will respond to herbal and dietary therapy and can be managed effectively. The longer the diarrhoea has been a problem, the less likely a cure will be effected, but it will be possible to at least get an improvement. Consider the Bowel Detoxification Program for chronic digestive tract problems.

Diet

Use a low-fat diet, especially if the pancreas is involved or there is poor fat digestion such as inflammatory bowel disease or small intestinal bacterial overgrowth. Low-fat recipes should be fed under the supervision of a veterinarian.

Colitis is thought to be immune mediated. Use a single protein source (moderate to high quantities of good quality protein are recommended) your dog has not been exposed to before, such as fish, cottage cheese, turkey or lamb or a commercial veterinary diet designed for the management of diarrhoea. This should be carried out under veterinary supervision and be fed for a minimum of six weeks. Feed several small meals daily rather than one or two large ones.

Preferably use rice as a grain source. Rice is gluten free, highly digestible and ferments less than other grains. It also contains substances that support repair of the cells lining the digestive tract.[187]

Avoid milk products that contain lactose such as milk and cheese.

Small quantities of dietary fibre (soluble and non-soluble) are generally beneficial, but excessive amounts can worsen the condition.

With bowel inflammation, the addition of oats to the diet may be beneficial as a source of L-glutamine that can assist with repair of the digestive tract.

Supplements

High doses of vitamins E and A, and selenium may be useful in reducing the inflammation of inflammatory bowel disease,[188] Vitamin B complex is important (especially where the small intestine is involved), glutamine helps promote recovery and normal activity when the intestine is inflamed,[189] Fructo-oligosaccharides, fibre from oat bran, psyllium, legumes, fruit, vegetables.

Probiotics such as powdered acidophilus, bifidus and other organisms, Multivitamin/mineral.

Glucosamine may be helpful in inflammatory bowel disease, chronic colitis and food allergies (aids in the repair of mucosal cells),[190] digestive enzymes, flax seed oil, vitamins C and E, dimethylglycine.

Herbs

Carob powder; Slippery elm powder; Ginger and turmeric as calminatives; Peppermint can help abdominal pain and other symptoms associated with irritable bowel syndrome;[191] Aloe vera for an inflamed bowel; Liquorice for inflammatory bowel disease, de-glycyrrhizinated liquorice helps restore damaged intestinal mucosa; Marshmallow for inflammation; Oak bark; Peppermint for ulcerative colitis; Red raspberry for chronic diarrhoea; Wild geranium for colitis with bleeding and inflammatory bowel disease.

Bach Flowers

Try walnut, crab-apple, star of Bethlehem, Rescue Remedy and olive.

Acupuncture

Acupuncture and Chinese herbs can be a very effective combination for chronic diarrhoea and bowel problems. Consider:

ST 36, ST 25, SP 6, BL 20, BL 21, BL 25, GV 14, GV 20, ST 37, ST 39.

Homeopathy

Merc. sol. for diarrhoea without pain, phosphorus when there is straining, podophyllum for watery diarrhoea

Biochemical salts

Iron phosphate 6x, nat. mur. 6x when diarrhoea alternates with constipation; kali mur. 6x for pale loose diarrhoea; nat. sulph. 6x for dark diarrhoea

Protein losing enteropathy due to problems of the lymphatic system or cancer need low-fat, high-protein, high-carbohydrate recipes. Medium chain triglycerides (such as coconut oil) are special types of fats available as 'body builder' supplements from health food stores. They may be useful in protein losing enteropathy and malabsorption syndromes. A suggested dose is 1–2 mls per kilogram per day.[192]

Some dogs (such as Irish Setters)[193] may be sensitive to gluten, so rice should be used—avoid oats, barley, rye, wheat, buckwheat and millet. Papain is an enzyme from papaya (commercially available) that helps digest wheat gluten and may help some dogs to tolerate gluten.

Inflammatory Bowel Disease such as colitis, proctatitis, lymphocytic–plasmacytic enteritis, lymphocytic-plasmacytic gastritis, histiocytic colitis may respond to a single protein source diet.

Yoghurt is sometimes recommended for therapy of chronic diarrhoea, but the bacteria in the yoghurt are largely destroyed by stomach acid, which limits the numbers that reach the gut. Therefore powdered probiotics products with concentrated numbers of these bacteria are recommended instead

Food Allergies *(See also* Skin disorders)

If the digestive system is overwhelmed or damaged, food is not dealt with normally. Allergies can occur at lining of the gut and when food particles enter the body and become recognised as foreign by the immune system. This can happen with intestinal parasites, intestinal infections, diarrhoea, following parvovirus, and when there is inflammation such as colitis. 'Leaky gut' syndrome is one manifestation where when the digestive tract is inflamed, the lining becomes more permeable to food proteins, which can then enter the blood stream.

Food allergy occurs when the body develops an antibody response to a component of the food, usually a protein. It is often a food that your dog eats regularly. Food intolerance occurs when there is a deficiency of an enzyme (eg lactase in milk intolerance) or when the food is high in histamine or other chemical substances (from the food or contaminants) that can exert an abnormal effect. Allergy and intolerance can occur with either food or food additives, including prepared or commercial food and home-made food.

Symptoms of food allergy include any or all of itchy skin, otitis externa (ear problems), vomiting, diarrhoea, more regular bowel movements, behavioural changes and (very rarely) seizures. A blood test is available that can assist in pinpointing what foods might be causing the problems. This can be done quickly and head you on the right path, but it is not 100 per cent reliable. Food intolerance and food allergy can usually be identified when the symptoms improve when the food is excluded, when symptoms recur on challenge with the food and generally your dog will show improvement when the foods are avoided altogether.

Options

1. Consider a food Elimination diet using a protein source your dog has not been exposed to previously. A homemade diet or veterinary low allergy diet can be

used. It is important that during the trial, no flavoured heartworm medications, or flavoured supplements including yeast are given. The diet must be fed for at least 6 weeks. Once symptoms have resolved, consider adding in one food type at a time each week. Avoid common food allergens such as dairy foods, wheat, beef, corn, tomatoes, nuts, and mushrooms.

2. Consider the Bowel Detoxification Program as another alternative approach.

Coprophagy

The only time when faeces eating is normal, is when a bitch eats her puppies' waste. It can be a behavioural problem or a symptom of pancreatic insufficiency, malabsorption, worms, diabetes or other problems. If an underlying cause cannot be found there are a few options:

1. It is possible that your dog's digestive system is not coping well with his current diet. You may need to switch to a meat-based dry food, or homemade diet and add dietary enzymes (especially if the pancreas is involved). Papain is useful. An improvement should be seen within seven days to two weeks as your dog adjusts. The stool eating should resolve. If this is not effective try the Bowel Detoxification Program.
2. Try distracting your dog. Keep him on a harness or leash and when you see him head for his target, redirect him.
3. Coprophagy might also be associated with adrenal gland depletion due to stress (*see* Adrenal Gland Health)

Constipation

Constipation can result from too many bones in the diet, hair, excess fibre, a lack of exercise, difficulty in moving around (such as severe arthritis), drugs (such as diuretics, antihistamines, iron supplements), diseases of the rectum or anus, trauma, spinal cord disease and other problems. It's therefore important to have the problem investigated to rule out underlying causes.

Recommendations

Address the underlying causes. Increase exercise, even in old dogs. A short walk can encourage toileting and increase regularity. Encourage regularity by being consistent with timing of feeding and walks. Encourage plenty of fluids by feeding moist foods and broths. Avoid using laxatives and paraffin or other mineral oils as they can reduce the absorption of fatty acids and some vitamins and minerals.

Diet

A diet high in fruit and vegetables will increase both fibre and water in the diet. Aim for a fibre content of between 7 to 15 per cent. Include at least 1 to 4 tablespoons of cooked pumpkin daily in the diet. Encourage drinking by using broth and soups.

Supplements

Fibre from psyllium and oat bran should be added daily.

Herbs

If necessary, laxative herbs can be used intermittently. These include *Cascara sagrada* or *Cassia senna*. Avoid aloe vera since it can be irritating when given internally. Essiac for chronic constipation; Liquorice for chronic constipation; Slippery elm is a safe herbal supplement and can be used intermittently to help regulate the bowels; Plantain for sudden constipation; Yellow dock.

Bach Flowers

Crab-apple

Acupuncture

Consider LI 4, LI 11, ST 36, ST 25, BL 25, CV 12.

Prolapsed rectum

Consider GV 20, BL 20, LIV 13, GV 1, CV 1.

Homeopathy

Stools very dry: sulphur; Small round hard faeces: nux vomica

Flatulence

Obvious flatulence can indicate poor digestion or excessive fermentation in the bowel. It may be a natural consequence with certain foods such as legumes and beans. If it is persistent and offensive then consider the following:

Recommendations

A change in diet may be helpful. A diet that is highly digestible (good quality premium diets) means less is left in the large bowel to ferment. It may also help to begin with a Bowel Detoxification Program. Exercise is important to stimulate elimination.

Diet

Avoid soy products, beans, legumes, cabbage, and onions. Include fresh apple, yoghurt, brown rice and vegetables.

Supplements

Probiotics, nutritional yeast, vitamin B complex, digestive enzymes

Herbs

Slippery elm, fenugreek, chamomile, parsley, peppermint, fennel

Bach Flowers

Crab-apple

Homeopathy

Distended stomach, bloating and stomach rumbles: lycopodium
Nux vomica after eating rich food, overeating or constipation

Biochemical salts

Sodium sulphate 6x

Chronic Vomiting

Occasional vomiting is not uncommon in dogs. If your dog vomits frequently or there are other symptoms, have your dog checked by your veterinarian. There are digestive tract problems and other non-digestive related disorders that can lead to chronic vomiting. Chronic vomiting can also be confused with regurgitation, where food is expelled from the food pipe (oesophagus). Sometimes vomiting can be continuous without affecting the overall health of your dog, in other words he appears quite bright and active. It is important to try and find out what is causing the vomiting. If nothing can be found consider:

Diet

Try an Elimination diet for four to six weeks to see if there is an improvement. Attempt to raise the food bowl off the ground to the height of the shoulders. (Place the bowl on a stack of newspapers.) Consider spreading the food over a larger plate, so that your dog doesn't vacuum the food in one gulp.

Supplements

Consider: Vitamin B complex, digestive enzymes, activated charcoal

Herbs

Peppermint; Ginger; Fennel; Chamomile; Catnip.

Nervous dogs may vomit from stress and may benefit from celery extracts, cardamon or fennel.

Pyloric valve dysfunction may benefit from alfalfa.

Valerian and skullcap help relax the oesophagus.

Acupuncture

Megaesophagus responds reasonably well to acupuncture, try: LI 4, LI 11, HT 9, PC 6, PC 9, ST 36, ST 40.

Chronic vomiting may respond to acupuncture try: PC 6, ST 36, SP 6, BL 20, BL 21.

Tendency towards gastric dilation try: ST 36, ST 44, PC 6, BL 17, BL 20, BL 21.

Bach Flowers

Rescue Remedy, crab-apple, walnut, olive, star of Bethlehem

Homeopathy

Vomiting with diarrhoea: arsenicum

Watery vomit especially after drinking: mercurius corrosivus

Yellowish liquid vomit: mercurius solubilus

Vomiting after eating: phosphorus

Liver Disease

Infections, cancer, parasites, viruses, toxins, trauma, other illnesses, drugs and some anaesthetics can all take their toll on the liver. Toxins that have been associated with liver-toxicity include drugs such as acetaminophen, corticosteroids, halothane anaesthetics, mebendazole, methoxyflourane, phenytoin, thiacetarsemide and trimethoprim-sulphadiazine antibiotics. Heavy metals, some insecticides, herbicides and fungal toxins are also harmful. Liver disease needs to be diagnosed by your veterinarian, and the underlying causes determined. Conventional treatment is usually necessary and can be supported with complementary therapy.

Recommendations

Diet is very important to minimise the work of the liver. One of the best supports you can provide is St Mary's thistle, well known for its liver protective and liver restoring properties. If possible reduce the use of chemicals in and around the home and on your dog. Under veterinary advice reduce drug use if possible. Encourage consumption of plenty of fluids to aid in detoxifying the body.

Diet

A highly digestible, moderate protein diet is generally recommended. Your veterinarian can prescribe a suitable commercial diet. Consider adding globe artichokes (*Cynara scolymus*) to stimulate the detoxifying action of the liver.[194] Also consider small amounts of fresh liver. Carrot, beets, cucumber, steamed vegetables, rice, eggs and apples are all helpful.

Supplements

Taurine is important for gall bladder function, antioxidants vitamins C, E, Beta carotene L-carnitine, flax seed oil, lecithin, zinc, vitamin B complex

Herbs

St Mary's thistle (*Silybum marianum*) for hepatitis, detoxification; it protects the liver and assists regeneration. Liquorice helps protect the liver from toxins; Bupleurum; Barberry; Dandelion stimulates bile flow; Astragalus; Reishi mushroom; Garlic; Yellow dock for heavy metal poisoning.

Bach Flowers

Crab-apple, agrimony, holly may be useful.

Acupuncture

Consider LIV 13, BL 18, BL 19, BL 20, ST 36, GB 34, GV 9, depending on Eastern diagnosis

Homeopathy

Nux vomica, lycopodium, phosphorus

Biochemical salts

Nat. sulph. 6x

Exercise

Provide mild exercise daily to help stimulate elimination of wastes and improve circulation.

PANCREATIC PROBLEMS

Exocrine Pancreatic Insufficiency

This describes the disease where the pancreas is unable to produce all the enzymes needed to digest food. Fat is the most difficult food to digest, so a poorly functioning pancreas leads to poor digestion, weight loss, a ravenous appetite, and stinky faeces. Usually life long supplementation with digestive enzymes is needed. Other complications such as diabetes can occur.

Pancreatitis

A more acute form of pancreas disease is called pancreatitis. Here the pancreas is very inflamed and there is some self-digestion by the enzymes produced. It is a very painful condition with vomiting and pain as the main symptoms. Pancreatitis is a condition that responds best to conventional medicine, including fasting, although some of the suggestions below will also apply for the recovery period.

Recommendations

The pain of pancreatitis can be relieved by acupuncture treatment in addition to conventional care. A controlled diet is the best way to minimise the symptoms of exocrine pancreatic insufficiency along with digestive enzyme supplements.

Diet

For chronic pancreas problems, a highly digestible, low-fat, low-fibre diet is recommended. Protein should be of high quality and easy to digest. The food should be fed in small amounts often rather than one big meal. Each meal should be supplemented with digestive enzymes. Low-fat recipes should be fed under the supervision of a veterinarian:

Supplements

Powdered digestive enzymes, Cobalamin, vitamins A, D, E, K (fat soluble vitamins may be low in a low-fat diet), vitamin B complex, zinc, copper, multivitamin mix, trace elements

Herbs

Oak bark and fringetree bark via enema for pancreatitis
St Mary's thistle for exocrine pancreatic insufficiency

Echinacea, pau d'arco or Oregon grape root if there is an overgrowth of bacteria
Dandelion, peppermint, barberry, liquorice for chronic pancreatitis

Bach Flowers
Rescue Remedy is appropriate for pancreatitis.

Acupuncture
For pancreatitis consider GB 34, PC 6, LI 4, LI 11, GV 14, PC 6, ST 36, BL 20, SP 6, BL 23.

For exocrine pancreatic insufficiency treat according to Eastern diagnosis and symptoms.

Homeopathy
Phosphorus may be beneficial, or remedies for vomiting and/or diarrhoea if necessary.

Biochemical salts
Nat. phos. 6x

Diabetes
Any complementary therapy for diabetes must be used under the guidance of a veterinarian. This is because they can be very effective and doses of insulin may need to be lowered. See either a holistic veterinarian, or work closely with your regular veterinarian. The best approach is a combination of good diet, maintaining a normal weight, nutritional supplements and herbs.

Diet is the cornerstone of good diabetes management. If using insulin, follow your veterinarian's directions. Several small meals each day may be useful. Regular exercise is also valuable.

Include liver and pancreas in the diet (extracts of pancreas were used before insulin for the control of diabetes).

Supplements
Chromium and vanadium are used for treatment of adult onset diabetes in people and may be a useful supplement for dogs with diabetes. Brewers yeast also contains chromium. Coenzyme Q may benefit diabetes,[195] niacin and zinc may be beneficial.[196] Digestive enzymes assist digestion.

Consider glucosamine, proanthocyanidins, fatty acids—flax seed oil, antioxidants vitamins C and E, L-carnitine

Fibre, flavinoids

Herbs
Bilberry (*Vaccinium myrtillus*) has had a long history of use in the folk treatment of diabetes in people. Bilberry reduces high blood glucose levels in normal and diabetic dogs[197] and bilberry extracts are widely used in Europe in the treatment and prevention

of secondary eye problems (diabetic retinopathy and cataracts) in people.[198] This is a very safe herb to give, with no known side-effects.

Fenugreek seeds have been shown to have anti-diabetic effects. Normal and diabetic dogs given defatted fenugreek seeds (a daily dose of 1.5–2 grams per kilogram) had reduced blood levels of glucose, glucagon, insulin and triglycerides.[199] Including fenugreek seeds or defatted fenugreek powder in the diet, may assist the regulation of blood glucose.

Garlic has shown blood sugar lowering properties;[200] it increases the half-life of insulin and improves circulation.[201]

Grape seed extract (*Vitis vinifera*) contains flavinoids which help protect blood vessels and the eyes from diabetes-induced damage.[202]

Gymnema sylvestre is a plant native to India used in Ayuvedic medicine for the treatment of diabetes in people. Extracts of the herb help glucose control in dogs (possibly by enhancing the dogs' own ability to produce insulin).[203]
Dandelion has a mild blood sugar lowering effect.

Ginger helps stimulate peripheral circulation and may benefit some animals with poor circulation (those with slow healing wounds, or older dogs).

Juniper berries

Ginseng (*Panex ginseng*) can help lower blood glucose.

Yarrow—one of its actives works like insulin.

Bach Flowers
Consider what stresses your dog may be under, start with hornbeam and olive

Acupuncture
Consider GV 14, LIV 3, LIV 13, GB 21, LI 11, ST 36, SP 6, SP 9. Chinese herbs would also be beneficial.

Homeopathy
Iris versicolor, phosphoric acid, uranium nit., syzygium

Biochemical salts
Nat. sulph. 6x, Nat. mur. 6x

Other
Secondary infections and other problems are common with diabetes. Acupuncture can be very helpful to maintain a strong immunity and overall health and reduce the risk of complications.

Weight control and regular exercise are important.

Ears and
Eyes

EARS

Ears are an extension of the skin and sometimes quite an extension! Different breeds are more prone to ear problems by virtue of their ear shape and size. Droopy ears or hair-filled ears are predisposed to infections simply because of the lack of ventilation. Chronic ear infections may also be a symptom that there is something else going on in the body such as a thyroid imbalance, skin allergy and even neck problems. In Chinese medicine, ears are associated with the kidneys, so chronic problems might be related. If the ear problem is one-sided it is possible there is foreign material such as a grass seed or dirt in the ear or an infection. If the ears have a lot of discharge or debris it is important that the ear is cleaned by your veterinarian before attempting conventional or complementary therapy.

Ear Infections

If your dog has had several bouts of infections or chronic problems, then a referral to a dermatologist is a good idea. The important thing is to not continue to treat with ear-drops and antibiotics if they are not working. It's also important not to put anything into the ear if the eardrum is damaged, as this could make things worse. A veterinary examination is important for this reason.

Complementary therapies that can support conventional treatment or can be used as alternatives in mild cases include the following

Supplements

Consider vitamins A, C and E, and zinc.

Herbs (taken orally)

Garlic; Echinacea; Fenugreek; Pau d'arco has antifungal and immune supporting properties and can be useful for yeast infections of the ear, when given orally; The Chinese herb Coptis is also useful; St John's wort for ear pain.

Acupuncture

Consider acupuncture as an adjunct for chronic ear problems.
Points for otitis externa BL 20, SP 6, KI 3, LI 11

Homeopathy

Consider: Hepar sulph. where there is a discharge of pus, and pain; Belladonna for red hot ears; Mercurius solubis for foul pus discharge; Graphites for sticky discharges; Psorinum for hot, itchy ears; Sulphur for hot itchy ears and when your dog seeks coolness

Biochemical salts

Potassium chloride 6x, Iron phosphate 6x, Potassium sulphate 6x

Ear cleaners

There are a number of commercial ear cleaners that can be obtained from your veterinarian or pet shop. For healthy ears with a little bit of wax, simply wipe the ear using a tissue and a dab of almond oil. Avoid using cotton buds, which may cause injury.

Vinegar rinse

Vinegar acidifies the ear environment and keeps bacteria and yeast under control. Use ⅓ apple organic cider vinegar (2 to 2.5 per cent acetic acid) with ⅔ water. Using a syringe gently douche the ear canal with between 1ml and 5ml of the solution. This solution can be used for long-term prevention of infections in dogs prone to mild ear infections. It is also useful to douche after swimming.

Gentle massage

Gentle massage of the base of the ear can help relieve discomfort and stimulate circulation to the area.

Ear Oil for Chronic Ear Infection

　　1 teaspoon mullein flowers
　　3 tablespoons of sweet almond oil

Place flowers in non-aluminium pan, add oil and warm for fifteen minutes, do not allow to boil.

Allow to cool, strain through muslin, and store in glass jar. Use a dropper to take three to four drops. Warm first to room temperature and instil in ears on a daily basis.

Mullein can also be useful against ear mites.

Golden seal (or Oregon grape root) can also be added to mullein for eardrops.

Garlic Oil
Take two garlic oil capsules and warm them in your hands. Pierce them one at a time and drip the oil into the ear.

Or peel four cloves of garlic and place in half cup of olive oil. Leave in the oil for one week. Remove the garlic and instil two drops of the garlic-infused oil into the affected ear daily.

Middle and Inner Ear Problems
Most middle and inner ear problems result from infections moving further into the body from otitis externa, or upwards from the throat; even chronic dental disease may be a contributing factor. These problems can cause upsets in balance, head tilt, vomiting, pain and also head shaking. Bacteria cause many of these problems and it may be necessary to treat these with a long course of antibiotics. If so, you can support your dog during the treatment. (*See* Antibiotics)

Supplements
Consider vitamins A, C and E.

Herbs
Antibacterial and antifungal herbs to support antibiotics; Echinacea; Astragalus; Golden seal (or Oregon grape root); *Gingko biloba* if balance affected; St John's wort for pain.

Bach Flower remedies
Scleranthus

Homeopathy
Hepar sulph. if recent problem, Merc. cor. if long-term problem

Biochemical salts
Kali mur.

Other
Consider pain relief if there is fever or your dog is dull and resents touching around the ear. Conventional painkillers are usually necessary.

Caution: Avoid putting anything into the ear unless advised by your veterinarian. If absolutely necessary, to clean or soothe, use warm saline only.

Deafness

Some dogs are born deaf and others may gradually lose their hearing with age. Mild infections or long-term problems may be a contributing factor. As deafness becomes apparent train your dog to respond to hand signals (Yes, dogs can learn sign language) and remember that a leash is very important for safety. You can also use a torch to flash once or twice to get your dog inside at night. Some dogs respond well to a companion dog that can act as another set of ears!

Some dogs benefit by:

Acupuncture: TH 21, SI 19, GB 2, TH 3, TH 5.

And also by the herb *Gingko biloba*.

Massage of the ears is a wonderful form of connecting with your dog, and may improve circulation and hearing.

Aural Haematoma

Aural haematoma is actually a large blood blister between the skin and the cartilage inside the ear. It is often triggered by head shaking, which ruptures tiny blood vessels. However , it may also be related to an immune problem in some dogs. If the blood blister is large, it will cause the ear to droop, and it needs to be drained (this usually requires anaesthetic and minor surgery). Otherwise the ear flap will block the ear passage from ventilation and possibly contribute to further problems. Also the blood will be slow to be reabsorbed, and a 'cauliflower' ear can form. If the blood vessel is only small, natural therapies may be a useful alternative. It is best for your veterinarian to assess how serious the problem is.

Supplements

Vitamins A, C, E, K

Herbs

Yarrow; Pau d'arco; Liquorice.

Arnica for bleeding in the short term; Phosphorus if condition worsens.

EYES

General Eye Health

Eyes are a reflection of general body health and vitality. They can also reflect poor health or imbalances elsewhere in the body. In Chinese medicine eyes are related to the liver, and imbalances in the liver can show up first in the eyes. General eye health can be maintained through good diet. Leafy green vegetables, parsley, blue berries, carrots, sesame seeds and sunflower seeds are all considered good for the eyes. Also consider the following for routine eye care:

Supplements

Zinc, bioflavinoids, pycogenols, vitamins A, C and D

Herbs
Parsley; Gingko (especially for retinal disease); Dandelion; Bilberry; Eyebright.

Eye washes
Calendula tea can be used to bathe eyes.
Salt water: 1 teaspoon in 1 cup of water
Eyebright infusion
Rosemary tea

Acupuncture
Acupuncture can be useful for eye problems in conjunction with conventional care. Local points can be used, and if there are underlying causes such as an immune problem, liver or other problem, acupuncture can be used to improve the balance and health of your dog.

Other
Artificial tears can be soothing for mildly irritated eyes.

If your dog suffers from any eye problem, veterinary attention must be sought. It is easy for mild problems to become serious. You can also request a referral to a veterinary ophthalmologist for specialist attention.

Cataracts
Most cataracts are inherited or occur with ageing, but diabetes, toxins, uveitis (inflammation in the eye) and other underlying problems can lead to cataracts. Surgery is successful for most hereditary cataracts and early treatment is best. However, if surgery is not an option for you here are some suggestions:

Diet
Incorporate yellow vegetables (containing carotenes) and green leafy vegetables in the diet, legumes (contain sulphur amino acids), eggs and fruit (for vitamin C), especially apples.

Supplements
Antioxidant vitamins early on will help delay or even prevent the formation of cataracts; vitamin E helps protect against free radical damage, Selenium can be helpful, vitamin C reduces the progression of cataract development in people[204] and may be beneficial in dogs, vitamin A and beta-carotenes are good antioxidants; zinc is important for normal lens function.

Pycogenols and Quercertin may be beneficial too.

Herbs
Bilberry; Cineraria; Gingko.

Biochemical salts

Nat. mur. for early cataracts, Silica for long-term cataracts

Other

The amino acids, cysteine, glutamine and glycine added to the diet help increase the levels of glutathione in the lens. Glutathione helps maintain a healthy lens.[205]

Eye Irritation

Red eyes can be a symptom of infection, allergy, injury or other problem and should be seen by a veterinarian. If it happens regularly check whether it is made worse by having the car windows wound down while driving, or if hair is irritating the eyes. It is quite possible that red eyes are a symptom of a generalised allergy too.

Wash Eyes with Eyewash

1 tablespoon of elderberry, chickweed, chamomile or eyebright in 1 cup of water. Boil water and flowers for 10 minutes. Cool, strain through coffee filter, and add ½ teaspoon of salt. Bathe three times daily.

   You can add artificial tears as a lubricant.

   Salt water (1 teaspoon salt in 1 cup of water).

Conjunctivitis

Conjunctivitis is an inflammation of the lining of the eyelids and can have a number of causes including viruses, bacteria, allergies and general irritation. It is important to have your dog examined by a veterinarian.

Supplements

Zinc , vitamins C, B complex

Herbs

Eyebright, chamomile teas applied externally; Fennel tea applied externally.

Homeopathy

Apis mel for mild conjunctivitis; Pulsatilla for green yellow discharge; Silicea for swelling

Other

Saline drops and salt-water washes can help relieve irritation. Avoid taking your dog outside where pollution, smoke, dust and allergens can make the condition worse.

Dry Eye

Dry eye or kerato conjunctivitis sicca is a deficiency of tears causing the eye to become dry. It can cause conjunctivitis. It can be associated with an underlying immune problem, drug use and other causes. Your veterinarian or a veterinary ophthalmologist might recommend surgery, or a drug called cyclosporine. Another option to consider is acupuncture, which has been used successfully to stimulate tear production. Artificial tears are another option, but they need to be given several times a day. Cod liver oil, rich in vitamin A can be instilled in the eyes as a lubricant, one drop three times daily under veterinary supervision. Additional attention should be given to the possible underlying causes.

Glaucoma

Glaucoma is an increase in the pressure in the eye. It can be inherited or caused by other eye problems and can cause blindness and pain if not treated aggressively and quickly, so it is essential that your dog is treated by a veterinarian as soon as possible. Glaucoma is generally progressive and must be treated medically. A veterinary ophthalmologist may also recommend surgery to help retain vision for as long as possible.

Other adjunctive help can be given through:

Diet
Include fresh foods such as carrot, beetroot, parsley, broccoli, leafy green vegetables, and cucumber.

Supplements
Vitamin C with bioflavinoids and rutin, pycogenols, fish oil and vitamin E, evening primrose oil,
vitamin B complex (especially B12), magnesium, Co enzyme Q10

Herbs (internal)
Coleus forskohlii (these eye drops have been shown to reduce eye pressure by 34%–40 % in people);[206] Bilberry and garlic; Ginger and turmeric; Gingko.

Homeopathy
Belladonna; Phosphorus.

The Immune System

The immune system is extremely complex, performing a variety of functions directed towards keeping the body healthy. The system is flexible (able to increase or reduce its response) and is able to respond to invasion by foreign agents (viruses, etc.) and internal agents (such as cancerous cells). However, because it is so complex it also has the potential to malfunction and trigger pathways that lead to inflammation and tissue destruction.

Immune disorders can be broadly classified into three major categories: immune deficiency, immune hyperactivity (autoimmunity, allergies and sensitivities) and cancer of the immune system. Immune disorders should be suspected:[207]

- when a disease is chronic with periods of relapse and remission
- where there are unusual infections or when normally harmless organisms become infections
- when infections fail to respond to conventional treatment
- when individuals react to vaccination either immediately or after a time
- when there are chronic low or very high white blood cell counts on blood tests[208]

Stress

Stress is a major factor affecting the health and well-being of your dog. How your dog reacts to stress is very individual and accounts for the diversity of stress-induced illnesses. Stress causes depletion of the adrenal glands due to the constant output of adrenaline and naturally occurring corticosteroids. These hormones reduce the activity of white blood cells and can cause the thymus gland to shrink. The thymus is very important in maintaining immunity. So stress can lead to immune suppression increasing susceptibility to cancer, infections and degenerative diseases.

Emotional stress is particularly important. For example, when your dog is depressed

or grieving there is an associated immune-suppression that causes a greater susceptibility to disease of any kind. For example, emotional stress can lead to the body being
attacked by infectious agents, and to cancer. The immune system may also attack itself
in the form of autoimmune disease.[209]

Similarly other causes of stress affect the functioning of the immune system, particularly if prolonged and without relief. [210] Stresses to consider include emotional stress,
nutritional stress, allergen overload, environmental pollutants, physical over-exhaustion,
extreme temperature variation, drug side-effects, low level radiation and electromagnetic pollution.[211]

Immune Support

Diet and nutritional supplements can be used to enhance and support the immune
system.

If your dog is chronically unwell it is important to improve the diet and include raw
foods especially fruit and vegetables. Look for pet foods with antioxidants and immune
supporting claims. Avoid chemical use in and around the home, and on your dog. Ensure
that your dog's teeth are clean and healthy (have them cleaned if necessary). Avoid
vaccination if your dog's immune system is at all compromised. Reduce stress as much
as possible. Provide plenty of fresh air and sunlight and gentle exercise. Daily grooming
and brushing is beneficial, as is the thymus thump. This is a gentle thumping action to
the thymus area, below the neck at the level of the shoulders. A gentle thump for five
minutes twice a day may help improve circulation and stimulate this important gland.

Diet

If there is weight loss associated with a generally compromised immune system,
consider increasing the protein content of the diet, by increasing lean meat content
or adding lean meat to a premium commercial diet. (*See* Diets for low immunity and
cancer.)

Supplements

Vitamin C and bioflavinoids (pycnogenols, proanthocyanidins), vitamin A is beneficial
for the immune system and may help prevent cancer,[212] Vitamin E enhances immunity,
hence preventing secondary infections,[213] B complex can be beneficial for stress,
allergies and infections and a healthy immune system,[214] Selenium protects the immune
system by preventing the formation of free radicals,[215] dimethylglycine may boost
immunity and may be helpful in allergies,[216] CO-enzyme Q10 benefits immune dysfunction and helps correct age-related decline in immunity,[217] Omega-3 fatty acids inhibit
tumor development and metastasis, help relieve allergic symptoms, and diminish
inflammatory responses.[218]

Others

- Five-mushroom extract is a useful immune stimulant.
- Probiotics enhance immunity, actively produce antibiotic substances and have

also been shown to be active against certain tumors.[219] Lactobacillus acidophilus improves white blood cell activity and results in improved immune defences.[220]

- Studies have shown that bovine cartilage may inhibit some cancers and halt growth of solid tumors. Both shark and bovine cartilage can improve immune function.[221]
- Digestive enzymes
- Glandulars especially thymus extracts and perhaps spleen extracts

Herbs

- Echinacea (*E. angustifolia*) has profound immune stimulating effects, hence its antibacterial, antiviral and immune-enhancing effects.[222] Echinacea is useful for infections and can be used topically for fungal infections. It also helps offset the effect of chemotherapy on the immune system, with treatment of cancer.
- Golden seal (*Hydrastis canadensis*) has remarkable immune stimulating effects by increasing blood to the spleen (improving activity and release of immune system compounds). It contains berberine, which also activates white blood cells (destroying bacteria, viruses, fungi and tumor cells). Alternatives include barberry and Oregon grape.[223] Active against infections, liver disorders and cancer, and it is an adjunct to chemotherapy.
- Liquorice (*Glycyrrhiza glabra*) induces interferon, which is antiviral. It helps prevent the suppression of immunity by stress and cortisone. Active against viral infections, inflammation, inflammatory bowel disease, and hepatitis.
- Korean ginseng (*Panex ginseng*) has immune stimulating activity. Avoid using it in acute infections; also highly concentrated ginseng can inhibit some immune functions.[224] Uses include aiding the recovery from disease or surgery, improving resistance to infection, as an anti-inflammatory (combine with liquorice). It may be useful in cancer and diabetes.
- Astragalus (*Astragalus membranaceous*) improves many immune functions and has been shown to possess antiviral and anti-tumor activity. Uses include prevention of infection in impaired immunity, chronic bacterial or viral infections, chronic and autoimmune diseases (especially nephritis), and congestive heart failure. It is not advisable to use it in acute infections.[225]
- Cat's claw (*Uncinaria tomentosa*) increases white blood cell ability to attack and kill abnormal cells. It is thought to have anti-cancer activity and is considered by some to be the most potent immune boosting herb, surpassing herbs such as echinacea and golden seal.[226] Active against infections, tumors, arthritis, allergies, dysbiosis, respiratory infections and parasites.
- Garlic can be used as an antimicrobial agent (bacterial and viral), for immune enhancement, for cancer prevention and for cardiovascular effects. It is also antifungal and exerts some anti-worm effects against roundworm and hookworm.[227]

Bach Flowers

Crab-apple, walnut, chestnut bud, olive, scleranthus, star of Bethlehem

Acupuncture

Acupuncture has numerous effects on the immune system. It has antiviral, antibacterial and anti allergy and anti-inflammatory properties. Acupuncture activates immune reactions and has a supportive role with conventional medicine or can be used on its own for milder problems. Generally one to two treatments are needed to improve immunity. Consider LI 4, ST 36, LI 11, GV 14, SP 6 and LU 7, GV 14.

Allergies (*See also* Skin and Food Allergies.)

Many dogs have an inherited tendency towards the development of allergies. Exposure to pollution, foods, cigarette smoke, chemicals, stress and other factors can also contribute to the development of allergies (or pseudo allergies which are sensitivities). Allergies can underlie a whole host of chronic diseases and should be suspected when symptoms do not respond well to regular treatment. Chronic ear problems, skin problems, constipation, diarrhoea, foot problems, red eyes, conjunctivitis, hyperactivity, seizures, some forms of arthritis and chronic discharges can all be manifestations of allergies.

The substances that cause allergies are called allergens. Almost any substance can become an allergen in a sensitive dog. The most common allergens though are flea saliva, dust mites, moulds, pollens, grasses and foods, especially protein sources. Insect bites, some additives such as sulphites, and some chemicals found in shampoos and soaps, paints, disinfectants, insecticides and household cleaning products can also be allergens.

It is important to try and identify what the offending agents are so that you can manage these and reduce reliance on drug therapy. Immune-therapy should be considered as an alternative to steroid use. Sometimes good management can mean your dog can be managed without the use of any drugs at all. But even if you are only able to reduce the duration of drug use or dosage, this is a positive step.

The allergic threshold

The body has an ability to cope with the presence of some allergens. The more allergens your dog is exposed to, the more likely his allergy threshold will be reached. When this happens he will have an allergic response. Anything you can do to minimise exposure to as many common allergens as possible will help to bring your dog below the allergy threshold.

Recommendations

1. Consider having allergy testing done to identify the allergens your dog is exposed to. Immune-therapy can be helpful in at least 50 per cent of dogs.
2. Consider an underlying dysbiosis or leaky gut.
3. Ensure excellent flea control.
4. Keep rooms free of dust and use dehumidifiers to reduce mould and dust.
5. Consider using dust mite insecticides or mite prevention covers to reduce the burden particularly in bedrooms and bedding. Wash bedding in hot water.

6. Thoroughly weed and tidy the garden.
7. Some dogs may benefit from booties (your veterinarian or pet shop can order them), when your dog has contact allergies to grass.
8. Some dogs can actually wear body 'suits' to help prevent exposure to contact allergens.
9. Consider a low allergy diet, even if tests don't show anything. It is still worth doing this if only to reduce the possibility of food sensitivities as contributing factors. This diet should be continued for at least six weeks.

Diet
Consider the Bowel Detoxification Program and begin on an elimination diet. Your veterinarian may be able to provide you with low allergy prepared diet food or you can make your own.

Supplements
Vitamins A, C and E, vitamin B complex, bioflavinoids, pycogenols, proanthocyanidins Selenium, zinc, flax seed oil and/or evening primrose oil, digestive enzymes

Herbs
Five-mushroom extract; Alfalfa; Liquorice; German chamomile; Burdock; Dandelion; St Mary's thistle.

Bach flowers
Crab-apple may be beneficial but consider any stresses that may be contributing to the allergy.

Acupuncture
Acupuncture reduces histamine-induced itchiness and may be beneficial to help regulate the immune system.

Homeopathy
Homeopathy may be beneficial in conjunction with dietary changes and herbs. Constitutional prescribing is important and is best carried out by a veterinary homeopath.

Sudden allergies
Bee stings and mosquito bites can cause swelling on the face or body. Apply a cold pack to the area. Homeopathic Apis mel can be useful.

Allergies from pets
It's not generally dog hair that causes allergies in people but proteins secreted by glands in your dog's skin onto the hairs and dander (small flakes of skin). When these settle in your eyes or nose or you inhale them, symptoms of allergies may appear.

Some suggestions

Keep your dog out of your bedroom (simply getting away from your dog for eight hours can substantially reduce symptoms for the rest of the time).

Make sure you use dust mite controls such as mattress and pillow covers.

Use special vacuum cleaners with filters or designed to remove animal hair.

Regularly steam clean carpets, furniture and curtains, and mop floors and wash pet bedding in hot water.

Wash your dog at least weekly.

Wipe your dog with a damp cloth once or twice daily to help remove the allergy-causing proteins.

Consider desexing your male dog, which can substantially reduce their allergy-causing potential.

Seek medical advice and complementary therapies for yourself.

Elimination Diet/Low Allergy Diets

In all cases of allergy a single source protein and carbohydrate diet is worthwhile trying. While food allergies might not be a contributing factor, simply improving the level of nutrition can have a marked effect. Likewise potential food sensitivities or intolerances may be reduced. Over time additional foods can be reintroduced. There are special veterinary diets specifically designed for this purpose, or you can make your own home-made diet. Remember to change diets over slowly to avoid digestive upsets.

Ideally your dog will need to be fed a diet with a protein source he hasn't been exposed to before such as fish, turkey or pork, and a carbohydrate source such as rice or potato. If you decide on a home-made diet, replace the bone-meal with calcium carbonate, and ensure the vitamin A source is consistent with the meat used, or use vitamin A supplements. If possible, and under supervision of your vet, suspend any flavoured medications including some heartworm preventions and supplements that may contain milk or other protein sources. Foods to avoid during the feeding trial include peppers, tomatoes, mushrooms, and seafood other than fresh or lightly steamed fish. Yeasts, raw hide chews and bones need to be avoided during the trial. It is also useful to provide filtered, spring or distilled water. This trial needs to be continued for a minimum of 6–12 weeks.

At about six weeks and provided your dog has improved, start introducing one food at a time with the existing diet. If your dog begins scratching again (it will usually be obvious within two days but can take up to twelve days for a reaction), you will know that your dog may have a sensitivity or allergy to that food. Wait one week and try another protein source. If no response then this food is probably OK. Wait another week and try another such as chicken. In this way you can build up a list of foods your dog can eat, and those he can't. Otherwise consider the following:

Home-made elimination diets[228]:

Short Term

- 250grams boiled or baked lamb (or other meat equivalent), pinch salt and 4 cups cooked rice (or other meat equivalent) for 8–10 weeks

- 250 grams boiled or baked lamb (or other meat equivalent), pinch salt and 4 cups cooked potatoes (or other meat equivalent) 8–10 weeks

Long Term

- 1.5 kg cooked potatoes, 250 grams cooked fish, 2tsp Calcium carbonate, 4.5 tbs oil, dash salt, mineral/vitamin supplement (4 days for 13 kg dog)
- 250 gram lamb, 2 cups cooked rice, 2 tsp oil, 3 tsp Dicalcium phosphate, ¼ tsp Potassium chloride, vitamin/mineral supplement (1 day for 13 kg dog)
- 10 cups cooked pasta, 11 boiled or poached large eggs, 1 cup creamed cottage cheese, 2 tsp Calcium carbonate, 3/4 tsp vegetable oil, ¾ tsp Potassium chloride, vitamin/mineral supplement (4 days for 13kg dog)
- 10 cups cooked rice, 250 grams turkey, 1.3 tsp Calcium carbonate, 1 tsp Dicalcium phosphate, 5 tbs oil, 1 tsp Potassium chloride, vitamin/mineral supplement (4 days for 13 kg dog)

Limitations of Elimination Diets

If symptoms improve by excluding foods then it is likely that your dog is food allergic or intolerant. It is common to try and challenge your dog with suspected foods to see if they react again. However, your dog might not react anyway if it is food intolerance rather than allergy. However, if you add that food again consistently to the diet, you may find the symptoms returning as it builds up in the system.

If your dog is sensitive to one or two of the foods in the elimination diet, no benefit may be seen. You may need to try another diet, which relies on different foods.

Ideally medications should be stopped too, especially if they contain protein sources such as beef, gelatine or cereal excipients or fillers.

Chemicals in the diet, such as pesticides on food, or plastic from food and water bowls or in water itself may not be excluded on the elimination diet and may be responsible for failure of the diet. Try and use stainless steel bowls, purified water and make sure you thoroughly rinse the dishwashing water from bowls.

Sensitivities and allergies can change with time. Some sensitivities may go away but new ones can be acquired. It is possible that your dog can tolerate a food once again after a couple of months if not eaten more than once a week; however, be aware that frequent exposure can lead to a build up of the food which might trigger a relapse of symptoms.

Autoimmune Disease

Autoimmune disease comes in many forms. The immune system acts like a patrol force guarding against bacteria and viruses but sometimes it short circuits and begins to recognise its own body cells or organs as 'foreign'. When this happens the immune system mounts an attack on its own body tissues. There are many possible triggers including genetic predisposition, infections (especially viruses), hormonal influences, stress, allergies and chemical sensitivities, and faulty digestion and in the case of autoimmune haemolytic anaemia (where the immune system attacks its own blood), vaccines have been implicated.[229]

Conventional treatment using corticosteroids or other immune-suppressive drugs is usually necessary. It is a fine balance between suppressing the immune system to stop it attacking itself, and opening a window of opportunity for infections to grab hold.

Recommendations

It is essential that any treatment be under the supervision of a veterinarian. Because there are so many forms of autoimmune disease, treatment has to take into consideration the organs and body systems involved in the particular disease. As much as possible we need to restore health to these organs and prevent further damage from the autoimmune process. The liver is the most vulnerable organ because it has to deal with the toxins and immune complexes carried in the blood. This can overwhelm the liver. Its ability to repair itself may not keep pace with the damage caused. Therefore the liver must be supported and protected no matter what type of autoimmune disease exists.

We need to treat the autoimmune disease and any factors that may be contributing to the ongoing process.

- Consider drug involvement; conventional drugs can be lifesaving, although they do have side-effects that need to be managed.
- Chemical overload: consider how you might avoid your dog's exposure to environmental pollutants, herbicides and pesticides in the garden, household cleaners and sprays, chemical residues in foods and food additives.
- Consider how you can reduce stress in the household.
- Consider whether there are low-grade chronic or reoccurring infections such as gingivitis or bad teeth.

It is important that any infections are treated with the most appropriate antiviral, antifungal or antibacterial drugs or herbs, along with supporting the immune system.

Diet

Consider a Bowel Detoxification Program.

Consider an elimination diet (single protein source) and using organic foods (chemical free).

Add spleen, fresh thymus or extracts.

Supplements

Consider those used for immune support.

Herbs

Five-mushroom extract

For liver support and protection: St Mary's thistle

Immune-suppressing action: *Stephania tetandra* and *Hemidesmus indicus*

Immune-stimulant action (take care): *Echinacea angustifolia/purpurea*

Anti-inflammatory action: *Allium sativum, Salvia miltiorrhiza, Rehmannia glutinosa*

Antioxidant herbs: *Gingko biloba*, bilberry

171

Acupuncture

Acupuncture can regulate the immune system and is anti-inflammatory. Consider LI 4, LI 11, ST 36, GB 14, BL 23, BL 54 once or twice weekly.

Immunomodulating points LI 4, LI 11, ST 36, GB 39, SP 6, GV 14, BL 11, 20, 23–28, CV 12

Immune-suppressing points BL 52, plus local points

Other

Because of possible genetic factors, breeding is not recommended.

Avoid vaccination where autoimmune disease or immune suppression exists.

Cancer

The diagnosis of cancer makes us feel helpless and fearful. This can be stressful and even lower our own immunity. Lucky for dogs that they don't understand the word cancer, at least they don't have the additional worry that we have. And yet they can easily sense the fear and distress that we might feel for them.

It's a fact that every day many of the millions of cells in the body go wrong. The immune system is well equipped to send fighter cells out to find and destroy these potentially cancer-causing cells. If cancer forms then many types can be treated very successfully with conventional treatment. It is also very important to support the rest of the body so that it has the best chance of self-healing.

The most important aspect of management of cancer is to have a diagnosis, so that you know what you are dealing with, and whether there are good indications to use a conventional approach that can include one or a combination of chemotherapy, surgery and radiation therapy. Your veterinarian may recommend that you consult with a veterinary oncologist who specialises in the treatment of cancers and is best placed to advise you of your options. Complementary therapies are very useful to provide support while undergoing treatment, or can be considered if you do not choose conventional options.

With malignant cancers the goal is usually to prolong life and provide a high quality of life. Canine lymphoma, osteosarcoma, malignant breast cancer, lung cancer, mast cell tumors and other forms of cancer can be treated in a humane way, provided they are treated early and preferably under the guidance of an oncologist. Conventional treatment usually increases survival time and the key is to get the best advice you can and get in early rather than later. Surgically reducing the size of tumors may be necessary if the growth is impinging on movement, causing pain or is affecting the functioning of the body.

If the cancer is one where conventional treatment cannot cure it or the side-effects are a concern, or simply that you choose not to pursue a conventional course of action then there are some options to consider. The main considerations are to support the body, minimise the impact of the cancer and promote health and quality of life as best we can.

Recommendations

Do not give up hope. Cancer is not a death sentence and although you need to know what your dog's chances are, every cancer and every dog is different. You need to decide what your goals are, and take into consideration the advice of your veterinarian, veterinary oncologist and your own interpretations to decide what you want for your dog. The combination of conventional and complementary care offers the best of both worlds. Many of the side-effects of conventional therapies can be reduced with complementary therapies. And when treatment is over, complementary care can keep your dog as healthy as possible. It is also a viable option if you decide not to treat, particularly if you are given a very poor prognosis. In this case complementary therapies can be used to support your dog.

Diet

There are veterinary diets that are available for dogs with cancer. Otherwise consider making your own home-made diet. These diets are high in fat and protein and low in carbohydrates and should be fed under the supervision of a veterinarian.

Beef and Pumpkin

Barley, cooked	1.3 cups	Bone-meal	1.5 tsp
Beef, raw, lean	375 g	Liver	50g
Vegetables, finely		Oat bran, raw	1 tbs
chopped or grated	½ cup	Pumpkin, cooked	½ cup
Flaxseed oil	1 tbs		

As much as possible feed the above ingredients raw, the whole lot can be mixed together, or components fed separately as you desire.

This recipe provides 1000 calories, energy from protein 41%, fat 34% and carbohydrate 25%, fibre 15 g.

Fish and Vegetables

Barley, boiled	¾ cup	Cod Liver oil	½ tsp
Broccoli, raw	2 pieces	Pumpkin, cooked	½ cup
Apple, raw	1 average	Fish, cooked	250 g
Vegetables, raw, finely		Oat bran	1 tbs
chopped, grated	½ cup	Rolled oats cooked	¼ cup
Flaxseed oil	1 tbs	Bone-meal	1.5 tsp

As much as possible feed the above ingredients raw, (the fish should be cooked) the whole lot can be mixed together, or components fed separately as you desire.

This recipe provides 1000 calories, energy from protein 41%, fat 33% and carbohydrate 26%, fibre 19 g.

Chicken (or Lamb) and Vegetables

Barley, boiled	¾ cup	Chicken, raw, lean	350 g
Broccoli, raw	2 pieces	Chicken liver	50 g
Apple, raw	1 average	(Or Lamb, raw, lean	1.5 cup
Vegetables, raw, finely		and lamb liver 50 g)	
chopped, grated	½ cup	Bone-meal	1.5 tsp
Flaxseed oil	1 tbs	Oat bran	1 tbs
Pumpkin, cooked	½ cup	Rolled oats cooked	¼ cup

As much as possible feed the above ingredients raw, the whole lot can be mixed together, or components fed separately as you desire.

This recipe provides 1000 calories, energy from protein 39%, fat 35% and carbohydrate 26%, fibre 19 g.

The lamb recipe provides 1000 calories, energy from protein 39%, fat 34% and carbohydrate 26%, fibre 19 g.

Anti-cancer foods that can be included in the diet include beetroot, broccoli, cooked tomatoes, parsley, legumes, berries, apples, pears, peaches, grapes, plums, cabbage, sage, garlic, yams, cauliflower, shitake mushrooms, green and orange vegetables, potatoes, rice, yoghurt, fish, carrots, watermelon, spleen, fresh thymus and extracts.

Supplements

Consider those used to support the immune system including:

Fish oil (3 grams per 15 kg bodyweight per day), antioxidants vitamins C, A and E, probiotics, Shark and bovine cartilage may inhibit some cancers and halt the growth of solid tumors;[230] digestive enzymes induce the production of tumor necrosis factor by white blood cells;[231] L-Arsparaginase may be beneficial in the treatment of lymphoma and leukaemia in animals;[232] omega-3 fatty acids—flax seed oil may help inhibit tumor development and spread of cancer;[233] fibre for bowel cancer.

Flavinoids, selenium

Herbs

Five-mushroom extract for anti-cancer properties
Essiac for anti-tumor effect
Cleavers for cancer of the lymphatic system
Red clover where there are single hard lumps like in breast cancer or in the lymph nodes
Astragalus to boost the immune system

Herbs with chemotherapy

Siberian ginseng (*Eleutherococcus senticosus*) for immunity and well-being
Echinacea can assist in offsetting the effects of chemotherapy.[234]
Ginseng (*Panex ginseng*) for chemotherapy and radiation, and it has anti-cancer properties.
Dandelion as a useful tonic when undergoing chemotherapy treatment
St Mary's thistle

Others

Cat's claw; Pau d'arco; Garlic aids in the prevention of some forms of cancer; Echinacea; Golden seal.

Bach Flowers

For stress, exhaustion or debility. Hornbeam, olive, crab-apple and others can be considered.

Acupuncture

Immunity is often reduced in cancer, and chemotherapy and radiation treatment can compromise it further. Acupuncture can have a primary role or be supportive in the treatment of cancer. It increases immune responses and reduces the effect of radiation therapy. It can also provide pain relief and help control secondary symptoms associated with cancer. Master points can be used to help stimulate the immune system. Ting points can be useful in treatment of certain forms of cancer.

Homeopathy

A veterinary homeopath can select the most appropriate remedies. Homeopathy is best used here in a supportive role:

Thuja 30c

Lymphoma, prostate, mammary gland and brain tumors: Conium

Benign breast tumors: Phytolacca

Bone cancer: Symphytum, silica calc. flor.

Bone cancer of the jaw: Hekla lava

Soft cancers, neuromas: Bellis perenis

Squamous cell carcinoma: Calc. flor.

Testicular cancer: Oxylic acid

Liver cancer: Hydrastis

Other

Direct application of heat or cold changes the environment of the cancer cells. Some veterinarians may use freezing agents to 'burn' cancers away, or heat probes to 'cook' tumors.

Gentle exercise is important to help oxygenate the body; oxygen is a powerful nutrient in itself.

Pain

Many types of cancer can cause pain. This can be difficult to detect in some dogs. (*See* Pain.)

Lymphatic System and Spleen Health

The lymphatic system flushes wastes from the body, filtering and engulfing foreign bacteria and harmful particles. The lymphatic system includes the lymph nodes (such as tonsils), lymphatic vessels and the spleen. The spleen destroys worn out red blood cells and sends healthy red blood cells out into the circulation to provide oxygen to the body. Lymphoma occurs when there is cancer in the lymphatic system (*see* Cancer).

A more common problem is lymphadenitis, which is inflammation of the lymph nodes. They are swollen and sometimes painful. This is usually the result of infectious agents establishing an infection in the very nodes that are meant to destroy them. It is often associated with a general infection with fever and loss of appetite.

Treatment relies on identifying the cause of the problem, and antibiotics are usually necessary.

Complementary therapies are very useful to support the lymphatic system and help boost the immune system (*see* Immune support).

Lymphatic function can be improved through increasing circulation of lymph. Exercise and massage are beneficial.

Diet
Consider the Bowel Detoxification Program. Consider raw spleen and thymus or extracts.

Supplements
Vitamins A, C and E; Zinc

Herbs
Herbs that increase white blood cell activity may be useful. These include golden seal (*Hydrastis canadensis*), Echinacea (*Echinacea angustifolia*) if there is bacterial involvement, and Korean ginseng (*Panex ginseng*).[235] Cleavers (*Gallium aparine*) has a particular affinity for the lymphatic system and can be used for swollen glands, tonsillitis, chronic cysts, and cancer of the lymphatic system, for lymphadenitis and unresolved infections around the head and neck. Astragalus to boost the immune system

Burdock root has a cleansing effect.

Spleen
Golden seal (*Hydrastis canadensis*) enhances blood flow through the spleen and increases white blood cell activity. Spleen and spleen extracts may be of benefit in improving immune function and have been shown to increase white blood cell counts in extreme deficiencies of white blood cells.[236]

Homeopathy
Calc. fluor. for very hard lymph nodes
Phytolacca for enlarged lymph nodes around the throat and mammary glands

Acupuncture
The spleen is a major organ in acupuncture and so acupuncture is very effective in treating problems of the spleen and lymphatic system in general. Spleen points on the spleen meridian and local points should be considered.

Other
To stimulate lymph flow, provide regular gentle exercise. Massage the body gently and pat gently all over the body to stimulate drainage. Start at the back feet and move towards the heart, and then start again at the front feet.

Infections and Antibiotic Use

Infections can involve bacteria, viruses, fungi and other organisms that cause inflammation somewhere in the body as the body tries to fight off the offending organisms. Fever is a common reaction that also assists the immune defence system. Antibiotics can be lifesaving in many instances such as meningitis and septicaemia, and a course of antibiotics may cure many infections. So veterinary advice should always be a priority.

The other way to treat infections or prevent them is to enhance the body's own immune system. Recurring or chronic infections may indicate a suppressed immune system and/or thyroid disease or some other underlying problem (such as atopy in skin infections). Recurring infections are not normal and they are an indication that the body is out of balance. Ironically this can also be caused by over-use of antibiotics, which in some circumstances can further compromise the immune system.

Complementary therapies can be used with antibiotics and if antibiotics are not effective, complementary medicine may provide an alternative approach.

Recommendations

Be prepared to search for underlying causes (*see* Chronic Disease) if your dog is not responding to a normal course of antibiotics. Many viral, bacterial and other infections will respond to boosting of the immune system using diet and supplements, and many herbs have both antibacterial and antiviral properties.

Diet

Consider improving the diet, by including fresh vegetables and fruits. During severe infection and inflammation the requirement for amino acids increases dramatically, so increasing the protein content moderately helps to fight off disease. Consider adding spleen and thymus extracts. Consider the Bowel Detoxification Program, dysbiosis and leaky gut especially if your dog has had numerous courses of antibiotics.

Encourage plenty of fluids by providing broths and soups to help with detoxification.

Supplements

Consider supplements to support the immune system such as vitamins A, C and E, dimethylglycine, evening primrose oil, flax seed oil, grape seed extract, vitamin B complex, zinc, Digestive enzymes can assist in reducing the effects of acute inflammation, which are pain and swelling, Probiotics can be used during, but especially after an antibiotic course to help restore normal bowel organisms, fructo-oligosaccharides and inulin and soluble fibre can also help restore the bowel following antibiotic use, bromelain (enzyme from pineapple) helps to reduce swelling, bruising, healing time and pain following infections, injuries and surgery.[237]

Herbs

Five-mushroom extract (especially useful for non-bacterial infections)

Echinacea (*Echinacea angustifolia*) has antiviral, antibacterial and immune-enhancing effects. It can be used for infections and wound healing.[238]

Golden seal (*Hydrastis canadensis*) is effective against staphylococcus, streptococcus, chlamydia and other bacteria, and has immune stimulating properties. Barberry or Oregon grape root are substitutes. They can be used for infections of the respiratory, gastrointestinal and genitourinary tract, as well as infectious diarrhoea (giardia).[239]

Liquorice (*Glycerrhiza glabra*) helps prevents the suppression of immunity by stress and cortisone and has antiviral properties.[240]

Astragalus (*Astragalus membranaceua*) has antiviral properties. It may be helpful for chronic bacterial and viral infections. It is not advised in acute infections.[241]

Cats Claw (*Uncinaria tomentosa*) improves the ability of white blood cells to kill abnormal cells and overcome infections.[242]

Garlic can be used as an antibacterial and antiviral herb, and it has some antifungal properties as well.[243] Works well with Echinacea.

St John's wort has antiviral action.

Cleavers for infections involving the lymphatic system and lymph nodes

Dandelion for low-grade infections

Pau d'arco for fungal infections

Bach Flowers
Consider crab-apple, walnut, olive, gentian, Rescue Remedy.

Acupuncture
Acupuncture can enhance the immune system, is antiviral, antibacterial and has anti-allergenic effects, as well as being anti-inflammatory. Consider: SP 21, BL 17, BL 20, BL 23.

Immune stimulating points include LI 4, 11, ST 36, GB 39, SP 6, GV 14, BL 11, 20, 23–28, CV 12.

Plus local points and affected organ points

For fever consider: LI 4, LI 11, ST 36, GV 20, GV 13, GV 14.

Points to enhance white blood cell function include LI 1, LI 11, GV 14.

Homeopathy
Aconite can be used at first signs of any infection.

Belladonna may be useful if infection is associated with high fever.

Bacterial nosodes and viral nosodes may be useful for specific conditions such as parvovirus, distemper, canine hepatitis, kennel cough, leptospirosis, Lyme disease and others. A veterinary homeopath can guide you to the best form of treatment and regime.

Treatment of external infections
A saline solution of 1½ teaspoons salt per 600 mls of water can be used to bathe infected areas. Epsom salt soaks can also relieve discomfort associated with foot pain.

For complementary treatment of external infections, *see* Wounds and Skin problems.

19

Glandular Health

Adrenal Gland Health and Stress

The adrenal glands are located just near the kidneys. One part of the gland produces cortisone (the natural anti-inflammatory hormone) and other hormones that also help sugar metabolism. The other part of the gland produces adrenaline and other hormones that affect metabolism to help cope with stress. During stress these glands become more active. Persistent stress can exhaust them, thereby affecting the health of the whole body. Also the use of corticosteroid drugs can lead to the glands becoming less active which affects metabolism and overall health as well.

Adrenal gland health can be achieved by minimising negative stresses, avoiding corticosteroid drugs unless absolutely necessary, and providing your dog with support, especially during periods of stress.

Adrenal stress may lead to lethargy, anxiety, fatigue, irritability, low immunity, dry skin and pica (abnormal cravings for strange things, such as wanting to eat faeces).

Diet

Diet is critical to the health of the adrenal glands. Nutritional stress leads to poor health. Fresh foods are important. High potassium foods such as fish, potatoes and avocados can be beneficial.

Supplements

Consider adding nutritional yeast, wheatgerm, flax seed oil, vitamin B complex, vitamin C, Digestive enzymes, Coenzyme Q.

Herbs

Siberian ginseng; Astragalus; Liquorice; Borage; Nettle

Acupuncture

Acupuncture can be used to balance the body and support the adrenals in times of stress.

Other

Moderate exercise is important to reduce stress.

Massage can be very beneficial and calming.

Behavioural enrichment—providing toys and chews can help reduce stress.

Addison's Disease

Addison's disease or hypo-adreno-corticism is when there is a deficiency of hormones produced by the adrenal glands. The adrenal gland is underactive. This can be caused by many problems including an immune-mediated disorder, tumors and also drug use especially following sudden withdrawal of corticosteroid drugs. Depending upon the underlying cause, it can usually be managed well with conventional medicine by replacing the hormones that the adrenal gland can no longer produce. However, there are some specific things you can do to support your dog if he is being treated for this condition:

Diet

A good diet is essential, consider upgrading to the best diet you can.

Supplements

In addition to those for the general support of the adrenal glands consider using glandular extracts of adrenal gland or fresh adrenals.

Herbs

Liquorice is excellent, but if used long term this should be blended with dandelion or supplemented with potassium. Siberian ginseng, nettle, panax ginseng

Bach Flowers

Consider any underlying stresses and select accordingly.

Biochemical salts

Nat. mur. 6x

Acupuncture

Acupuncture and Chinese herbs can be used successfully to support this condition: GV 14, LI 11, SP 6, LI 4, ST 36 and others.

Cushing's Syndrome

This condition is almost the opposite of Addison's Disease, and occurs where there is over-production of adrenal hormones. Immune suppression, tumors or excessive use of corticosteroid drugs may cause Cushing's Syndrome. Lifelong therapy is usually needed and sometimes surgery is required too. In addition to the general support of the adrenal glands consider:

Diet
Many dogs with this condition are overweight, so weight loss must be monitored carefully. High potassium foods are important (try vegemite, wheat bran, parsley), and good quality protein such as eggs and fresh meat will help. Sometimes these dogs also have diabetes, so a high-fibre diet would be appropriate.

Supplements
Potassium, vitamins A, C, E and selenium

Herbs
Lovage root; Dandelion; Siberian ginseng; Astragalus

Also consider St Mary's thistle to help minimise side-effects of conventional medications, particularly mitotane and ketoconazole.

Bach Flowers
Hornbeam and olive for fatigue.

Consider any other stresses and select accordingly (*see* chapter on Bach flowers).

Biochemical salts
Nat. mur. 6x

Corticosteroid Use
Corticosteroid-type drugs are very commonly used. Used appropriately and for short periods they can be very useful. But long-term dependence on these drugs is potentially dangerous. These drugs can suppress the immune system, lead to Addison's Disease and/or Cushing's Syndrome, diabetes, skin infections, skin thinning, and liver disease. Because they affect the functioning of the adrenal glands they affect the whole body, not just the symptoms that are being treated.

Alternative day therapy using tablets, rather than regular injections is the safest way to use corticosteroids for longer periods. Although injections are more convenient they tend to shut down the normal functioning of the adrenal gland so that it becomes even more dependent on the drug. However, by giving tablets (at the lowest dose possible) every second day the adrenal gland can still function by itself. If your dog needs to be treated with corticosteroids make sure there are no other options, especially if the treatment is for more than two to three weeks.

General support of the adrenal gland is important. (*See* above)

Corticosteroid Use and Herbal Treatment
If you are using corticosteroids or after finishing a course of corticosteroids consider:
- Liquorice (*Glycyrrhiza glabra*) increases the anti-inflammatory effect (prolongs the half-life) of corticosteroids and also reduces histamine release. [244] It can be

given to aid the withdrawal of corticosteroid drugs and to extend the effects of steroid drugs. Do not use for more than three weeks (unless prescribed) and avoid where there is high blood pressure, or where diuretics are being used.
Suggested dose 0.5 ml / 15 kg daily.

- St Mary's thistle (*Silybum marianum*) assists in restoring the liver following corticosteroid use, also use it if there is a possibility of chemical pollution (drugs, anaesthesia, etc.). It has potent antioxidant activity, anti-inflammatory and liver-protective properties.
Suggested dose 1 ml per 10 kg daily

- Bupleurum (*Bupleurum falcatum*) has both anti-inflammatory and immune-modulating activity. It appears to induce the secretion of natural corticosterone in the body and increases its anti-inflammatory activity. Side-effects include a sedative effect in some patients and increased bowel movements and flatulence in larger doses.[245]
Suggested dose 1 ml per 10 kg of 1:2 liquid extract to reduce the dose of cortico-steroids or as an alternative to corticosteroids.

- Rehmannia (di Huang) *Rehmannia glutinosa* is anti-inflammatory in autoimmune disease and allergies and supports the adrenal cortex; it can protect against the suppressive effects of corticosteroid medication.
Suggested dose 2 ml per 10kg 1:2 liquid extract. No adverse effects expected.

Consider using Siberian ginseng (*Eleutherococcus senticosus*) and/or Korean ginseng (*Panex ginseng*) for anti-inflammatory properties and to support a debilitated dog.

Acupuncture
Acupuncture can also boost the immune system and reduce inflammation. While the effect of acupuncture can be diminished with concurrent use of corticosteroids, it is still worth treating in order to reduce the dependence on drugs and assist immune function. Chinese herbs can also be prescribed as another long-term alternative.

Thyroid Health and Disease
The thyroid is like the thermostat of the body and regulates metabolism and the energy of the body. If it is depleted or deficient, the whole body becomes lethargic and low in energy. Hypothyroidism is the most common hormonal problem of dogs and may in some instances be associated with vaccination.[246] It may present as a whole range of symptoms from dry scaly skin, infertility, constipation, and regurgitation to behavioural changes such as aggression, hyperactivity and fearfulness. Conventional treatment is successful as a rule, and usually requires hormone supplementation for life. However, you can assist your dog's health with the following suggestions:

Recommendations
Weight reduction is important and should be under the supervision of a veterinarian. The dose of thyroxin hormone will need to be monitored carefully.

Diet
Watch calories since weight gain can be a problem. Include fresh greens daily in the diet. If possible include fresh thyroid gland or extract. Vitamin A rich foods such as yellow vegetables, eggs, carrots and dark green leafy vegetables are beneficial. Avoid brussels sprouts, broccoli, turnips, pine nuts, and millet, soy products and cabbage that contain anti-thyroid substances. Also include foods that are high in selenium such as eggs, meat and brazil nuts.

Supplements
Garlic, digestive enzymes, coenzyme Q10, vitamins A, C and E, vitamin B complex, Thyroid glandular products, evening primrose oil. Kelp may or may not be helpful. There is some concern that kelp might enhance autoimmune activity against the thyroid gland.

Herbs
Garlic, cayenne to stimulate circulation, dandelion, Siberian ginseng

Bach Flowers
Hornbeam and olive may be helpful for lack of energy.

Acupuncture
Acupuncture and Chinese herbs are a valid option in the treatment of this problem alongside conventional therapy. They will help regulate the immune system and balance the energy in the body.

Homeopathy
Nux vomica 30c, thuja 30c, Arsenicum alb., causticum, sulphur, thyroidinum

Biochemical salts
Nat. mur. 6x

Other
Exercise is important to oxygenate and stimulate circulation.
    Chiropractic adjustment may be helpful.

Pain and
Inflammation

Pain is vital for survival and protects against physical threats to the body,[247] which is why dogs will rest or lie still to avoid further damage. Your veterinarian should treat acute pain. However, chronic pain saps strength and spirit and can make life miserable and is more difficult to control. The most difficult thing about pain in dogs is recognising it, and symptoms vary considerably.[248] Dogs can lick and bite or scratch at the source of pain. They may become quieter and less alert, sometimes unwilling to move or constantly shifting their position. They may stop eating or grooming. If the pain is severe they can appear restless or have changes in their sleeping patterns. They may be more anxious or fearful than usual. They may shiver, pant and guard the area that hurts. Some dogs will whimper, and even growl when approached or touched, sometimes they appear to be aggressive. We can anticipate pain if your dog requires surgery, has been injured badly or has chronic low-grade pain due to arthritis or cancer. Your veterinarian will prescribe drugs for acute and chronic pain relief and you can consider these suggestions.

Recommendations

It is important to know what is causing the pain, so that it can be corrected or managed. Sometimes it can be difficult to locate where the pain actually is in some dogs. Trigger points are muscle spasms that can cause pain and are often not easily found. A veterinary acupuncturist will look for them routinely. Pain can also be referred, so that foot chewing may arise from pain in the shoulder for example. Whatever the nature, it is important not to merely mask it, but to try and resolve it. For short-term pain relief until you can see your vet, consider using Aspirin. There are far better veterinary analgesics, but if you are stuck then Aspirin is an effective analgesic for painful muscular or skeletal problems. The dose rate is 10 mg per kilogram body weight every 8 to 20 hours[249] administered with food. See your vet as soon as you can. For chronic pain consider the options below, either in combination with conventional medicine or as alternatives. Natural remedies work gently and safely, although they can take longer to be effective.

Diet

Include fresh vegetables and fruits in the diet. Some dogs in pain have a reduced appetite so consider broths and increasing the meat (protein) content of the diet.

Supplements

Digestive enzymes (following injury). Digestive enzymes, especially protease enzymes, break down large protein molecules. Taken on an empty stomach they can be absorbed into the blood stream. Here they can assist in reducing pain and swelling. They can improve recovery time following surgery and they can also aid in the elimination of chronic inflammation.

Vitamins A, C and E, dimethylglycine; bromelain (enzyme from pineapple) helps to reduce swelling, bruising, healing time and pain following infections, injuries and surgery,[250] Evening primrose oil, flax seed oil, grape seed extract; D-phenylalanine, an amino acid, may reduce pain in some dogs (300 mg per 20 kg with food daily, for three weeks); glucosamine and chondroitin for arthritis

Herbs

Turmeric (*Curcuma longa*) has anti-inflammatory properties comparable to phenyl-butazone and cortisone in acute inflammation, but is only half as effective in chronic inflammation[251] without the side-effects.

German chamomile (*Matricaria chamomilla*) has been reported to reduce inflammation, spasms and pain.[252]

Roman chamomile for spasms and pain, it is also gentle for stomach pain and colic.

Calendula can be rubbed into scars if they are tender.

Arnica is useful for bruising and sprains when used externally.

Black cohosh may assist arthritis, muscular and neurological pain.

Essiac is useful for cancer pain.

Ginger for colic, fibrositis and muscle sprains

St John's wort for spinal pain, arthritis, pain associated with nerve damage, pain of toes, tail and dew claws and depression

Valerian may reduce pain and is also calming.

Devil's claw for arthritic pain and mild pain from other causes

Passionflower (*Passiflora incarnata*) assists with gut-related spasm and pain.

Bach Flowers

Rescue Remedy can be helpful.

Acupuncture

There have been many studies evaluating the effectiveness of acupuncture for relief of both acute and chronic pain. A review of twenty-four studies in humans found that acupuncture was 70 per cent effective when compared to placebo.[253] Acupuncture can mask pain and provide almost immediate relief of most types of pain, and so it is important to have a diagnosis before treatment.

Consider:

Neck pain: BL 11.

Lower back pain: BL 40, KI 7, BL 23, BL 60.

Abdominal pain: ST 36, CV 12, BL 20, SP 6.

And local points for joint, abdominal and other pain.

Chiropractic adjustments might also be beneficial depending on the condition.

Homeopathy

In conjunction with other therapy, consider using Arnica or hypericum three times a day.

Biochemical salts

Mag. phos. 6x

Other

Comfortable bedding, softly spoken words, and quality time together can be very comforting for dogs in pain. It's also important to consider their other needs, especially if they are less mobile. Assisting them with regular toileting is important. Help them up and assist them to get to the garden by using a towel as a sling underneath their belly. Massage their belly daily. Grooming works wonders. Gentle exercise, if possible is wonderful. Gentle massage and hands-on healing therapies are also particularly beneficial for dogs to help them relax and reduce pain.

Wounds, Stings and Trauma

Dogs seem to be prone to all sorts of wounds through their daily busy lives. Cuts, bites, injuries, sprains and insect stings are all relatively common. If there is trouble to find, you can be sure it's a dog that will find it! First aid should be administered until veterinary attention can be sought. Minor wounds can be treated at home, but if the condition worsens, or your dog is in pain or off his food, take your dog to your veterinarian as soon as possible.

Recommendations

Make sure you have a first aid kit and a guide in a convenient place, so that should you be faced with a problem, you will be well prepared to deal with it. Most veterinary practices have after-hours services to help deal with emergencies. Conventional emergency treatment is very effective and complementary care can be given as well.

Supplements

Vitamins A,C and E, digestive enzymes, sunflower or flax seed oil; glucosamine for injuries of tendons, ligaments, cartilage

Herbs

Calendula (*Calendula officinalis*) in ointment or salve or spray is good for red, swollen wounds with pus, also slow healing wounds and minor burns.

Yarrow (*Achillea millefolium*) is good for injuries that are deep, or bleeding, as well as bruises.

Arnica is a herbal remedy, which—applied externally—is particularly indicated for bruises and sprains.

St John's wort (*Hypericum perforatum*) is useful for cuts that involve damage to nerves, particularly on the lower limbs where tendons and nerves have been injured, or the toes and feet, as well as minor wounds and clipper rash.

Aloe vera is excellent for burns and minor wounds.

Burdock with yellow dock, red clover or cleavers can be used externally on ulcers and minor wounds.

Minor skin wounds and cuts benefit from chickweed and marshmallow combined in a salve externally.

Echinacea can be applied externally for wounds, abscesses and burns.

Golden seal or Oregon grape root is best for clean wounds.

Plantain, fresh pulverised leaves or tincture (diluted) is good for dog bite wounds, insect bites and wounds.

Rose hips help soothe and heal wounds and scars, burns and insect bites.

Slippery elm (mixed with a little water) can be applied to wounds, abscesses, bites and minor burns.

Honey can be useful for minor wounds.

Bach Flowers

Rescue Remedy may be useful to calm a dog in shock and also for yourself.

Acupuncture

Laser therapy can stimulate healing of wounds, infected wounds and burns. Acupuncture around scars and wounds can also stimulate healing.

Homeopathy

For injury and bruises arnica can be used until veterinary attention is found.

Mild insect bites respond well to Apis mel.

Burns may be assisted with cantharis and urtica.

Cuts can benefit from calendula.

Other

Lavender oil can be applied safely to wounds and cuts to speed healing and provide antibacterial action.

Snake Bite

Snake bite: Echinacea inhibits hyaluronidase and may be beneficial as an adjunct to snake bite treatment.[254]

Recovery from Surgery or Hospitalisation

It's a fact of life that just about all dogs will undergo some form of anaesthesia and surgery at least once in their lives, if only for neutering or dentistry. Surgery can repair broken bones, remove cancerous growths and correct deformities that hinder health or normal functioning. But surgery and any major medical treatment are always stressful on the body.

If surgery or major medical treatment is not urgent you may wish to consider your options. Most veterinary hospitals have the facilities to offer complete medical and surgical services. However, you may also ask for a referral to either a medical or surgical specialist, or a holistic veterinarian who may offer you other options. There is usually more than one approach for such problems. You should feel comfortable with your veterinarian and the care of your pet. Most practices these days are happy to show you around the hospital, which can be helpful to alleviate any concerns you might have before leaving your pawed friend.

If you have some advance warning that surgery or major medical treatment needs to be done, there are some things you can do to strengthen your pet, reduce stress and improve the chances of rapid recovery, repair and healing. But if the treatment or surgery is unexpected, you can also aid recovery with these few simple ideas:

- Before going into hospital your veterinarian may want to take a blood sample to look at how well your pet's body is functioning. This is especially important for older animals or very sick animals. Blood tests can help determine what type of anaesthesia and fluid therapy may be best and whether any other therapy is required to minimise the risks and enhance the recovery period.
- From a holistic perspective it is best not to have your pet vaccinated at the time of surgery. If vaccination were due, you would be better to have the vaccination done some weeks before surgery or at least a month after surgery.
- Before going into hospital you can help your pet by strengthening the immune system, providing nourishing nutrition and encouraging weight loss if your dog is overweight.
- You can aid the immune system by giving your pet vitamin B complex and C with vitamin bioflavinoids to enhance tissue health.
- On the day before surgery, ensure that your pet has plenty to drink during the day and a light meal before bedtime. An empty stomach is usually required for surgery, so unless your vet has told you otherwise, no breakfast in the morning. Make sure your pet has gone to the toilet before hospitalisation.
- You may wish to give your pet a few drops of the Bach Flower Rescue Remedy every 15 to 30 minutes before leaving for the hospital. Make sure to take along a familiar smelling toy or T-shirt or something to comfort him while he's in hospital.
- If your pet has special dietary requirements, or you like to feed him only particular types of foods, make up a batch to take along with you. This will help if your dog is picky after surgery and may be very important if he has no appetite for a strange food in hospital.
- The less nervous you are about the surgery, the less nervous your pet will be. So try to remain calm. If you are at all worried, then do speak to your veterinarian to allay any fears.

- Following surgery or major medical treatment, make sure you take the time to visit your pet, especially if she is in hospital for any length of time. And be prepared to spend some time there. Pets love nothing more than a visit from their people, and appreciate a good groom and even a feed when you are there. Just make sure you call to schedule a visit.
- When you take your pet home, follow your veterinarian's advice, and if you're not sure, call the practice to clarify any questions. It is really helpful in the first few days to spend considerable time with your pet. They enjoy a gentle massage twice daily, some TLC (tender loving care) and any assistance you can provide. If you practise Reiki or any other form of hands-on healing now is the time to employ your skills, but if not, then don't underestimate the power of gentle stroking and massage and healing intent.
- Pain management is very important. Follow your vet's instructions and supplement this care with suggestions under the pain control section.
- Feed your dog lightly on the first couple of days, you may wish to add a little organ meat like liver to his diet to improve palatability, and continue with the vitamin supplements and encourage plenty of drinking. Chicken broth always goes down well. Your vet may advise a special diet, because many procedures increase the body's need for protein and energy. Make sure your pet is warm and comfortable and that he is encouraged to use a litter tray (if immobile) or go outside several times during the day.
- Digestive enzymes and probiotics can also be beneficial following surgery. And if your dog has to have antibiotics then these are especially important. You can also continue with the Rescue Remedy if your pet seems at all uncomfortable or depressed. Don't hesitate to call your vet if your pet seems any worse or has new symptoms.
- Vitamin E, calendula cream and aloe vera gel are all helpful for healing scars and lesions, or puncture wounds. Glucosamine sulphate or Perna sea mussel are particularly useful following any joint, bone, tendon or ligament surgery. You should always check with your vet before surgery or medical treatment whether it is OK to give any other supplements or substances.

General anaesthetics suppress immunity and may take a while to leave the system; use St Mary's thistle, ginseng (*Panex ginseng*), dandelion and echinacea.

Acupuncture
Acupuncture can be used before and after surgery to relieve pain, discomfort and nausea.

Homeopathy for convalescence
Arnica for bruising and pain
Staphysagria for trauma
Cinchona for convalescence
Phosphoric acid

Muscles, Bones and Joints

The musculo-skeletal system comprises the skeleton, muscles, tendons and ligaments. The most common sign that something is wrong is lameness with an altered gait, stiffness and reluctance to move. The musculo-skeletal system can be affected by poor diet, calcium imbalances, hormonal imbalances, prolonged use of corticosteroids and non-steroid anti-inflammatory drugs, food allergens, injury and 'wear and tear'. The musculo-skeletal system responds well to acupuncture, chiropractic and massage as well as good nutrition.

Arthritis, Osteoarthritis, Degenerative Joint Disease and Osteochondrosis

Any dog that suffers from ongoing lameness or stiffness may have arthritis (also called osteoarthritis and degenerative joint disease). And unfortunately arthritis is common in older dogs. It is usually due to injury or a lifetime of wear and tear on the joints of the body. But younger dogs can have arthritis too, either because of injuries, infections, poor nutrition and also developmental disorders such as osteochondrosis (a problem of the cartilage lining the joints), hip dysplasia and elbow dysplasia. Obese dogs, working dogs and athletic dogs may be more prone to arthritis because of the extra loads on their joints. Dogs with Cushing's Syndrome and diabetes may also be susceptible because of the metabolic processes that affect the bones.

Sometimes what appears to be arthritis can in fact be 'trigger points'. These are like muscle cramps that can resemble the symptoms of arthritis. They can usually be treated effectively with acupuncture. Whatever the age, it is important to establish the possible underlying factors that can be contributing to the problem.

Your veterinarian can assess the condition and may advise surgical or medical treatment of the problem. However, one of the most important things you can do to help relieve these joint problems long term is making sure your dog is a normal weight.

Many dogs also find great relief following a course of acupuncture. Usually a course of acupuncture is needed over a period of time, with 'top ups' as necessary. Some forms of arthritis can also benefit from chiropractic manipulation, particularly if the pain is associated with the back and spine, although these will often benefit from acupuncture too.

Arthritis may also respond to a change in diet. Some dogs will have improvement on a single-protein source diet, such as a balanced chicken food, or balanced lamb food. One of the theories behind why this may work is that arthritis may be related to food sensitivities in some dogs. Likewise there are a number of dietary supplements that may benefit dogs with arthritis.

In the meantime if your dog is experiencing pain, he may benefit from conventional drugs prescribed by your veterinarian or alternatively herbs. Other methods of alleviating discomfort include gentle massage and warming of the joints. Providing a heating pad or a hot water bottle in winter is greatly appreciated by older pets. It is important to encourage exercise (swimming is excellent) to keep joints mobile. Old dogs enjoy a short walk each day, even if it is a slow one. Walks help to keep noses and brains active and every dog enjoys a walk.

Recommendations

Long-term use of corticosteroids such as prednisolone should be avoided unless it is the last resort, due to high incidence of adverse side-effects and possibility of accelerating joint damage.[255] Care must also be taken with the use of non-steroid anti-inflammatory drugs (NSAIDS) because there is some controversy as to whether they can in fact cause more damage to joint tissues.[256] In addition some NSAIDS can adversely affect the kidneys, liver, brain, immune system and blood.[257] So it's important to avoid long-term reliance on these drugs.

Diet

Prevention of developmental bone problems that can lead to arthritis depends on limiting food and also restricting jumping and exercise while puppies are growing. For large breed dogs, and those susceptible to inherited forms of arthritis and developmental problems consider meal feeding rather than leaving food out all of the time (ad libitum). In a five-year study, dogs fed ad libitum dry dog kibble were significantly heavier, and had increased frequency and severity of osteo-arthritis compared to meal fed dogs (25 per cent less calories were consumed).[258] Reducing calories has a protective effect against arthritis.

Some dogs have both skin and arthritis problems. They may benefit from the Bowel Detoxification Program.

Consider an elimination diet or a veterinary diet formulated to help arthritis. Some dogs will respond to the diet over four to six weeks. Consider the diet you are feeding now. Include raw fruit and vegetables to increase vitamin C, and other important anti-oxidants. Avoid potato, tomato, eggplant, chili, capsicum and dairy products, which have been known to aggravate arthritis in people. Reduce red meat and increase white meats including cod, tuna, salmon and mackerel, which can be fed three times a week to increase fatty acids. Other good foods include tripe, oats, mussels, and calf trachea and apple pectin.

Supplements

Glucosamine aids cartilage repair and is safe. It decreases pain and improves joint function[259] and /or:

- Chondroitin sulphate inhibits the enzymes that destroy cartilage and helps improve nutrient supply to the joints.
- New Zealand Perna green-lipped sea mussels contain some 10 per cent glycosa-minoglycans.
- Bovine cartilage or shark cartilage
- Combinations of glucosamine, chondroitin sulphate and manganese

Manganese, magnesium and zinc are beneficial, omega-3 fatty acids, flax seed oil and cod liver oil, vitamins C and E, dimethylglycine, methylsulphonylmethane (msm), pro-biotics, digestive enzymes or apple cider vinegar with meals.

Herbs

Devil's claw eases pain.

Ginger is anti-inflammatory and reduces pain.

Celery (*Apium graveolens*)—also helpful if arthritis is associated with depression

Bladderwrack, kelp (especially if the dog is also obese) and it can be used externally on joints as well.

Echinacea (*Echinacea* spp.), where infections are also involved.

Turmeric (*Curcuma longa*) has anti-inflammatory properties comparable to phenyl-butazone and cortisone in acute inflammation, but is only half as effective in chronic inflammation[260] (however, without the side-effects).

Boswellia, alfalfa, dandelion root, yellow dock

Acupuncture

If on steroids wean over four weeks while treating, then a further three to four treatments while off medication.

Consider:

Arthritis that is worse with cold: ST 36, LI 11 plus local points and moxa.

Arthritis that is worse with damp and more stiff than painful: SP 6, SP 9.

Arthritis with hot painful joints: LI 11, GV 14, LI 4, ST 44.

Arthritis where pain changes from one place to another LI 11, BL 11, GV 14, GB 39, TH 5

PLUS Local points:

Hind legs: BL 23, BL 40, BL 60, BL 11

Spine: BL points forward and behind painful area, BL 23
Knee/stifle: BL 21, ST 36, ST 35, SP 9, GB 34
Hip: GB 29, GB 30, BL 48
Shoulder: LI 11, BL 11, LI 15, LI 16, TH 14
Elbow: LI 11, LI 4, LI 10, HT 3, LU 5
Wrist/carpus: LI 4, LI 6, TH 5

Homeopathy

Rhus. tox. for creaky joints, worse in cold damp weather, stiff on rising but improves as warms up and moves around.

Ruta grav following sprains, ligament damage, cruciates.

Bryonia when arthritis is worse with exercise and warm weather.

Causticum for the older dog, where arthritis is improved with heat.

Calc. fluor. if due to growth problems

Biochemical salts

Calc. fluor. for chronic arthritis

Ferrous phosphate for acute arthritis

Bach Flowers

Try agrimony, beech, gorse, impatiens, oak, willow, and rock water.

Other

Pentosan polysulphate is a synthetic glycosaminoglycan mimicking chondroitin sulphate available by injection or capsule. It is a relatively safe medication that can provide excellent pain relief and improve mobility. Your veterinarian can provide this treatment.

For pain control consider:

Chiropractic

Chiropractic should be considered for chronic arthritis that leads to changes in gait and changes in the biomechanics of the spine, resulting in wear and tear of other joints.

Massage

A total of 20 drops of either or all of juniper berry, rosemary, lavender, thyme, ginger, in 100 mls of sweet almond oil can be mixed. Massage a teaspoon of this into the affected area when necessary.

Hip Dysplasia

Hip dysplasia is one of the most common skeletal diseases of dogs. It is considered to be an inherited disorder causing laxity of the hips. Rapid growth, diet and exercise can affect the progression of the disease and how it manifests.

Conventional therapy as a rule consists of medical therapy (analgesics and anti-inflammatory drugs), although these usually only provide temporary relief. There are several surgical options, from complete hip replacement to actually removing the joint altogether. Consider a referral to a veterinary surgical specialist to give you the options, costs and expected outcomes.

Recommendations

To avoid hip dysplasia, the best thing you can do is to make sure that your puppy has sound parents. Get some advice from your veterinarian, and preferably a couple of breeders before taking a puppy home. Limit feeding and restrict exercise to allow the bones and joints time to grow SLOWLY; this will go a long way towards preventing the expression of the disease. Hip dysplasia may take several years to be manifested in terms of lameness.

If you already have a half-grown or an adult dog, then weight control is equally important. A lighter dog will have less load on the joints.

Exercise should be regulated to reduce further damage and pain. Swimming is an excellent form of exercise and physiotherapy should also be considered. Passive movement of the joints will help to keep them mobile and the muscles toned. Gentle stretching and flexion and extension of the joints should be done daily. Your veterinarian or animal physiotherapist can show you how.

Diet

Weight control and diet are important. (*See* Arthritis)

Supplements

Supplements listed under arthritis are appropriate.

Herbs

Herbs listed under arthritis may be beneficial.

Acupuncture

Consider these points: BL 11, BL 40, GB 34, GB 30, GB 29, KI 3.

For dogs with chronic pain also consider the possibility of gold bead implants. The success of this procedure is higher in younger dogs. Of 250 dogs treated with gold bead implants 99 per cent of dogs younger than seven years, 80 per cent between seven and twelve years and 50 per cent of dogs older than twelve years showed a major improvement in mobility and movement.[261] Certified veterinary acupuncturists can provide this procedure.

Homeopathy

Consider:
Calc. phos. for lean dogs
Calc. carb. for more solid dogs

Biochemical salts

Calc. fluor. 6x

Calc. phos. 6x

Other

Chiropractic may be beneficial.

Epsom salt hydrobath in warm water is comforting for some dogs.

Lyme Disease

Lyme disease is a type of 'bacterial', tick-borne disease. It causes recurring bouts of arthritis and lameness, though dogs can also develop heart, kidney and nervous system symptoms. Prevention is better than cure and avoiding tick infestation is important. The disease is thought to be exotic in Australia, although there have been diagnoses made in people. So it is possible that it occurs. Vaccination is available for dogs in the USA, although there is some controversy as to the effectiveness and safety of the vaccine.

Lyme disease usually responds to antibiotic treatment; however, the disease can recur. Natural therapies that address the disease by enhancing the immune system, seem to be helpful.

Recommendations

Consider the suggestions in Immune Support.

Acupuncture is worthwhile to stimulate the immune system too, consider: LI 4, LI 11, ST 36, GV 14, BL 23, BL 40.

Consider the suggestions for arthritis, including the supplements and diet.

Trigger Points

Trigger points are hard nodules that occur within muscles or tissues surrounding the muscle. They can cause referred pain elsewhere in the body. Dogs with trigger points often have a history of six months to several years of chronic lameness or pain, which is unresponsive to corticosteroids, anti-inflammatory drugs, painkillers and acupuncture. Sometimes the trigger points can occur with arthritis and sometimes after excessive jumping and play; however, fatigue, stress, trauma, viral infections and strain may also be involved.

In dogs there are nine places where trigger points often occur (triceps, infraspinatus, quadriceps, pectineus, peroneus longus, iliocostalis lumborum, semitendinosis, semimembranosus, tensor fascia latae and gluteus medius muscles). There are other possible points including the extensor carpi radialis. They can vary in size from a few millimeters to several centimeters.[262]

If a trigger point is detected (and there is often more than one) they can be treated under sedation or anaesthesia. The points have to be needled by a veterinary acupuncturist or injected, and often a muscle twitch is observed. About 60 per cent of dogs will respond in 3–4 treatments a week apart.

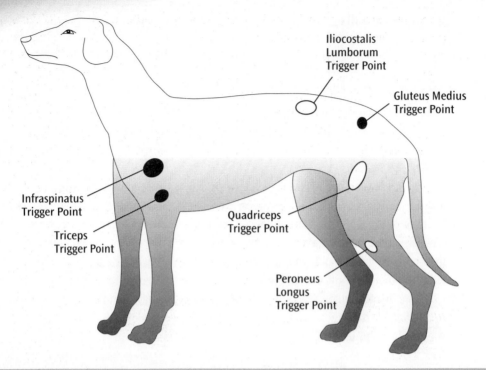

Iliocostalis
Lumborum
Trigger Point

Gluteus Medius
Trigger Point

Infraspinatus
Trigger Point

Triceps
Trigger Point

Quadriceps
Trigger Point

Peroneus
Longus
Trigger Point

Figure 6. Common sites for trigger points

For trigger point treatment, consider the suggestions for arthritis, particularly acupuncture and the supplements.

Leg Injuries

Fractures, sprains, torn ligaments (like anterior cruciates), pulled muscles and other injuries are common in dogs. They need veterinary attention and care to help minimise pain and potential complications. There are some complementary therapies you can consider to speed up the repair and healing of your dog.

Recommendations

Most dogs will require rest to allow time for the injuries to heal. Physiotherapy (and hydrotherapy) with gentle movement of the limbs can be beneficial. Talk to your vet about what you can do at home to improve the return of normal function.

Massage is useful in some situations to relax your dog, reduce pain and increase circulation to the area but if the area is swollen or painful it's best to leave it alone. Massage around surrounding areas with warm flax seed oil or wheatgerm oil.

Prevention of leg injuries is better than cure. Consider minimising off leash exercise and any exercise that has jumping activity (Frisbee catching for example) and rough play with other dogs. Encourage swimming both as another form of exercise and in the recuperation and strengthening of your dog's limbs.

Support bandages may be useful to provide extra comfort for your dog. Your veterinarian can help you with this.

Diet
Cut back on the amount you are feeding while your dog is resting and not exercising. This will help prevent weight gain.

Supplements
Vitamins C and E are helpful.
Glucosamine is useful for any injury of joint, tendon, ligament and muscle.
Consider other supplements listed under arthritis.

Herbs
Consider any of the herbs listed under arthritis and also under pain.
St John's wort salve can be applied externally.
Comfrey can be applied externally to fractures (under veterinary supervision).
Arnica gel can be applied externally to bruises and sprains.

Bach Flowers
Consider Rescue Remedy and other remedies specific for your dog.

Acupuncture
Acupuncture is very useful to help reduce pain and inflammation and speed healing with any injury.

Homeopathy
Ruta for torn or pulled ligaments and tendons
Arnica for dislocations, bruises and sprains
Symphytum for fractures

Other
If your dog has a sprain or injured ligament or tendon, consider ice packing after you have had him examined by a vet. Use a bag of frozen peas or similar around the affected area, and leave in place for 20–30 minutes. Remove for 15 minutes and repeat the process for two to three hours. This helps minimise bleeding and swelling. Apply alternating hot and cold packs the next day to stimulate the circulation and reduce pain. Allow your dog to rest.

Spinal Problems
A range of signs may indicate a problem in the spine. These include: lick granulomas (they often appear on the legs, but can relate to pressure on nerve roots), suddenly yelping in pain without other symptoms, incontinence, neck stiffness, when your dog

is unable to jump into the car or onto the bed, foreleg lameness where the pain cannot be found, hip pain, stiffness in moving, a hunched back and pain along the back (including resenting being touched around the base of the back).

Spinal disorders include disc disease, spondylitis, spondylosis, paralysis, intervertebral disc disease, fibrocartilaginous embelopathy, degenerative myelopathy, cancer in the spine, haemorrhage in the spine and infections in the spine.

Recommendations

Your veterinarian will usually conduct a neurological exam and possibly take some radiographs. A referral to a veterinary neurologist or specialist surgeon may be necessary.

Complementary therapies especially acupuncture and chiropractic, diet and supplements can be very useful in reducing pain and delaying progression of any disease.

Diet

If your dog is overweight, weight reduction will benefit most dogs with spinal problems. Provide the best diet you can, but keep in mind that your dog's energy requirements may be less than normal if exercise is reduced.

Supplements

Consider the following supplements to help support the spine, as well as those listed under arthritis.

Glucosamine, Flax seed oil, Grape seed extract, Lecithin, vitamin C.

Herbs

Herbs for arthritis and also for pain control may be beneficial.

Oats for depression and inflammation associated with the spine

Skullcap for spinal problems; this also combines well with valerian.

St John's wort for disc and spinal pain, and nerve damage

Bach Flowers

Rescue Remedy

Acupuncture

Acupuncture is especially helpful for most spinal conditions (*see* below); however, a diagnosis is essential before commencing treatment.

Homeopathy

Consider: Nux vomica; this may help back pain. Also hypericum, causticum, Conium mac., Arnica, Plumb. met.

Massage

For herniated discs, rub tincture of golden seal over area three times daily.

For backs in general, gentle massage using flax seed oil, sesame or wheatgerm oil is warming and soothing.

Disc Disease, Protrusion; Prolapsed, Slipped Disc

Conservative therapy of disc problems consists of painkillers, rest (confined for four weeks), corticosteroids and muscle relaxants. Approximately 30%–50% of mildly affected dogs may respond to this treatment. Surgical treatment consists of removing some of the bone or disc material around the spine to relieve the pressure on the spinal cord. Approximately 85 per cent of dogs can respond to surgery.[263]

Cervical, thoraco-lumbar and lumbo-sacral disc disease responds well to acupuncture. One study reported 83 per cent success with thoraco-lumbar disc disease (63 per cent had received prior medical treatment with no response for two weeks) with an average of three to four treatments a week apart.[264] In another study 69 per cent of dogs with cervical (neck) disc disease responded well over two weeks.[265] Acute spinal disc prolapse needs to be assessed quickly. Depending on the severity of the symptoms, acupuncture may be used to alleviate pain and inflammation either with or as an alternative to conventional medicine or surgery.

Cervical Disc Disease

Corticosteroids to reduce inflammation are really only useful if used within eight hours of the spinal injury or disc prolapse. They will also reduce the effectiveness of acupuncture.

There are three basic levels of symptoms:

Level 1 where there is just neck pain

Level 2 has neck pain and the front legs are weak with reduced proper placement of the feet. Acupuncture works very well for level 1 (approximately 80 per cent respond to 3–4 treatments over 1–2 weeks) and level 2 (approximately 67 per cent respond to 5–6 treatments over 3–4 weeks). Approximately 33 per cent of dogs treated with acupuncture for cervical disc disease relapse within 3 years. Dogs that don't respond to acupuncture for level 1 and 2 may benefit from surgery. Dogs may be treated with acupuncture and conservative therapy and then surgery can be considered if this is ineffective.[266]

Level 3 cervical disc disease has neck pain and front and hind leg paralysis with or without deep pain sensation. These dogs are best helped with surgery (within 24 hours) and then acupuncture can help to relieve pain and promote recovery. Acupuncture treatment will vary depending on the site of the disc problem

Thoracolumbar Disc Disease

There are four levels of symptoms:

Level 1—There is back pain present, the dog moves slowly and avoids stairs or jumping up.

Level 2—There is back pain and the hind legs are weak and uncoordinated and the back paws knuckle over.

Level 3—Dogs have paralysis in their back legs and cannot stand up but have pain perception.

Level 4—Dogs are like level 3 except they have no pain perception in their feet, although they are in severe pain over the back. These dogs should undergo prompt (within 24 hours) surgical decompression. Acupuncture can be used if more than 24 hours have passed.

Acupuncture

Approximately 90 per cent of dogs with level 1 thoracolumbar disc disease recover after 2–3 treatments over 1–2 weeks. Approximately 90 per cent of dogs with level 2 disease recover after 3–4 treatments over a 3-week period. Approximately 80 per cent of dogs with level 3 disease recover after 5–6 treatments over 6 weeks. 10 per cent won't recover and 10 per cent only partially. Less than 25 per cent of dogs with level 4 disease recover after ten or more treatments over 3–6 months. Acupuncture is only half as effective as prompt surgical decompression for level 4 disease.[267]

Acupuncture treatment will vary depending on the site of the disc problem.

Acupuncture points

Consider:

GB 34 and two local BL points.

GB 34, GB 30, BL 60 and local BL points.

BL 40, BL 60, GB 30, GB 34, ST 36 plus local points.

Acupuncture varies from daily to weekly, the greater the pain the more frequent the treatments.

Use SI 3 and BL 62 bilaterally (right foreleg first then left hind for females and left foreleg first and right hind for males) for 5 to 10 minutes to open the spinal channel first, then:

Local points along the BL meridian plus:

BL 40, GB 34, BL 60, ST 36 for lumbar spine.

GV 14, BL 40, GB 34 for thoracic spine.

LI 4, LI 11, SI 3, ST 38, BL 10, GB 20, BL 11, TH 15 for cervical spine.

Dachshunds

Dachshunds are prone to disc problems, but respond well to acupuncture.

BL 67, BL 40, GB 34, ST 36, BL points forward and behind the lesion. Sedation may be necessary. Avoid barbiturates as this will reduce the effect of the acupuncture.

Wobbler Syndrome, Cervical Vertebral Instability

Wobbler syndrome describes a condition in dogs where there is compression of the spinal cord around the neck region. Conventional treatment depends on when it is first diagnosed. Surgery and the use of glucocorticoids early on is one approach. Mildly affected dogs may respond just to glucocorticoids. Weight control and restricted exercise is also recommended.

Consider the supplements and suggestions recommended for spinal conditions.

Acupuncture

Acupuncture is another option. Success of acupuncture depends on the age of the dog, and severity of disease. Young dogs seem to improve better than old dogs. In dogs with severe spinal cord compression approximately 30%–40% of dogs can be helped with at least eight treatments. Approximately 70%–80% of dogs with milder compression will respond to some degree. The more hunched up, knuckling of paws and flexion of the neck, the less favorable the outcome.

Points to consider include:

SI 3, BL 64, GV 14, Bai Hui

GB 34, BL 60, ST 36, LI 4, LI 11, ST 36

Degenerative Myelopathy

Degenerative myelopathy or degenerative radiculo-myelopathy of German shepherds (and German Shepherd crosses) is a disease of the spinal cord where the sheath surrounding the spinal cord progressively deteriorates. This means that the transmission of nerve impulses becomes gradually worse. Initially dogs with this disease show progressive weakness and incoordination in their back legs, later there is knuckling of the feet, swaying of the hind legs and sometimes incontinence. This disease looks very similar to disc disease and also arthritis so needs to be diagnosed carefully.

Most dogs with this condition do not seem to be painful or uncomfortable. One of the problems is that the muscles of the hind legs gradually waste away, so even though dogs with this condition walk 'funny' they should still be encouraged to exercise. The stronger and more active your dog is, the longer he will be able to continue moving about.

In conventional medicine there is very little that can be done unless there is concurrent disease like arthritis or disc disease. Corticosteroid use may worsen muscle atrophy and should not be used.

This is basically a non-treatable disease in conventional medicine. However, besides exercise and diet, complementary therapies may be used to help prolong health and delay progression of the disease.

Diet

Keep your dog lean and consider a weight control diet if he needs to lose weight.

Supplements

Flax seed oil or olive oil are a source of omega-9 fatty acids which may be useful for demyelination of the nerve sheathes; lecithin (or choline), vitamin B complex, vitamin E, glucosamine, *L. carnitine*

Herbs
Gingko, Turmeric

Acupuncture
There may be temporary improvement with acupuncture, especially electro-acupuncture. However, the longer the problem has existed, the less effective acupuncture is. Points to consider include BL 67, GB 44, ST 45 and nail beds. Acupuncture is worth trying, though many dogs improve for a week to three weeks then get worse again and need repeated treatments.

Bach Flowers
Consider using flower essences depending on your dog's state.

Homeopathy
Remedies will depend on individual symptoms, Conium mac may be useful.

The Cardiovascular System

Heart Disease

Dogs can suffer several forms of heart disease. The most common are congenital heart defects, degenerative valve disease (typically in small breeds), dilated cardiomyopathy (typically in large breeds) and heartworm disease. In valvular heart disease the valves inside the heart are faulty, making the pumping action of the heart weak. In the dilated heart disease there is an enlargement of the heart, but the walls of the heart are weak and floppy, again the pumping action is compromised. In heartworm disease, the worms block some of the major vessels making it more difficult for the heart to pump effectively. In all cases the heart is often starved of oxygen, as is the rest of the body, which is why these dogs are often short of breath and can't tolerate exercise well.

Severe forms of these diseases lead to congestive heart failure where breathing problems, coughing, intolerance to exercise and lethargy are seen. A referral to a veterinary cardiologist is often worthwhile, particularly if there are complications or your dog doesn't respond well to treatment.

It has been proposed that some heart disease may be a consequence of infections, poor nutrition or immune mediated disease. From a holistic perspective some other considerations are a possible association with dental disease, lack of exercise (poor oxygenation and sluggish circulation), emotional stress and free radical damage.

Conventional medicine is usually very effective in early stages of the disease and some newer medications can help delay the progress of heart disease. Complementary medicine can be used to help protect and support the heart while your dog is on medication.

Recommendations

While there are a variety of drugs that are safe and effective, sometimes an individual dog responds poorly or cannot tolerate the side-effects. Acupuncture is one of the best adjuncts to conventional medicine, alongside diet and supplements. Acupuncture is also very useful for shock, heart failure and arrhythmias (where the heartbeat is abnormal).

Mild, regular exercise will help oxygenate the body and stimulate circulation and should be considered if at all possible.

Diet

If your dog is overweight, it is very important that your dog loses weight slowly and carefully to reduce the load on the heart. This should be done under veterinary super-vision. There are special veterinary diets available for heart disease although most prescription veterinary diets are low in salt (the main concern). If your dog has early congestive heart failure, reducing sodium to below 90 mg/100 kcal may be useful. In more advanced stages reduce the salt to below 40 mg/100 kcals. With home-made foods, a low sodium diet is also recommended (use potassium chloride salt). Fresh green vegetables, potassium-rich foods such as broccoli, spinach, peas and potatoes and fruit, fish, oat or rice bran, brown rice and other grains are good. Consider adding fresh heart to the diet as well.

Supplements

Taurine can be helpful in dilated cardiomyopathy as an antioxidant (500 mg each 8–12 hours) especially for cockers, corgis and dachshunds.

L-Carnitine (1–2 g twice or three times daily) particularly for boxers

Antioxidant vitamins C, E, A (with bioflavinoids), Coenzyme Q10, Potassium chloride, dimethylglycine, sunflower or flax seed oil, selenium, vitamin B complex, magnesium.

Also lecithin, wheatgerm, kelp and nutritional yeast

Herbs

Hawthorn (also combines with garlic and dandelion for chronic heart disease)
Cayenne pepper to stimulate circulation and reduce fluid accumulation, ginger
Dandelion is a powerful diuretic like the drug furosemide.
Siberian ginseng, Gingko biloba, Garlic

Acupuncture

Acupuncture has powerful effects on the heart.[268] Initially start by treating with PC 6, PC 7, PC 9, BL 15 for first few treatments then move to HT meridian HT 7 or HT 9.

Cardiomyopathy

Conventional drugs can often be reduced after a couple of weeks of acupuncture. Consider the points HT 7, KI 7, LU 5, BL 13, BL 14, BL 15, BL 16, ST 36, PC 6.

If there is cyanosis or blueness in the tongue include SP 6 and SP 10.

Mitral Valve Insufficiency

Here there is often fluid accumulation in the chest. BL 13, LU 5 and KI 7 can help remove this fluid either alone or with the aid of diuretics. HT 7, BL 14, BL 15 and BL 17 are also useful. Treatment is usually weekly for 3–6 weeks then once a month or as needed.

Heart Failure

These dogs have often not responded to increasing doses of diuretics and other drugs. If acupuncture is tried your dog will require treatment approximately three times a week; if an improvement is not seen in a couple of weeks then the prognosis is very poor. The points would include LU 5, LU 7, KI 7, HT 7, BL 13, BL 14, BL 15, BL 16 and LIV 8.

Heartworm Disease

Conventional treatment sometimes includes the use of arsenic-based drugs. Acupuncture can help reduce the side-effects of this treatment. Consider the points HT 7, LI 4, LI 11, ST 36, LIV 8. Globe artichoke can be given to reduce side effects of arsenic-based drugs.

Homeopathy

Homeopathy should be administered under the care of a veterinary homeopath.

Consider: Digitalis helps to strengthen the heart; Crataegus; Spongia if coughing.

Biochemical salts

Calc. fluor. 6x

Kali phos. 6x for arrhythmias

Heartworm Prevention

In areas and situations where your dog is at risk of contracting heartworm you basically have three options:

1. Use standard veterinary heartworm-prevention drugs. These have proven effectiveness and are regarded as safe for most breeds of dogs.
2. Use nothing, and test your dog for heartworm every six months. If your dog is positive, conventional treatment is best.
3. Use heartworm nosodes, which are harmless, but do not have proven effectiveness. Therefore your dog should be blood tested every six months as for option 2. I have seen several patients who were on nosodes that developed heartworm disease, so I do not recommend this therapy for prevention.

Although anaemia is a symptom and not necessarily a cardiovascular problem (e.g. it can be caused by poisoning, liver disease, chronic renal failure, etc.), for convenience it will be included in this chapter. For the same reason hyperlipidaemia, a metabolic fat disorder with a number of different causes, will be included here as well:

Anaemia

Anaemia is a deficiency of red blood cells or haemoglobin (the oxygen-carrying part of the red blood cell). There are different causes and different types. Any anaemia should be investigated to identify the cause.

Recommendations

Food and herbal sources of iron are helpful. Some mild exercise can help increase oxygenation and energy levels. It is also important to feed good quality protein to support the making of blood in the body.

Diet

Include fresh liver daily (50 grams per 1000 kcals of energy needed by your dog) for four to six weeks. Molasses, beets, brown rice, eggs, mussels, oats and wheatbran help. Manganese-rich foods such as legumes and eggs assist with iron uptake. Broccoli, sunflower seeds, vegetables, fruits, sesame seeds are all beneficial.

Supplements

Vitamin B complex, Folic acid 50–300 micrograms twice daily, vitamins C and E, nutritional yeast, wheatgerm

Herbs

Dandelion (*Taraxacum officinale*) is a very rich source of vitamins, minerals, iron and other nutrients. It has a long history of use in the treatment of anaemia, probably because of its nutritive content.[269]

Parsley; Alfalfa; Yellow Dock; Pau d'arco; Siberian ginseng.

Acupuncture

Acupuncture according to symptoms and Eastern diagnosis, GB 34.

Biochemical salts

Iron phosphate

Hyperlipidaemia

Hyperlipidaemia is a condition describing a high fat level in the blood. It can be a disease or secondary to other problems such as pancreatic disease, diabetes, thyroid disease and liver and kidney disorders.

Dietary management is important to avoid acute pancreatitis, seizures and nervous problems associated with high blood fat. Supplementing with fatty acids ironically can improve the condition, but this should be done under the supervision of a veterinarian.

Diet

A low-fat diet is important, and this is sometimes enough to manage the condition. Adding fibre is also useful. If your dog is overweight consider a weight loss program.

Supplements

Consider Oat bran, Pectins, Carnitine, Chromium.

Herbs

Garlic; Turmeric; Reishi mushroom extract

Other

Exercise your dog lightly.

Reduce stress.

CHAPTER

The Nervous System, Epilepsy and Strokes

The Nervous System

The nervous system is the first system to be affected by stress and tension. There are also many conditions that affect the nervous system. However, some general suggestions apply.

Recommendations

Your veterinarian may refer you to a veterinary neurologist for complicated disorders. Whatever the diagnosis, complementary therapies may be useful to support your dog during treatment and recovery. Acupuncture and chiropractic can be particularly helpful.

Diet

Diet improvement is important for nervous system health. Fresh greens, vegetables, and sulphur foods such as oat bran and celery are beneficial. B vitamin foods such as leafy greens, sesame seeds and rice are also good. Seeds, nutritional yeast, carrots and wheatgerm oil are also beneficial. For chronic disease consider the Bowel Detoxification Program, especially if your dog has received several courses of antibiotics or other drugs.

Supplements

Lecithin (choline), flax seed oil, vitamin B complex, vitamin C, flavinoids, nutritional yeast, magnesium

Herbs

Gingko biloba for head tilt, stroke, blindness, seizures, dementia, ageing

Oats for epilepsy, tremors, depression, and inflammation associated with nervous system

Skullcap for epilepsy and seizures, also spinal problems. Combines well with valerian.

St John's wort for nerve damage and depression

Valerian for nervousness and excitability, may reduce pain.

Valerian also for epilepsy and dogs with muscle tremors

Chamomile for calming

Acupuncture

Acupuncture can be useful for many conditions affecting the nervous system. Points selected will depend upon the condition and TCM diagnosis.

Bach Flowers

Consider star of Bethlehem, scleranthus (especially for one-sided conditions) and others according to your dog's needs.

Homeopathy

Consider: Hypericum if there is nerve damage; Passiflora is soothing; Causticum, Hypericum, Phosphorus, Gelsemium for paralysis.

A veterinary homeopath can prescribe the most appropriate remedy for your dog.

Biochemical salts

Mag. phos. 6x

Head Tilt and Ataxia

Consider the suggestions above.

Acupuncture may be useful, points include GV 20, GB 20, LI 4.

Vestibular Syndrome in Old Dogs

This is an abnormality of the inner ear that occurs in some old dogs. They have problems with their balance, are sometimes disoriented, and often have a head tilt and irregular eye movements. Normally this condition improves by itself, with improvements beginning within 72 hours, and recovery taking as long as two to three weeks. This process can be speeded up with acupuncture using the points GB 20, GV 14, LI 4, LI 11, PC 6, LU 7 and gingko biloba.

Nerve Paralysis

Provided the nerves are not cut, nerve paralysis can respond to acupuncture. Consider acupuncture points along the nerve path and electro-acupuncture to stimulate nerve regeneration. If the nerve is severed completely the outcome is likely to be poor.

Facial Paralysis

Consider the suggestions above and also acupuncture. Points to consider include:
GB 20, GB 14, ST 2, ST 4, ST 6, LI 4 for 3–4 treatments.

Epilepsy and Seizures

Sometimes dogs develop tolerance or resistance to medication, so that seizures are not well controlled or the dose needed to control the seizures may make the dog lethargic. Often medication is required for life; however, if your dog is seizure free for six to twelve months, very careful reduction of dosage under veterinary supervision may be attempted[270]. Phenobarbital medication is used commonly and if seizures are not adequately controlled, potassium bromide is often added. If this is ineffective or unsatisfactory, acupuncture should be considered.

Epilepsy may be associated with allergies, and there is some evidence that nutrition and supplements can help control and minimise epilepsy in dogs.[271]

Recommendations

Do not change dosage of any medications without consultation with your veterinarian.

Keep a journal of your dog's seizure activity noting times, duration, and unusual factors, looking for triggers. Provide moderate exercise and beware of swimming in case your dog seizures in the water.

Diet

Consider a low allergy or elimination diet. Also consider the Bowel Detoxification Program.

Supplements

Dimethylglycine has been used in treating epilepsy;[272] vitamins E and C, proanthocyanidins, Flax seed oil, lecithin, magnesium, tyrosine (10–20 mg/kg), taurine (10–20 mg/kg)

Herbs

Gingko biloba; Valerian; Skullcap; St Mary's thistle is useful to help protect the liver if on phenobarbital.

Bach Flowers

Rescue Remedy should be kept on hand for you and your dog. It can be distressing to see your dog seizure.

Acupuncture

Acupuncture is not usually considered a substitute for conventional medication but it may help to control the seizures and allow a lower dose of medication.

In an acute episode consider the points GV 26, GV 20, PC 6, KI 6, BL 62, GV 16, GV 20, GV 26, GB 20

For more chronic epilepsy consider an ear tack at Shen Men point in both ears.[273]

Gold seeds are another option and can be implanted in the body at BL 4, BL 6, BL 9, GB 14, GB 20, GV 20. Approximately 50 per cent of dogs have reduction in severity and frequency and lower phenobarbital dosage with this regime. It is important not to reduce the dosage of phenobarbital until an improvement is seen. If medication is tapered off too soon the condition could worsen.

Homeopathy
The most appropriate remedy should be selected by a veterinary homeopath.

Other
If on conventional medication it's important to consider regular blood tests to assess the dosage of medication and also the impact on liver enzymes. Desexing may reduce seizure activity in some dogs. Reduce stress. Chiropractic treatment may help as well. Also consider craniosacral therapy.

Head Injuries and Brain Problems
Trauma, bleeding inside the brain, or growths can affect brain functioning. Conventional treatment is essential. Complementary therapies can be used in the recovery period, which can take from several days to several months.

Diet
Review diet and upgrade if possible.

Supplements
Consider lecithin, kelp, vitamin C, vitamin E, flax seed oil, grape seed extracts, selenium.

Herbs
Gingko biloba; St John's wort; Passionflower.

Bach Flowers
Rescue Remedy

Acupuncture
Consider the points GB 20, GB 14, ST 4, ST 6, LI 4, LI 11, ST 36.

Homeopathy
A veterinary homeopath can prescribe the most appropriate remedy for your dog.

The Respiratory System

The respiratory system includes the nose, windpipe (trachea), bronchial tubes and lungs. Dogs, like people are susceptible to viruses and infections, airborne allergens and toxins particularly if they are stressed or in smoky environments or if their immunity is low.

Nasal Discharges and Sinusitis

Nasal discharges can be related to foreign bodies, dental problems, allergies, tumors and viruses. It is important that a diagnosis is made so that any underlying disorders are uncovered. Sinusitis can be due to viral or bacterial infections, often triggered by allergies. Poor circulation and lack of exercise can also be contributing factors.

Recommendations

Nasal secretions clear more easily when your dog is well hydrated. Encourage plenty of fluids (broths and moist foods). Take your dog into the bathroom while you shower and allow the room to fill with steam. You don't need to put your dog under the water for the steam to help loosen the congestion in the nasal passages. Do this for at least fifteen minutes a day for acute conditions, and ten minutes a day for chronic conditions.

Use an oil vaporiser and oils of eucalyptus, thyme, pine and lavender (all or any) so that your dog can inhale the essential oils. These oils help clear congestion and have antimicrobial properties.

Diet

For chronic nasal discharge or sinusitis consider the diets to improve immunity.

Supplements

Vitamins C and A, zinc, vitamin B complex

Herbs

Echinacea, Thyme, Elder flower, Eyebright, Pleurisy root, Nettles, Chamomile

Acupuncture

Acupuncture can be a very effective therapy for sinusitis, both in clearing the passages, its anti-inflammatory effects and immune stimulating effects. Consider the points LI 20, LI 4, LI 11, BL 13, BL 18, BL 25, and ST 36. Be warned, stimulation of LI 20 in particular, can lead to lots of revolting sneezing, but it helps clear the passages.

For upper respiratory tract infection with thick yellow discharge consider GV 14, TH 15, LI 4, LI 11, ST 40.

For upper respiratory tract infection with fever and thin discharge LI 4, LU 7, GB 20, GV 16.

Homeopathy

Pulsatilla for profuse pale discharge
Silicea for chronic sinusitis
Kali bich. for yellow discharge
Or another remedy prescribed by a veterinary homeopath for your dog.

Biochemical salts

Potassium chloride 6x
Iron phosphate 6x

Bronchitis

Bronchitis (persistent coughing) is an inflammation of the tubes (bronchi) leading from the windpipe down to the lungs. Pneumonia refers to an infection or irritation of the lungs. Kennel cough is usually an infection of the windpipe and bronchi. In healthy dogs these problems usually follow a viral infection or irritant such as pollution, cigarette smoke or noxious fumes. Stress, fatigue and low immunity can also be underlying contributing factors. Your vet may prescribe decongestants, antibiotics and mucous loosening medications.

Recommendations

Make sure your dog is not exposed to smoke or smog. Allow him to have plenty of fresh air and gentle exercise. Avoid very cold air and be careful of air pollution that can make bronchitis worse.

Try 'steaming' your dog in the bathroom as above, followed by gentle, very gentle rubbing and patting over the chest area with a cupped hand to help loosen mucous.

Use an oil vaporiser and oils of eucalyptus, thyme, tea tree, mullein, pine and lavender. These oils help clear congestion and have antimicrobial properties.

Diet

Encourage drinking by offering broths and soups.

Immune support should also be considered.

Supplements

Vitamin C with bioflavinoids should be started immediately to reduce the course of the symptoms. If started later it should reduce the severity of the disease. Vitamin A, zinc, dimethylglycine

Herbs

Liquorice (*Glycyrrhiza glabra*) acts as an expectorant (promoting the removal of secretions and phlegm from the airways) and has antiviral and antibacterial properties for dry, non-productive cough.

Echinacea (*Echinacea angustifolia*) has antiviral and antibacterial properties.

Catnip for bronchitis associated with fever

Fennel is helpful as an expectorant.

Mullein (lungwort), good for kennel cough and tracheitis and dry, non-productive cough.

Garlic is antibacterial and antiviral, and an expectorant.

Ginger as a general tonic and warming expectorant.

Golden rod for upper respiratory infections, with echinacea gentle and safe.

Golden seal for kennel cough

Thyme for dry coughs and kennel cough to reduce spasm.

Acupuncture

Acupuncture can relieve symptoms by improving overall health and treating the underlying causes.

For chronic coughs and chronic allergic coughs try LU 7, LI 4, LI 11, BL 13, BL 38, BL 14, LU 8, LU 9.

Treat once or twice weekly for up to six weeks, the course may need to be repeated.

Kennel cough, consider: LI 4, LI 11, CV 17, CV 22.

Homeopathy

If the heart is involved try spongia.

Aconitum for rapid onset of cough

Lycopodium for difficulty breathing

Causticum for hard cough and gagging

Byronia for harsh dry cough

Hepar sulphurus for coughing aggravated by cold
Phosphorus for coughing which is exhausting

Other

Some dogs appreciate a hot water bottle applied to the chest or back to help ease discomfort.

Inhalation of peppermint and eucalyptus oils help loosen mucous and dilate airways.

Pneumonia

A wide range of infections or chemical irritants can precipitate pneumonia. Antibiotics may be absolutely life saving when the infection is bacterial, but viral infections are a lot harder to treat conventionally. Pneumonia may be a result of lowered immunity, a preceding bacterial or viral infection, sensitivities to chemical irritants or pollution, allergies, stress and fatigue, especially if exercised in very cold weather.

Recommendations

Follow the same recommendations as for bronchitis. Complementary therapies are most useful to assist return to health.

Diet

Consider immune support recommendations. Encourage plenty of broths and soups to increase fluids.

Supplements

Vitamin C with bioflavinoids should be started as soon as possible. Vitamins A and E, zinc, dimethylglycine, coenzyme Q10, flax seed oil

Herbs

As for bronchitis. When temperature is normal, consider:
Immune enhancing herbs
  Echinacea
  Astragalus
Tonics such as Panax, Siberian ginseng
Thyme, fennel

Acupuncture

Acupuncture can relieve symptoms by improving overall health and treating the underlying causes.

For pneumonia, points to consider are BL 13, BL 14, BL 15, BL 17, GV 11, GV 12, GV 14, SP 21, SP 20, SP 6, SP 9, GB 21. Treat once or twice or more often depending on symptoms.

Homeopathy

If heart is involved try spongia.

Aconitum for rapid onset of cough

Belladonna for high fever

Lycopodium for difficulty breathing

Causticum for hard cough and gagging

Byronia for harsh dry cough

Hepar sulphurus for coughing aggravated by cold

Phosphorus for coughing which is exhausting

Or a remedy prescribed by a veterinary homeopath

Other

Some dogs appreciate a hot water bottle applied to the chest or back to help ease discomfort.

Behavioural Problems

Behavioural problems are many and varied. Underlying many behavioural disorders is the issue of stress. The stress may be emotional, mental, environmental, nutritional or unknown in origin. Overwhelming stress can be a major contributing factor to any chronic disease as it affects the immune system. A proper diagnosis and appropriate behavioural modification is essential for success. Your veterinarian can help you with most behavioural problems; however, a referral to an animal behaviour specialist can be very worthwhile particularly if you don't seem to be making progress or the problem is serious.

Early socialisation is critical to the normal social development of puppies. Attending puppy parties, and being exposed to varied experiences early in life can prevent or reduce fears, phobias and other behavioural problems later on. Basic and Obedience training is very beneficial and it's never too late to start. Ensure your dog receives plenty of exercise. This will help keep him stimulated and healthy and can reduce some of the symptoms associated with stress and boredom.

If you have a problem with your dog, the first thing to consider is to avoid reinforcing inappropriate behaviour. If your dog receives attention (whether good or bad) this will reinforce in his mind that if he continues with that behaviour he will get your attention. Ignoring your dog and rewarding him for appropriate behaviour is a better approach. Distracting your dog when the behaviour is inappropriate may also work. Avoid punishment because this will be even more stressful and probably worsen the problem.

Sometimes behaviour-modifying drugs can be very effective and safe and can be used to assist while training and other therapies take effect. Diet, supplements and Bach Flower remedies can also assist the process. Acupuncture can be another effective form of treatment for behavioural problems that are unresponsive to conventional treatments.

Tellington Touch (using the circular TTouch) is especially good for behavioural problems. Here are some suggestions to consider alongside regular veterinary care.

Diet

Diet can play a role in behavioural disorders. This is because the quality of the diet, especially proteins and the nutritional balance can affect the nervous system and hormonal system. It has been suggested that a diet that is very high in carbohydrates (cereals) may lead to lower serotonin levels in the brain, which might contribute to aggression and 'nervousness'.[274] However, recent research suggests that aggression (in particular dominance aggression) may benefit from a change from a high protein diet to a low protein diet and dogs with territorial aggression may benefit from a low protein diet supplemented with tryptophan.[275]

It is also possible that an elimination diet may lead to improvement in some dogs. In human medicine a diet devoid of gluten and casein (wheat and milk products) leads to considerable improvement in symptoms.[276] Sometimes food sensitivities and allergies can play a role in anxiety. Consider a single source protein, low allergy diet using a protein your dog hasn't been fed before such as fish, for at least three weeks. Also consider a natural, raw food diet on a single-protein source for three to six weeks.

Provide raw meaty bones for behavioural enrichment. Add vegetables and greens to the diet.

Supplements

Lecithin, flax seed oil, vitamin B complex (especially B3 for anxiety), multiple vitamin, mineral complex, magnesium, nutritional yeast, evening primrose oil

Herbs

Oats for nervousness
Siberian ginseng for nervous tension, restlessness
Valerian for excitability and nervousness, and it may help curb aggression.
Passionflower for calming and agitation
Gingko biloba for stress and anxiety
Skullcap for nervousness and stress
Hypericum for depression and grief
Chamomile for calming
Kava for anxiety, phobias, insomnia

Bach Flowers

Bach Flowers offer a gentle and safe adjunct to any behavioural modification program, and can help reduce stress and anxiety in some dogs.[277] They are certainly worth trying, but not as an alternative to a good diagnosis and appropriate behaviour therapy.

For the nervous dog try aspen, larch, mimulus, sweet chestnut and Rescue Remedy

For the grieving dog try star of Bethlehem, walnut, honeysuckle, gentian and chestnut bud

For dogs going into boarding consider walnut, chestnut bud, honeysuckle, olive, gentian, white chestnut, star of Bethlehem

For lack of confidence try walnut, chestnut bud, larch, centaury

For a stressful environment try walnut, crab-apple, wild rose and mustard

For training, and during behavioural modification programs consider walnut, chestnut bud, clematis, impatiens, olive, wild oat

Acupuncture

Acupuncture is very useful for behavioural problems. In Chinese medicine these disorders are considered a disturbance of 'Shen' or a disturbance of the heart and mind. This can occur when there are prolonged states of emotion that can then affect the organs of the body, the heart and energy of the body. There are specific points that can be used to balance and harmonise the body. This in turn alleviates the symptoms and condition.

For behavioural disturbances consider HT 7, HT 8, HT 9.

Plus:

For anxiety in general consider PC 6, GV 20, or gold bead GV 20.

For show ring shyness try BL 23, BL 52.

For anxiety try PC 7, PC 6, KI 9, CV 4.

For aggression consider PC 6, LIV 3.

For depression consider PC 6, GV 20, SI 3, BL 62.

For poor training try GB 40, GB 13, GB 34, GV 20.

For grief use LU 7.

Touch therapies

Tellington Touch and other forms of hands-on work are very good supports for dogs with behavioural disorders. They are gentle, peaceful and easy to learn, and you can play a major role in providing relaxation therapy. They can help your dog to relax, to connect and to learn.

When your dog is stressed he will look to you for support. Remain relaxed and try blinking your eyes slowly, yawning and avoiding his eyes and look away from him and the thing he is worried about. Hopefully he will take your cue that it isn't something to get distressed about.

Body and neck massage and brushing can be soothing and calming. But this should not be used as a 'reward' during inappropriate behaviour. Chiropractic assessment and adjustment may be useful for some behavioural problems.

Homeopathy

Homeopathy offers additional support during behavioural modification. Some remedies to consider include:

Aconite for panic or acute fear or nervousness that begins after a fright.

Fear of thunder or loud noises consider belladonna, nux vomica, gelsenium, phosphorus or causticum.

Consider argentum if fear results in diarrhoea.

For jealousy consider lachesis.

For separation anxiety consider phosphorus, pulsatilla, Arsenicum album.

For a dog that is hyperexcitable consider belladonna, nux vomica.

For hysteria consider aconitum, belladonna, chamomilla.

For show fright try gelsemium or pulsatilla.

For grief and hysteria consider ignatia.

For grief and depression consider nat. mur.

For hyperactivity consider belladonna, sulphur, nux vomica, pulsatilla, Arsenicum album, nat. mur.

Biochemical salts

Magnesium phosphate 6x, or silica 6x for anxiety or stress

Relaxation

Soft music and massage can help relax your dog. Aromatherapy oils like lavender can also be beneficial.

Nervousness and Anxiety

Nervousness and anxiety can underlie fear aggression, separation anxiety and a host of other behavioural disorders and can be a constant source of stress for your dog. Sometimes anti-anxiety drugs may need to be used. If the anxiety is mild then complementary therapies can be considered either on their own or in conjunction with conventional treatment. However, it is also important to reduce or eliminate the anxiety through modifying your dog's behaviour. This can be a process of desensitisation where you gradually introduce the cause of stress in a supportive environment, so that your dog becomes tolerant of it. You might consider removing causes of stress by providing company and a secure environment. It is also important to provide regular exercise, especially in the evening, before bed, and play and touch therapies can do much to help relieve anxiety.

Bach Flowers

Consider larch, star of Bethlehem, mimulus, aspen, Rescue Remedy.

Barking

Barking is one way dogs communicate but can become a nuisance when excessive. Barking can be reduced or stopped but only when we understand what is underlying the barking. Many dogs are bored and understimulated all day and so they like the sound of their own voice for company. Maybe this dog can't see the source of that interesting noise or smell and is barking to find out. Perhaps he is telling everyone that there is a strange person or dog in the neighbourhood. Or perhaps it is a symptom of separation anxiety. Each of these situations will be treated differently.

- Reward your dog when he is quiet and completely ignore him when he barks, wait for a quiet spell then give him some attention. If your dog is barking because he is anxious, yelling at him to stop will only increase the anxiety and reinforce his behaviour.
- Anti-barking devices such as citronella oil collars can also be more stressful for some dogs but may be necessary in situations where anxiety is not an underlying problem.
- Providing a companion animal may or may not be a good idea, try a part-time companion to start with.
- Behavioural enrichment toys and large raw meaty bones may be useful to keep him busy.

It is important to seek advice for the best results. Your veterinarian may provide guidance or assist you in finding someone who can help you solve this problem.

Bach Flowers

Try cerato, heather, vervain, chestnut bud, walnut.

Separation Anxiety

Separation anxiety affects many dogs. Dogs are meant to be part of a pack, even if that means their people are that pack. So when a dog is left alone all day, and isolated, he may either accept the situation and rest all day, or he may become extremely anxious, whimpering, barking, howling, whining, panting and may even go to the toilet inside the house. He may even begin to destroy furniture or the garden in his frantic attempts to escape to find his 'pack'. It is the urgency and sense of panic that distinguishes separation anxiety from poor house training, watchdog barking or playful destruction. It can be difficult to know if your dog has separation anxiety, though one way to find out is to leave a video camera or tape recorder on, before you leave the house.

Conventional treatment for separation anxiety usually includes a short course of anti-anxiety medication and behaviour modification techniques to help desensitise your dog to being left alone. For example consider a series of planned departures from home, making each one slightly longer. It's also important to avoid emotional departures and arrivals, which may heighten your dog's feeling of being left behind. Feed your dog just before you leave and make a quiet exit. When you come home, ignore your dog for ten minutes or so, and when he is quiet and settled, then greet him. Encourage relaxation and exercise. If your dog has separation anxiety or you suspect it, talk to your veterinarian about finding help. A referral to a behaviour specialist may be necessary.

Bach Flowers

Consider aspen, mimulus, heather, red chestnut, star of Bethlehem, wild oat.

Fear

Fear affects many dogs. It can be learnt (from previous bad experiences) or it can be part of the breeding or socialisation that your dog received as a pup. Fear of certain types of people including children, fear of vets and fear of loud noises are quite common. But some dogs are generally anxious and fearful most of the time, as though it is part of their personality. Such dogs might urinate, attempt to escape or even bite when fearful.

For many of these dogs, a short-term or long-term course of anti-anxiety medication may be necessary to help reduce the fear and anxiety. This alone will make it easier to train your dog to accept the fear-inducing event more calmly. If your dog is afraid of the veterinary clinic such medication may help you to reintroduce your dog slowly. Regular visits, from stopping in the car park, to entering the building, to waiting in the waiting room can be built up slowly over time, in a process of desensitisation. Similarly you can reintroduce your dog to those things or animals or people he is most fearful of. Yelling or punishing your fearful dog will only make the situation worse. If your dog nips or bites when he is afraid it is very important to seek behavioural counselling to reduce the danger of your dog biting anyone. Your veterinarian or behavioural specialist can assist you.

Bach Flowers
Consider aspen, mimulus, Rescue Remedy, star of Bethlehem, walnut.

Thunder and Loud Noises
Thunder, fireworks or other loud noises affect many dogs. It is an irrational fear that can worsen over time. One of the suggested methods of assisting this problem is to play CDs with thunder and other noises on it to desensitise dogs. However, this doesn't always work. Severely affected dogs may benefit from anti-anxiety medication for short periods, or in anticipation of stormy weather to help them. It's also worth considering whether petting and soothing your dog when she is distressed is a good idea. This is because your dog may interpret this as praise for her behaviour. It would be better to attempt to distract her by offering a raw meaty bone, or a game or to encourage her to stay in a secure spot. Your veterinarian can provide you with more guidance or a referral to a behavioural specialist.

Bach Flowers
Try aspen, mimulus, Rescue Remedy, larch, rock rose.

Aggression
Aggression is a serious problem, and needs to be identified early. Dogs may be aggressive because they are fearful, they may be defending their territory, they may be exerting dominance behaviour over their people or it may be that the behaviour is encouraged as 'good watch dog' behaviour.

If your dog has indicated ANY aggression towards children or other people or even yourself, seek veterinary advice and professional counselling straight away. At worst, your dog may seriously injure someone, you may be sued, and your dog may be destroyed.

If your dog is identified as aggressive or shows symptoms of aggressive potential, your dog should be on a leash at all times, and may need to be muzzled when outside his own environment. He should never be left unsupervised, particularly with children. It just isn't worth the risk. Even if your dog is an angel with you, you should not put at risk other people or animals.

Conventional treatment includes prevention (reducing the risk of any injury), behaviour modification and sometimes medication.

Bach Flowers

For fighting between pets try: chestnut bud, walnut, willow, holly, beech.

For unpredictable animals try: aspen, elm, mustard, scleranthus, sweet chestnut, Rescue Remedy.

For aggression: beech, cherry plum, mustard, holly, walnut, wild rose.

For fear aggression: mimulus, aspen, Rescue Remedy, rock rose.

Obsessive–Compulsive Disorders

Behaviour that is repetitive, seems to have no purpose or is odd may be symptomatic of obsessive-compulsive disorder, especially if it occupies your dog's time a lot, or causes you or your dog distress. A chemical imbalance or frustration may be the cause of your dog's obsessive tail chasing, snapping at imaginary bugs, repetitive barking, and self-mutilation or staring into space. Conventional treatment includes the use of medication along side stress reduction, enriching the environment and not reinforcing the behaviour with attention. Sometimes simply reducing stress is enough. A referral to a behavioural specialist is usually necessary to unravel this problem.

Bach Flowers

Consider walnut, scleranthus, chestnut bud.

Urinating Inappropriately

Urinary tract problems, inadequate house training, marking or anxiety may cause inappropriate peeing. Dogs may urinate when greeting you or when they are scolded. This is usually submissive urination, where your dog is telling you that he is lower in the pecking order, and this is his way of showing his lower status. Punishment merely confuses him, and makes him feel even worse. Instead it should be avoided and prefer-ably ignored. If your dog pees when he greets you, ignore him completely when you enter the home. Puppies in particular are prone to this problem but often grow out of it as they mature.

Dogs that urinate on the stereo or your favourite shoes can be very annoying. In this case your dog is marking his territory in order to tell others that he or she is important. Entire male dogs are more likely to do this than desexed males, or females, although female dogs in heat may also urine mark. In this case limit access to parts of the home and exert your dominance (go through doorways before the dog, have the dog sit before being rewarded with food or petting). Desexing may also be considered. If your dog shows other evidence of territorial dominance, then obedience training will also be beneficial. Most dogs respond to desexing and to behavioural modification and medication is rarely needed.

Dogs can also wee inappropriately if they are confused or fearful, when they don't know what is expected of them, and you are yelling at them, and if they are very stressed or distressed. The first step then is to find out what the cause is. Your veterinarian can help you uncover the underlying cause.

Bach Flowers
Depending on the underlying cause consider walnut, larch, mimulus, aspen, beech.

Urinary Tract

The urinary tract consists of the kidneys, which filter the blood, the passages between the kidneys and the bladder, the bladder, and the urethra through which urine passes from the bladder outside.

Changes in urination can alert you to a problem. If there is straining, repeated attempts, or changes in the normal flow or colour, then it's important that you have your dog checked by a veterinarian immediately. When you arrive at the vet's, ask for a dish and take your dog for a short walk to collect a sample of urine. When he or she urinates, quickly place the dish in the way of the stream. It is a skill that may take one or two attempts! If this doesn't work, your vet or vet nurse can assist.

Chronic bladder problems can result from infections, environmental and food allergies, lowered immunity and chronic constipation. Stress can be another contributing factor.

Bladder Infection—Cystitis

Bladder infections must be treated because they have the potential to become chronic and even spread to the kidneys. Some bladder infections can also lead to the development of bladder stones. Often a long course of antibiotics is necessary. However, if infections are persistent and you want to provide extra care here are some suggestions:

Recommendations

Encourage plenty of drinking, by providing broths and soups as well as the usual diet.

Diet

Reduce weight if your dog is overweight. Encourage urination by taking her on frequent small walks.

Supplements

Cranberry extract is reasonably palatable for dogs and can be sprinkled on the food. Use 1 capsule twice daily for dogs 40 kg, and 1/2 capsule twice daily for dogs 20 kg. Some dogs will drink cranberry juice (make sure it's sugar free) diluted with water (50:50). Although not researched for dogs, cranberry helps prevent *E. coli* bacteria from attaching themselves to the bladder wall so helping to prevent infection and stop the growth of bacteria.[278] It is also high in vitamin C and acidifies urine. Barley can also be soothing, place 30 grams of barley in 1 L of water and boil, until the fluid is reduced to 500 mLs. Serve at room temperature.

Juniper berries are very useful for infections too. Add three to six daily.

Vitamins A and C with bioflavinoids, zinc, lecithin, nutritional yeast, flax seed oil

Herbs

Cleavers (anti-inflammatory and reduces spasm)

Couchgrass for inflammation of the urethra, bladder, kidney, also bladder stones, and prostate gland

Liquorice and dandelion for chronic bladder infections.

Marshmallow for inflammation

Cystitis and prostate infection, use yarrow.

Cystitis, consider echinacea and dandelion.

Golden rod for urinary tract retention and bladder problems in older dogs

Juniper berries for urinary tract infections

Others include St Mary's thistle, nettle, parsley, cornsilk and buchu, gravel root, stone root, hydrangea.

Bach Flowers

Consider crab-apple and Rescue Remedy for discomfort.

Acupuncture

Consider BL 23, BL 28, SP 6, ST 36, BL 32, CV 3, CV 4, CV 9.

Homeopathy

Sudden onset, painful cystitis: Aconitum

When accompanied by stones or crystals: Sarsaparilla

Blood in urine and constant urge to urinate: Cantharsis

Biochemical salts

Ferr. phos. 6x, Potassium chloride 6x

Other

If giving antibiotics twice daily, or once daily consider giving them last thing at night to keep the antibiotics in the bladder for as long as possible. Consider the suggestions for complementary antibiotic therapy.

Bladder Stones—Urolithiasis

Bladder stones vary in their composition and their underlying cause. It is important to know what type of stone is present so that the right diet and medicines can be used. In some cases surgery is necessary to remove stones. Other times diet and medical therapy can resolve the problem.

Recommendations

It is important that your dog's condition is monitored carefully because the stones can change over time, and you can get rid of one problem and find another takes its place.

Diet

In general the diet can be altered to minimise the risk of stone formation. Animal-based protein diets help maintain an acidic urine, while plant-based diets help maintain an alkaline urine. In many of these cases the diet doesn't cause the problem, but the composition of the diet can contribute to the minerals in the stones. There are many veterinary diets that can be used depending on the diagnosis. Sometimes they only need to be used for a short time, until the stones are dissolved (if possible) and other times your dog will need to stay on the diet to prevent recurrence. Encourage plenty of fluids, making broths and stews to increase fluids and help dilute the urine in the bladder.

Struvite

This is the most common type of bladder stone. Special diets are available that help reduce the size of bladder stones, and then minimise the risk of them recurring. Antibiotics are usually necessary. Acidifying diets with restricted magnesium are beneficial.

Calcium oxalate

Avoid calcium supplementation, dietary oxalate (e.g. spinach) and vitamin C in the form of calcium ascorbate. Consider a low to moderate protein diet and low salt to minimise the risk of reformation of stones. Encourage plenty of fluids. Veterinary diets may be prescribed. Canned and fresh foods contain more moisture than dry foods. Supplement with vitamin B complex (B6 2–4mg per kilogram daily). Potassium citrate (a urinary alkaliniser) may be needed if stones persist.

Calcium phosphate

A diet formulated to prevent calcium phosphate is available through most veterinary practices. Canned and fresh foods contain more moisture than dry foods and are recommended. Avoid supplementing with calcium and phosphorus and restrict bone consumption.

Cystine

Special diets are available through your veterinarian to help in the treatment of this problem, along with appropriate medication. Potassium citrate may be necessary as a urine alkaliniser.

Urate

A low purine (low glandular meat) diet that is alkaline is important to help reduce and prevent urate stones.

Xanthine

This type of stone can occur when dogs are treated with allopurinol, a drug designed to prevent urate bladder stones. Treatment relies on surgical removal, discontinuing the drug, and using a low purine diet.

Supplements

Glucosamine for chronic bladder inflammation may be helpful.

While vitamin C does not cause bladder stones, avoid high doses of vitamin C (acidifies urine) in all but struvite stones.

Flax seed oil, vitamin E and betacarotene, vitamin B complex

Herbs

Urate stones in Dalmatians: cherries (fresh or canned half a cup daily), blueberries and other dark red-blue berries are rich in proanthocyanidins that can help reduce uric acid levels. Use burdock and ursa ursi.

Grape seed extracts and hawthorn extracts may help.

Hydrangea for urinary stones associated with bacterial (struvite) cystitis

Marshmallow, gravel root, corn silk and stone root

Chamomile tea added to food

Cleavers, couch grass, uva ursi and juniper are all appropriate herbs.

Bach Flowers

Consider Bach Flower remedies depending upon the nature of your dog and how he is coping with the problem.

Acupuncture

Consider BL 23, BL 28, SP 6, SP 9, ST 30, ST 36, CV 3, CV 4, CV 6, BL 24, BL 25, BL 27 to help relieve pain and discomfort, and aid dissolution and prevention of recurrence.

Homeopathy

According to constitution consider:

Lycopodium where there is also bleeding

Thlaspi bursa for phosphate stones

Benzoic acid for urate stones

Calc. carb. for an overweight dog

Calc. phos. for a thin dog

Incontinence (Bladder)

Incontinence is not uncommon in middle-aged to older neutered female dogs, though young females and old neutered dogs can also be affected. Causes are many, including chronic bladder problems, infections, cancer, deformities, nerve function disorders, urine retention and others. The underlying cause has to be found so that the appropriate therapy is given. Many dogs will respond to conventional medicines. These include hormones and other drugs that although effective, may in some dogs have side-effects. Complementary therapies can be helpful alongside conventional medicine or for those dogs that don't respond. Some forms of incontinence may respond to an elimination diet where bladder irritation may be related to food sensitivity or allergy. Consider the following:

Recommendations
Encourage your dog to drink plenty of fluids and to go to the toilet often. In the evening, cut back on fluids, offering only small amounts. Take her outside before bedtime, and first thing in the morning. Encourage exercise, which will help keep her toned and fit. If she is overweight, consider a weight reduction program, this may reduce the problem. Consider the use of absorbent dog diapers or bedding at night.

Diet
Obesity can increase the risk of incontinence, so weight reduction is important.

Supplements
Cranberry, digestive enzymes, kelp, vitamins A, C and E, flax seed oil

Herbs
St John's wort; Marshmallow; Uva ursi; Nettles; Bachu; Dandelion; Gingko biloba; Saw palmetto for male dogs.

Bach Flowers
Crab-apple, larch, star of Bethlehem, olive and others can be considered.

Acupuncture
In young dogs about 70%–80% respond to acupuncture. Incontinence can be associated with speying and the scar along the midline. Some of these dogs respond to needles circling the scar tissue.

Also consider BL 52, BL 23, BL 28, SP 9, SP 6, KI 3, KI 7, CV 3, CV 4, GV 4.

In older bitches this treatment may only last two to three months.

For older dogs also moxa GV 4

Homeopathy
Consider:

Causticum in older dogs

Conium

Oestrogen for a neutered bitch

Agnus castus for old male dogs

Other

Massage and brushing is important, as is bathing, to help your dog to feel better.
Chiropractic adjustments may assist some dogs.

Kidney Disease

Kidney disease can be sudden and life threatening or chronic, persisting for months to years. There are many underlying causes including infections, toxins, chemical and environmental pollution, chronic drug usage, lowered immunity and others. Because the kidneys are the main blood-filtering organ in the body (along with the liver), malfunction of the kidneys leads to a build-up of unfiltered wastes in the bloodstream. Signs include a great thirst, increased urination, weight loss, lethargy and even vomiting. Constipation and diarrhoea may also be present.

Recommendations

Regular monitoring of kidney function is recommended. This requires a blood test and a urine test. This shows how well the kidneys are working and whether diet and therapy need modification. Complementary therapies can help delay progression of disease and reduce dependence on medication. But they must always be used under the guidance of a veterinarian.

Diet

A low to moderate protein diet with restricted phosphorus and sodium is beneficial. There are veterinary diets designed for kidney problems and also homemade low protein diets. The key to good management is to monitor kidney function. Restricting protein severely may not be necessary and may lead to weight loss and protein loss. It's important your dog has plenty of fluids to help 'flush' the kidneys. Include fresh kidneys in the diet and fresh foods, vegetables and fruits. Include garlic, bananas, watermelon, sprouts and leafy greens if possible.

Supplements

Essential fatty acids in fish oil, sunflower oil, safflower oil, flax seed oil, L-carnitine, vitamin B complex, vitamin C low dose, zinc, potassium

Herbs

St Mary's thistle; Echinacea if there is infection; St John's wort if incontinent; Liquorice root; Dandelion; Cleavers.

Bach Flowers

Consider hornbeam, olive and crab-apple, they may be beneficial.

Acupuncture

Consider BL 23, KI 1, GB 25, KI 3, KI 7, SP 6, BL 58, ST 36.

Homeopathy

Constitutional remedies are best.

Consider:

> Phosphorus for acute kidney disease
>
> Kali chloratum
>
> Mercurius solubilus
>
> Nat. mur.

Other

Massage and gentle exercise help keep the circulation going, which in turn assists the kidneys. Consider the possibility of discomfort; some dogs enjoy a warm wheat bag or hot water bottle (wrapped) across the lower back.

Reproductive System

Female Reproduction

Infertility and reproductive problems are not uncommon these days. Diet, stress, infections, drug use and environmental pollution, build-up from pesticides and herbicides and other factors can influence reproduction.

Maintaining a Healthy Pregnancy, Whelping and Lactation

Most bitches require little assistance during their pregnancy. However, there are situations where some complementary therapies may be considered.

Diet

The calories your bitch needs will increase by 10 per cent each week after week 5. (*See* Chapter 3 on nutrition.) Consider feeding smaller meals more often. Provide a nourishing diet and consider incorporating more dry food towards the end of the pregnancy. This means less food (with a full abdomen) but more calories for energy, foetal growth and milk production. Encourage plenty of fluids such as soups and broths. Spinach contains lots of folacin, pumpkin contains zinc, and leafy greens, green grasses, and brown rice and yoghurt can be added to the diet.

Supplements

Consider a multivitamin and mineral mix, betacarotene and vitamin C, and niacin in particular.

Kelp, natural vitamin E or wheatgerm capsules, zinc, evening primrose oil or flax seed oil.

AVOID over-supplementing with calcium. A balanced diet should be sufficient. In dogs prone to milk tetany (eclampsia) seek guidance from your veterinarian. Over-supplementing can be a predisposing cause.

Herbs

Red raspberry tea can be given during pregnancy from the end of the first trimester. It strengthens and tones the uterus and aids whelping.

Peppermint can assist digestion, especially if there is loss of appetite. Note it is usual for the appetite to go just before whelping.

Echinacea may be used as a substitute for antibiotics during pregnancy.

Chamomile may be used as a gentle sedative for anxious mothers to be and for digestive and bowel problems.

Black cohosh can be given during labour to aid uterine activity.

For false labour consider blue cohosh tea to help normalise the cycle.

Fennel, St Mary's thistle (milk thistle) and marshmallow increase milk flow.

Parsley can be given at weaning to help dry up milk.

AVOID. Many herbs have the potential to induce abortion in pregnant bitches, only use herbs under the guidance of a veterinary herbalist. Avoid aloe vera, barberry, buchu, cascara, golden seal, juniper, lovage, mistletoe, wormwood, pennyroyal, rue, yarrow, senna, wild ginger.

Homeopathy

Consider giving Caulophyllum for the three weeks before (dose twice weekly) then during the birth process.

Consider Calcarea phosphorica for calcium metabolism.

Arnica can be given after whelping to reduce bruising and swelling.

Bach Flowers

As needed, consider the nature of your bitch and what flowers would be most appropriate for her. If she is anxious try larch and star of Bethlehem; if she is fearful, try aspen and mimulus; if she panics, try star of Bethlehem and rock rose; for most cases include Rescue Remedy.

Acupuncture

Acupuncture is usually not considered during pregnancy; however, it may be useful for:

Prolonged labour: LI4, LIV 3, KI 8, SP 4, SP 6, CV 2, CV 3, CV 4, CV 5

For bitches with a history of miscarriage, to help prevent it, consider points: ST 36, BL 23, BL 47, Bai Hui, HT 7, KI 9, PC 6 and SP 6, LI 4.

Biochemical salts

Calc. phos.. 6x throughout pregnancy

Female Infertility

Diagnosing the cause of infertility can be difficult. Older bitches (over six years of age) are likely to have a degree of endometrial hyperplasia and may be more predisposed to infertility and infections. Thyroid disease, abnormal ovarian functioning and improper time of mating can all be causes of infertility too. So it's important to know the underlying cause. If the underlying cause cannot be found, then the following may be beneficial:

Diet
Adequate nutrition is very important. If your bitch is grossly underweight or overweight this can also affect fertility.

Supplements
Antioxidants, vitamins A, C and E, vitamin B complex, flax seed oil or sunflower oil, zinc, essential fatty acids
(In addition, for males include carnitine and chromium.)

Herbs
Ginseng (*Panex ginseng*) for improving fertility (males and females)
Vitex agnus castus for improving fertility in females

Acupuncture
Acupuncture may be useful, but success depends on the underlying cause.
Chinese herbs may also be useful, and work well with acupuncture.
Anoestrus, consider LU 7, KI 6, BL 23, BL 25, GV 1, GV 2, GV 4, SP 6, Bai Hui.
Infertility, consider LU 7, KI 6, ST 36, BL 11, ST 37, ST 39, BL 23, SP 6, in males add ST 30.
For reproductive tract infection, consider ST 36, BL 20, BL 23, BL 25, CV 1.

Homeopathy
Consider sepia, pulsatilla, platina.

Biochemical salts
Nat. mur. 6x

False Pregnancy
False or pseudo pregnancy is not uncommon in entire bitches. It looks like the real thing, except there are no puppies. It usually occurs some two to three months after the last heat and is considered a normal phenomenon, so treatment is not usually necessary. The false pregnancy will usually resolve in two to three weeks by itself, but if it is considered a problem and recurs repeatedly then speying is often recommended. Alternatively various drugs can be used to halt the false pregnancy.

The major problems associated with false pregnancy are the enlargement of the mammary (breast) tissue and self-suckling.

Some complementary therapies can be considered:

Acupuncture
Consider one treatment using points SP 6, BL 22, BL 23.

Homeopathy

Consider sepia and pulsatilla.

If she is producing milk, consider urtica.

Mastitis

Bacterial infection of the mammary glands is potentially life threatening and can lead to septic shock. It can be caused by trauma inflicted by the puppies' teeth or nails, poor hygiene or an infection from somewhere else in the body. The puppies will need to be hand raised or placed on a surrogate bitch. Breeders' clubs will be able to put you into quick contact with a suitable bitch if you are prepared to do some phoning around. Meanwhile your bitch will need to be treated. Usually antibiotics are necessary and can be life saving.

Complementary therapies include those for infections and:

Diet

Encourage plenty of fluids. Consider feeding her small meals often of calorie-rich food.

Supplements

Vitamins C, E and A

Herbs

Echinacea, Calendula, Galium internally

Ginger externally

Homeopathy

Consider belladonna, bryonia and phytolacca.

Biochemical salts

Ferr. phos. 6 x initially, then change to silica 6x if the glands harden.

Other

Compress of boiled and cooled (but still warm) cabbage leaves

Pyometra or Infection

When dogs are on heat, they are naturally meant to get pregnant. Repeated cycles of being on heat without pregnancy and repeated use of hormones in previous cycles can lead to changes in the lining of the uterus predisposing it to infection. Pyometra refers to the uterus being infected, and this can be a life threatening condition leading to septic shock.

Desexing is considered the treatment of choice; however, conventional medicines may be used if you really want to breed from your bitch later. Just remember that if there are already changes in the lining of the uterus, the chances of her getting pregnant are significantly reduced anyway. Antibiotics are usually life saving in this condition.

Complementary therapies that might be useful include:

Herbs

In addition to antibiotics, echinacea, golden seal and rosehips may be used.

Acupuncture

If the cervix is open, acupuncture can stimulate drainage of the infection

Stimulate BL 31–34 for 30 minutes

Also consider BL 20, BL 22, BL 23, BL 28, BL 31–34, SP 6, GV 3.

Homeopathy

Consider sepia.

Male Infertility

There are a whole range of factors that can lead to infertility including hormone abnormalities, poor mating management, trauma, environmental damage, stress, heat stress, prostate disease and others.

Provided the underlying causes can be found and dealt with, increased fertility may take some two to three months to return. Reduced stress and good quality nutrition will assist.

Diet

Improving the diet and including fresh vegetables (leafy greens) and pumpkin will be helpful.

Supplements

Consider:

Zinc, manganese, vitamins C and E , vitamin B complex, lecithin, kelp, evening primrose oil, carnitine and chromium.

Herbs

Ginseng (*Panex ginseng*) for improving fertility

Acupuncture

Acupuncture may be useful, but success depends on the underlying cause.

Chinese herbs may also be useful, and work well with acupuncture.

Infertility, consider LU 7, KI 6, ST 36, BL 11, ST 37, ST 39, BL 23, SP 6, ST 30.

For reproductive tract infection, consider ST 36, BL 20, BL 23, BL 25, CV 1.

Prostate Disorders

Prostate problems affect many male dogs particularly those that are not desexed. Middle-aged to older entire dogs are likely to have some degree of prostate enlargement. Castration actually reduces the risk of this enlargement and also reduces the risk of infection and cancer of the prostate gland. Castration is a common form of therapy to resolve enlarged prostate glands although hormones may also be used. Antibiotics are necessary if there is an infection because there is a danger that the infection may become an abscess.

Recommendations

A diagnosis is important to avoid missing cancer of the prostate gland. Therapy will depend on the cause of the problem but complementary therapies can support your dog during therapy.

Diet

Add fibre to the diet to help prevent constipation and make toileting easier. Include wheat germ, pumpkin seeds, oat bran, and nutritional yeast, lecithin and sesame seeds on a rotating basis each day.

Supplements

Zinc, vitamin B complex, vitamin C, flax seed oil

Herbs

For prostate infection and benign enlargement, use saw palmetto, hydrangea, nettle, horsetail.
For prostate infection affecting the urinary tract, use couchgrass and yarrow.
For enlarged prostate or inflamed prostate, use hydrangea.
If there is infection, use echinacea and pau d'arco.

Bach Flowers

Crab-apple may be beneficial.

Acupuncture

Consider the points BL 23, BL 28, BL 39, CV 3, CV 4, LIV 5, ST 29, GV 1, CV 1, KI 3, KI 7.

Homeopathy

Consider thuja, Agnus castus, Sabal serrulata, clematis.

Other

Prostate enlargement and infection can be uncomfortable, pain management is important.

Health
Maintenance

Guidelines for Vaccination

Vaccination is one of the most common veterinary procedures undertaken in dogs. There is no question that it is important in preventing and controlling infectious diseases. Go to any country where vaccination is not practised and you will see the suffering of local dogs with canine distemper, hepatitis, parvovirus and others. But what about your dog? What is the likely risk of your dog contracting one of these diseases in your own home town? And must you have your dog vaccinated every year?

The practice of annual vaccination is a long held one without any basic scientific rationale[279] and is currently under review. The issue is twofold. First, the annual recommendations are just a recommendation, not an absolute, and are based on duration of immunity studies that traditionally only go out to one year. Second, there are a number of vaccine-associated adverse events that can occur. Recent research suggests that duration of immunity delivered by some vaccines is much longer than one year. As a result, many veterinarians are adopting new protocols. It is important that dogs receive their initial vaccinations (a two- or three-shot series) and booster twelve months later, then every three years thereafter unless required by law. Vaccination sets up a template in the immune system, so that should your dog be exposed to the disease, his immune system can quickly churn out lots of appropriate antibodies to fight the infection. It's important to remember though that some vaccines, such as kennel cough may actually require more frequent administration to obtain significant protection.

Vaccination targets the immune system and should only be administered to healthy dogs. It has been shown that the immune response of dogs with atopy (skin allergies) is exaggerated by vaccination,[280] so may worsen the condition. Vaccination has been associated with autoimmune haemolytic anaemia[281] and thyroid disease as well as other adverse effects. It is important to question whether it is appropriate for you to vaccinate your dog if his immune system is at all compromised. Seriously consider whether your dog will benefit from vaccination if he is very old, has concurrent disease, atopy, chronic disease, immune deficiency, autoimmune disease or debilitation. Consider carefully if he is very stressed (such as undergoing surgery) or has concurrent drug administration (including glucocorticoids and some anaesthetic agents) that can affect the immune response to the vaccine. Also try and avoid vaccination one month before oestrus for bitches, and immediately after, as well as during pregnancy and lactation. It may be useful in these situations to delay vaccination until your dog's health and hormonal status is back to normal.

It's important to realise that vaccination is part of the overall approach to health, it does not always provide protection from infection or signs of disease, and vaccination does not necessarily provide absolute protection. Certain diseases are more prevalent in some areas than others. Your veterinarian can advise you what vaccines may be more important for your dog, particularly if there are outbreaks. Other diseases rarely occur, and apart from initial vaccination, you might consider boosters every couple of years rather than yearly.

There are some risks associated with vaccination, including immediate reactions such as pain, fever, and stiffness as well as some more alarming associations such as seizures and the development of autoimmune disease. Considering the number of dogs that are vaccinated, these reactions are considered rare, but they can still happen. There is also the possibility of long-term effects in some dogs, sometimes referred to as vaccinosis. Little study has been done on this, but it is recognised by many holistic veterinarians as being a major underlying factor in the development of degenerative diseases, due to the amount of foreign materials injected into the body over time (including the substances carrying the vaccine in solution).

You should speak to your veterinarian about any concerns and have her explain the risk of exposure to infectious diseases in your area, possible adverse reactions and benefits of vaccination and then you can decide whether to go ahead or not.

Guidelines

1. Only have your dog vaccinated if your dog is absolutely healthy. If he has a minor problem, have it sorted out and wait at least two weeks after the problem has resolved before revisiting your veterinarian for vaccination.
2. Your veterinarian can advise you about the risk of particular diseases in your dog's environment. It is possible to vaccinate against single diseases rather than multiple vaccination.
3. Some vaccines are for diseases not considered potentially fatal. An example is kennel cough. If your dog contracts kennel cough he will generally get better in five to seven days, meanwhile the cough can be helped with herbs or in some cases antibiotics. If you are going to vaccinate, do it one month before going into kennels or boarding, as the protection wanes quickly. Also realise that the vaccination only protects for one or two of the several organisms causing the coughing disease, and your dog can still get 'kennel cough'.

4. In some countries it is illegal not to vaccinate for rabies. If this is the case, ask your vet if she can give your dog's rabies vaccine at least three weeks after the regular vaccination.

5. In countries where vaccination for Lyme disease is available, it is important to weigh up the benefits against the potential side-effects of this vaccination,[282] ask your veterinarian about the risks and benefits.

Alternatives to Conventional Vaccination

Personally I recommend that puppies receive their initial vaccination series (starting a 6–8 weeks of age), then 12 months later. I weigh up the risk and benefit for each individual dog and vaccinate accordingly with the minimum of vaccine components. However, I am reluctant to vaccinate any dog that I believe is not well. You can also talk to your veterinarian about the possibility of vaccinating for diseases separately rather than altogether, selecting the higher risk diseases for your dog.

Another option available in some places is to have serum antibody titres measured. Titres can tell whether antibodies exist, though it is not a reliable indication of whether there is enough protection. It is certainly an option though if you are reluctant to vaccinate.

Avoid over-vaccination by discussing any concerns, benefits and risks with your veterinarian. Apart from laws that require vaccination in some countries, you can decline vaccination as long as you are aware of the risks and you have talked this through with your veterinarian.

Non-vaccination is another option, with the risk obviously, that your dog is more likely to contract the disease if he is exposed. Sick, debilitated and very old dogs should not be vaccinated. Any dog with a chronic, long-term problem affecting his health should not be vaccinated. Also certain breeds such as Akitas, Weimaraners, Harlequin Great Danes, albinos and coat-diluted Shetland sheep-dogs appear to be at greater risk of vaccine reactions.[283]

Nosodes are also considered an alternative if vaccination is not appropriate (if the dog is immune-suppressed or has concurrent disease or has previously reacted to vaccination). They can also be used in puppies before their first vaccination, and can be used in conjunction with vaccination. While some veterinarians suggest that nosodes may be useful as an alternative to vaccination, there is an absence of convincing research to prove that they do prevent disease. A few studies have shown that nosodes may reduce the severity of disease and also may help prevent the spread of disease such as kennel cough.[284] However, there is also a study with canine parvovirus nosodes that showed the nosodes were completely ineffective. Therefore they should not be used as a sole means of protecting your pet.

It is important to remember that nosodes are not vaccinations even though they are sometimes termed homeopathic vaccinations. They do not work in the same way. What is perhaps more useful is the use of constitutional homeopathic prescribing and good nutrition to increase the overall health, immunity and vitality of your dog.

Another option is to vaccinate and use homeopathic remedies at the same time to reduce possible side-effects and to help prevent long-term effects or vaccinosis. Again this has not been researched convincingly. However, the remedies are considered safe when used like this. They include:

Thuja 200c: give one dose with any vaccine given except rabies (at the same time or same day).

Lyssin 30c: give one dose at the same time as rabies vaccination or on the same day.

Other vaccinosis remedies include sulphur, silicea, malandrinum and mezureum.

Worming Your Dog

Worm infestations can range from unnoticeable to serious and even life threatening in a puppy or debilitated dog. Worms live, feed and breed in the digestive tract. Vomiting, diarrhoea, dragging the bottom on the ground, licking of the bottom, ravenous appetite, weight loss and anaemia are all possible symptoms. But worms can also be more insidious. Many of the immature stages of the worms migrate through various body tissues such as the lung and liver and even the central nervous system. They contribute to poor health and debility in susceptible dogs, and can undermine the health of seemingly healthy dogs.

Recommendations

Most of the current veterinary worming products available for dogs are considered safe and effective. They don't necessarily remove 100 per cent of the worms, but they will reduce the burden significantly. They don't stop your dog picking up new worms through faeces, bugs, birds, rabbits, raw meat and other sources the very next day. This is the reason why worming is recommended routinely even in healthy dogs every three months, or more regularly in some situations.

There are some other options to routine worming. You can have a faecal test done every three months. Your veterinarian can check for the presence of worm eggs and even advise you which worms are present. If your dog appears to be worm free (especially if at low risk from contracting them), then it's possible you may not need to worm at all. Part of this 'low risk' is in maintaining good flea control (fleas carry tapeworms), removing dog poo daily from his environment and feeding commercial diets or cooked meat. If your dog has a large worm burden, treat with conventional worming preparations according to your veterinarian's advice.

Supplements to help prevent worm burdens

Garlic exerts some activity against roundworms and hookworms[285] and can be included daily in the diet; vitamin B complex.

Herbs

With any of these remedies, consider having a worm test done before and after the treatment. You may still need to give conventional treatment.

Cucumber juice is a traditional remedy for tapeworms (mix 100 grams of mashed/grated cucumber with honey and water for a 15 kg dog).

Pumpkin seed tea acts as a cathartic to help expel tapeworm, but can cause diarrhoea. Pumpkin seeds, dried, 2–6 teaspoons can have a mechanical cleansing effect on the bowel.

Pau d'arco

Bach Flowers

Crab-apple is appropriate plus remedies depending on symptoms.

Homeopathy

Roundworms—China or Chenopodium

Tapeworms—Filix mas or Granatum

Biochemical salts

Nat. phos. 6x

Flea and Tick Control

Fleas are not always obvious, and if a dog is constantly grooming himself, there may be no evidence of fleas. To check whether your dog has fleas, moisten a white paper towel and place this underneath your dog. Brush your dog so that the dander falls onto the paper. You might see little specks of black that turn red with moisture. This is a positive test for fleas.

No one would argue that natural control of fleas and prevention is much better than reliance on chemical control. A truly natural approach would be to leave the fleas on the dog, but this isn't satisfactory either. So fortunately there are a couple of conventional veterinary flea products that are safe and effective (applied as a spot on the skin and they are not absorbed into the body). Your veterinarian can recommend the safest ones that have been proven to work. Start the flea control in spring. This approach will mean fewer chemicals need to be used.

Recommendations:
- Always read labels on products and follow manufacturer advice.
- Avoid taking your dog into long grassed areas during tick season. Groom your dog daily, checking ears, under the tail and between toes. Keep lawns mowed short. Use a tick product in areas where paralysis ticks or disease carrying ticks are prevalent. Check your dog daily.
- Over 90 per cent of the flea population in the home is not on the dog, but in the form of eggs, larvae and pupa. These immature stages are usually resistant to insecticides that kill adult fleas. Therefore you have to treat your dog, other pets, the home and the dog's environment. There are veterinary products that can help control these other life stages.

- Begin flea control in spring. Wash your dog's bedding in hot water. Clean and vacuum the house thoroughly, particularly where the dog spends most of her time. Also under furniture, cushions, and where other pets like to sit. Consider steam-cleaning carpets too. Clean the car, garage, laundry and anywhere else your dog goes. Consider fogging the house with an insect growth regulator. It is important to follow safety directions. Ask your veterinarian for a safe product. On the same day, send your dog out to be washed, or do it yourself, and apply a flea product.
- If you want to avoid chemicals altogether you will need to keep your dog confined to the house, clean and vacuum weekly the entire home and garage, wash bedding weekly, flea comb and remove fleas daily.
- You can also go the low chemical approach by using insect growth regulator foggers in the home and use a safe product recommended by your vet on your dog.

Alternative Flea Products

- Desiccants on the whole should be avoided unless specifically designed for flea control in homes with pets.
  - Borax and borax powders are toxic to dogs as well as fleas.
  - Borates are also effective but can be toxic if inhaled or ingested.
  - Diatomaceous earth can be very irritating to breathe.
- Rotenone is naturally derived from derris root. It is, however, more toxic than some synthetic flea products and is poisonous if it enters waterways or ponds.
- Limonene and other citrus extracts are natural flea repellents that should not be used on puppies. They have been known to cause poisonings especially if combined with other flea products.[286]
- Electronic Flea Collars are usually not effective.[287]
- Parasitic Nematodes are tiny worms that eat flea larvae. They might be useful if your dog has a favorite patch in the garden somewhere.[288]
- Pyrethrum is derived from the chrysanthemum flower and is one of the safest insecticides around, available in both the natural and synthetic form such as permethrin. They are often combined with piperonyl butoxide, which makes it more effective. You will find these compounds in many of the veterinary products.
- Insect Growth Regulators are not natural, but are probably the best products for preventing fleas. They are basically insect hormones that stop the flea from developing. They are safe and effective and usually have a long lasting effect.

Diet

A dog that has an excellent diet will be in a healthier condition and less likely to be affected by fleas. So consider upgrading your dog's diet.

Supplements

Garlic, yeast and vitamin B have been touted as anti-flea, but scientific studies have not demonstrated that they control fleas.[289]

Repellant herbs

Lavender can be sprinkled around the bedding, or a lavender pillow can be made.

Plant fennel near the kennel.

Sage and Wormwood can also be grown near the kennel.

Acupuncture

It is very difficult to acupuncture fleas.

Aromatherapy

Cedar, citronella, lavender, geranium and eucalyptus oils help repel fleas but should be used in a very diluted form. Add 10 drops total (of one or more oils) to 20 mls of almond oil, and use 1 drop per kg of dog by massaging into the coat twice weekly. Alternatively add 10 drops to 100 mls of water in a spritzer and spray on twice weekly. (Shake before use.)

Wash bedding in hot water and rinse in cold water adding 10 drops of eucalyptus or lavender oil.

Flea repellent oils that can be added to shampoo include lavender, rosemary and eucalyptus 10 drops per 100 mls.

Homeopathy

Pulex may be beneficial, but not in my experience.

Removing fleas

In smaller dogs, flea combing is one means of catching fleas without using flea control products. Comb the dog thoroughly on a daily basis. Insert the flea comb into a dish containing hot water and liquid detergent to kill fleas, and then dip the comb into cool, clean water before continuing the hunt.

Removing ticks

Tick poisoning from the paralysis tick can be life threatening and some ticks also carry disease so contact your vet immediately for advice. Use tweezers or a tissue to prise the tick out. Grasp it at the base of the body as close to the skin as possible and pull it out gently and slowly. Try to avoid crushing the tick. If the tick's head doesn't come out, keep an eye on the area over the next few days. It will generally fester out of its own accord. If there is a lot of swelling or pain or your dog behaves unusually then seek veterinary attention. You can keep the tick for later identification in a jar. Observe your dog closely over the next few days; take your dog to the vet if you have any concerns.

Ageing

The quality of our dogs' lives is most important. We can't help ageing, it's a natural process but we can influence its progression. The most important things you can do are to provide an excellent diet, supplements, regular exercise and veterinary check-ups. Don't forget that love and involvement in family activities keeps life interesting and stimulating for older dogs. Just because they slow down, doesn't mean we should let them lie!

Recommendations

Old dogs generally have a lower metabolism, decreased oxygenation of their blood, and a reduced immune function so regular check-ups are important. Consider six-monthly check-ups and routine blood tests to detect any early problems. Have any lumps checked out, as cancer is more common in older dogs. If there is any weight change, change in appetite, change in thirst or reluctance to exercise have your dog checked. Many old dogs have bad teeth. Consider a dental clean (under anesthetic), it is one of the best things you can do to improve your dog's health.

Regular exercise is important for old dogs. A twenty-minute walk at least daily will help keep him alert and stimulated. Consider a weight loss diet if he is overweight. Elevate food and water dishes if your dog has arthritis, it might make him more comfortable. Ramps rather than steps can also be helpful for older animals.

Regular acupuncture 'tune-ups' can keep old dogs happy and healthy by boosting the immune system and balancing the body. Acupuncture can also reduce any discomfort associated with early arthritis.

Consider another pet. There is nothing so sure to awaken the spirit of an older dog than a puppy or kitten. It's amazing how many times a younger animal will take care of the older one, acting as his ears and eyes when necessary.

Diet

Healthy longevity can be enhanced through improving the diet. Quality is vital and quantity needs to be reduced in general. Providing your dog is healthy, feeding smaller meals more often may be beneficial. Provide plenty of fresh vegetables, leafy greens, beetroot, broccoli, pumpkin, sweet potato and fruits. You may need to consider reducing the number of bones he gets if he is at all constipated. Good quality protein is very important. Consider a top quality geriatric diet available through your veterinarian. These often contain antioxidants to support good health.

Supplements

Antioxidants vitamins A, C and E, lecithin, coenzyme Q10, digestive enzymes, flax seed oil, evening primrose oil, pycogenols, vitamin B complex, multivitamin and mineral supplement, vitamin B complex, zinc

Herbs

Gingko biloba helps maintain blood and oxygen flow to the brain and is useful where older dogs are depressed, slow to respond, or showing signs of dementia, deafness or dullness.

Siberian ginseng as a tonic

Astragalus to support the immune system

Oats for debility, depression

Ginseng (*Panex ginseng*) in low doses as a tonic

Rosemary, an antioxidant, in small amounts

Bach Flowers

Bach flowers can be helpful if your dog is depressed or anxious.

Olive; Hornbeam; Gorse; Mustard

Acupuncture

A regular 'tune-up' for general health or treatments for arthritis or stiffness will not only improve your old dog's health but her vitality as well.

Points to consider include:

ST 36, LI 11, GB 34, GV 14, BL 23, BL 21

Longevity points: LI 4, LI 11, ST 36

Also LU 7, PC 6, BL 40, SP 6.

Rotate through these points to avoid over stimulation.

Plus use points for arthritis or other conditions

For geriatric deafness include SI 19, TH 5.

For a dog that is dying or close to death, the points LU 7, PC 6, LI 4, ST 36 will hasten the process and reduce suffering.

Other

Older dogs may need some help with their grooming. Brush her daily, and wipe eyes, nose and bottom with a damp tissue. Keep nails trim. Make sure the teeth are healthy and if not, plan to have them cleaned. Bad teeth will compromise your dog's health and longevity.

Weight Control

Being a little bit overweight is not that harmful, but your dog is likely to continue to put on more weight over time. An overweight dog is usually not a healthy dog. An overweight dog moves slower, gets tired out more quickly, is more prone to other health problems and if obese also suffers reduced immunity. Obesity increases the load on various systems making fat dogs more prone to arthritis, cardiovascular disease, heat stress, diabetes and liver disease. Provided weight loss is carried out sensibly and slowly, your dog can regain vitality and improved health. You will be rewarded with a healthier happier dog.

The safest approach to weight loss is to control the number of calories you feed your dog. To begin with, aim for a 15% reduction in weight as your goal. Calculate your dog's current weight less 15%, and then you and your vet can assess whether more weight loss is necessary. A weight loss of up to 15% can be achieved over twelve to fifteen weeks by feeding about half the calories your dog would require at his new target weight.

Energy Requirement for Weight Loss

Before starting any weight loss plan it is advisable to first see your veterinarian, in case your dog is overweight because of a medical condition. In this case it may be dangerous for you to attempt weight loss without veterinary supervision. To work out the calories your dog requires in order to lose weight, first find out what the target weight should be. From the following table, and given your dog's current weight, you can see the target body weight you are aiming for and the energy (calorie) allowance needed each day to help reduce weight by about 1 per cent per week (a safe weight loss). If your dog is very overweight, we still aim for the first target weight. When his weight has come down, look for the next new target weight (current less 15 per cent) and go from there.

It may be necessary to reduce these levels even further depending on the dog's response. If there is no weight loss then a further reduction of 10 per cent by volume of food should be made.

Because you are going to feed less food, it's not a simple matter of halving the existing diet. You will also halve the protein, vitamin, mineral and fat components, which can lead to deficiencies. It's important to use a diet formulated for weight loss to ensure that nutrient requirements are still met. Veterinarians and pet food stores stock weight control products and products designed specifically for weight loss. Alternatively you can make your own diet based on good quality protein (low in fat, but do include half the oil supplement) with plenty of fresh fruit and vegetables.

It's important to remember that dry dog foods contain about four times the calorie content volume for volume as tinned or

TABLE 4 RECOMMENDATION FOR WEIGHT LOSS [290]

Current Body Weight (kg)	Current Body Weight (lb)	Target Body Weight (kg)	Target Body Weight (lb)	Energy Allowance for safe weight loss (kcal/day)
2	4.4	1.7	3.7	74
4	8.8	3.4	7.5	124
6	13.2	5.1	11.2	168
8	17.6	6.8	15.0	208
10	22.0	8.5	18.7	247
15	33.0	12.7	28.0	334
20	44.0	17	37.4	414
25	55.0	21.2	46.6	490
30	66.0	25.5	56.0	562
35	77.0	29.7	65.3	630
40	88.0	34	74.8	697
45	99.0	38.2	84.0	761
50	110.0	42.5	93.5	824
55	121.0	46.7	102.7	885
60	132.0	51	112.2	946

fresh foods. So the first thing to consider would be to cut back on the dry food. You can calculate the calories you are feeding your dog by knowing the calorie content of the dog food, and/or using a calorie counter designed for people.

Diet
The following recipe has been used successfully on many occasions:

Weight loss diet
> 350 g lean chicken breast or fish
>
> 1.5 cups cooked Basmati rice
>
> 1.5 cups of vegetables (including half a cup of pumpkin or sweet potato)
>
> 30 g liver
>
> 2 teaspoons of sunflower oil
>
> 1 teaspoon of calcium carbonate

Cook ingredients, then mix together adding oil when cool.

Snacks:
> 50 grams of dry food
>
> 1 apple.

This recipe and snacks provides 1500 calories. If your dog needs 500 calories per day on the weight loss diet, this plan provides for three days of food.

Alternatively see the low-fat, and low-fat high-fibre recipes.

If your dog is suffering other health problems you could begin with the Bowel Detoxification Program.

Supplements
L-Carnitine may assist weight loss; chromium, flax seed oil, multivitamin and mineral supplement, vitamin B complex, kelp

Herbs
Consider:
> Cayenne pepper for sluggish, overweight dogs with heart problems.
>
> St Mary's thistle
>
> Parsley fresh
>
> Brindleberry
>
> Alfalfa

Exercise
Daily exercise is the key to permanent, painless weight control. But if your dog is very overweight, this has to be done slowly and carefully, building up over time. As your dog loses weight she will have more energy, so you can begin to extend your walks further. Exercise helps to increase metabolism, which helps to replace fatty muscles

with strong lean muscle, and this in turn speeds up metabolism making weight control even easier.

Family

It is really important that family and friends understand how important it is for your dog to reach a healthy weight. They need to understand that anything extra that they give can sabotage all your good efforts and undermine your dog's health. If they must feed your dog or give her snacks, make sure it's from the allowances you have set. Pieces of popcorn (no butter), rice cake, carrot and apple make good snack substitutes.

Further Information

Useful Contacts

The internet provides incredible resources for those seeking more information. But beware, the best information comes from official organisations rather than just any old website. Don't believe everything you read, and check with your veterinarian before using any treatment or product with your pet. Internet information cannot take the place of a hands-on approach by your vet.

To find a holistic veterinarian who uses complementary or alternative medicine:

Australia/NZ

Contact your local Australian or New Zealand Veterinary Association for referral

Dr Barbara Fougere	www.Naturalvet.com.au	Sydney 02 95554249
Holistic Veterinarians	www.ava.com.au	
Veterinary Acupuncture	www.ava.com.au	
Veterinary Chiropractic	www.hume-phillips.com/avca	

USA

Contact your local Veterinary Association or

www.AHVMA.org for a directory of holistic veterinarians

www.altvetmed.com for general information on alternative veterinary medicine and directories

Veterinary Chiropractic	www.animalchiropractic.org
Veterinary Acupuncture	www.ivas.org
	www.aavma.org
	www.chi-institute.com
	www.aava.org
Veterinary homeopathy	www.theavh.org

UK

Contact the British Veterinary Association for referrals.

Veterinary Homeopathy   www.bahvs.com

Worldwide Veterinary Holistic Organisations (has contact lists to find veterinarians)

Veterinary Acupuncture   www.ivas.org

Veterinary Herbal Medicine   www.vbma.org

Veterinary Homeopathy   www.bahvs.com

Further Reading

Our Relationships with Dogs

Newby J., *The Pact for Survival: Humans and their Animal Companions*, ABC Books, Sydney, 1997.

Schoen A., *Love, Miracles and Animal Healing*, Simon and Schuster, New York, 1996.

Sife W., *The Loss of a Pet. The Human Companion Animal Bond: How Pets Enrich our Lives*, Macmillan Publishing, New York, 1993.

General Books on Complementary and Alternative Medicine

Anderson N., Peiper H., *Are You Poisoning Your Pets?*, Avery Publishing, Garden City Park, 1996.

Florence T. M., Setright R. T., *The Handbook of Preventive Medicine*, Kingsclear Books, Sydney, 1994.

Gerber R. (MD), *Vibrational Medicine*, Bear and Company, New Mexico, 1996.

MacDonald Baker S., *Detoxification and Healing*, Keats Publishing, New Canaan, 1997.

Micozzi M. S. (MD), *Fundamentals of Complementary and Alternative Medicine*, Churchill Livingston, Melbourne, 1996.

Murray M. and Pizzorno J., *Encyclopedia of Natural Medicine*, Prima Publishing, California, 1991.

Puotinen C. J., *The Encyclopedia of Natural Pet Care*, Conn Keats Publishing, New Canaan ,1998.

Schoen A. and Wynn S. (eds.), *Complementary and Alternative Veterinary Medicine*, Mosby, New York, 1997.

Shwartz C., *Four Paws, Five Directions: A Guide to Chinese Medicine for Cats and Dogs*, Celestial Arts, Berkley California, 1996.

Volhard W. and Brown K., *The Holistic Guide for a Healthy Dog*, Howell Book House, New York, 1995.

Nutrition

Balch J., Balch P., *Prescription for Natural Healing*, Avery Publishing, 1990, 1997.

Burger I. (ed.), *The Waltham Book of Companion Animal Nutrition*, Pergamon Press, Oxford, 1993.

Case L., Carey D., Hirakawa D. et al., *Canine and Feline Nutrition*, Mosby, Sydney, 2000.

Hanssen M., *Additive Code Breaker: Everything You Should Know about Additives in Food*, Lothian Publishing, Sydney, 1984.

Howell E. (MD), *Enzyme Nutrition: The Food Enzyme Concept*, Avery Publishing Group, Wayne NJ, 1985.

Kelly N. and Wills J. (eds), *Manual of Companion Animal Nutrition and Feeding*, British Small Animal Veterinary Association, London, 1996.

Leung A., *Encyclopedia of Common Ingredients Used in Food, Drugs and Cosmetics*, J. Wiley and Sons, New York, 1980.

Lewis L. D., Morris M. L. et al., *Small Animal Clinical Nutrition*, Mark Morris Associates, Topeka Kansas, 1987.

McCluggage D., *An Introduction to Clinical Nutrition: Healing with Nutrition*, AHVMA Annual Conference Proceedings, Vermont, 1997.

Murray M., *Encyclopedia of Nutritional Supplements*, Prima Publishing, California, 1996.

Pitchford P., *Healing with1 Whole Foods*, North Atlantic Books, 1993, uses Western and Chinese approaches to nutrition.

Wright J. V., *Healing with Nutrition*, Rodale PA, 1984.

Herbs

Bone K., *Clinical Applications of Ayurvedic and Chinese Herbs*, Phytotherapy Press, Warwick, Queensland, 1997.

British Herbal Pharmacopoeia, BHMA, Cowling, 1983.

Duke J. A., *Handbook of Medicinal Herbs*, CRC Press, Boca Raton FL, 1985.

Hoffman D., *The New Holistic Herbal*, Longmead Elements Books, Shaftsbury, 1988.

Mills S. and Bone K., *Principles and Practice of Phytotherapy*, Churchill Livingstone, Sydney, 2000.

Mills S. Y., *The Dictionary of Modern Herbalism*, Healing Arts Press, Rochester VT, USA, 1988.

Mowrey D. B., *The Scientific Validation of Herbal Medicine*, Keats Publishing, New Canaan, 1986.

Murray M., *The Healing Power of Herbs*, Prima Publishing, California, 1995.

Bach Flowers

Vlamis G., Graham H., *Bach Flower Remedies for Animals*, Words Distributing Co., Forres, Scotland, 1999.

Acupuncture

Frank E., 'Myofascial Pain Syndromes Due to Trigger Points', in *Australian Veterinary Acupuncture Association Annual Proceedings*, NZVA–AVA Conference, Christchurch, June 1996.

Maciocia G., *The Foundations of Chinese Medicine: A Comprehensive Text for Acupuncturists and Herbalists*, Churchill Livingston, Melbourne, 1989, pp. 127–43.

Schoen A., *Veterinary Acupuncture Ancient Art to Modern Medicine*, Mosby, Sydney, 1994 (pp. 5-19), 2001.

Touch Therapies

Fox M., *The Healing Touch: The Proven Massage Program for Cats and Dogs*, Newmarket Press, New York, 1991.

Tellington Jones L., Taylor S., *The Tellington Ttouch: A Revolutionary Natural Method to Train and Care for Your Favorite Animal*, Penguin, New York, 1995.

Homeopathy

Boericke W. (MD), Materia Medica *with Repertory B*, Jain Publishers Ltd, New Delhi, 1993.

Day C., *The Homoeopathic Treatment of Small Animals: Principles and Practice*, The C. W. Daniel Company Ltd, Essex, UK, 1990.

MacLeod G., *Dogs, Homeopathic Remedies*, C. W. Daniel, Essex, 1990.

Vithoulkas G., *The Science of Homeopathy*, Grove Weidenfeld, New York, 1980.

Aromatherapy

Battaglia S., *The Complete Guide to Aromatherapy*, The Perfect Potion Pty Ltd, Sydney, 1995.

Grosjean N., *Veterinary Aromatherapy*, Saffron Weldon, Suffolk, 1994.

Chiropractic

Rivera P. L., *Introduction to Veterinary Chiropractic*, Proceedings of the American Holistic Veterinary Medical Association, Annual Conference, Burlington Vermont, 1996.

Tellington Touch

Tellington Jones L., Taylor S., *The Tellington Touch: A Holistic Approach to Training, Healing and Communicating with Animals*, Cloudcraft Books, England, 1992.

Hands-on Healing

Brennan B. A., *Hands of Light: A Guide to Healing through the Human Energy Field, A New Paradigm for the Human Being in Health, Relationship, and Disease*, Bantam, New York, 1988.

Conventional Medicine

Ettinger S. J. and Feldman E. C. (ed.), *Textbook of Veterinary Internal Medicine* (4th ed.), Saunders Philadelphia, 1995.

Griffin C. E., Kwochka K. W., Macdonald J. M. (eds), *Current Veterinary Dermatology*, Mosby Editions, St Louis, 1993.

Kirk R. W. (eds), *Current Vet. Therapy*, W. B.Saunders, Philadelphia (vol. X) 1989, (vol.XI) 1992.

Robinson W. F. and Huxtable C. R., *Clinico-pathologic Principles for Veterinary Medicine*, Cambridge University Press, Sydney, 1990.

Rollin B. E., *The Unheeded Cry: Animal Consciousness, Animal Pain and Science*, Oxford University Press, Oxford 1989.

Tilley L. P. and Smith F. W., *The 5-Minute Veterinary Consult*, Williams and Wilkins, Sydney, 1997.

References

Chapter 2, Health and Disease

1 Rohrs, M., September 1987, 'Domestication of wolves and wild cats: Parallels and differences in nutrition, malnutrition and dietetics in the dog and cat', Proceedings of an international symposium, Hanover; English version Edney A. T. (ed.), Waltham Center for Pet Nutrition.

2 Newby J., 1997, *The Pact for Survival: Humans and Their Animal Companions*, ABC Books, Sydney.

3 Davies K. J. A. 1995, 'Oxidative stress: The paradox of life'. In: *Biochemistry Society Symposium*, vol. 61, pp. 1–31, Portland Press, London.

4 Machlin U. 1993, 'Antioxidant vitamins: Role in disease prevention', *Pet Food Industry*, vol. 35, no. 6, p. 4.

5 Kronfeld D. S. 1983, in 'Nutrition', *Proceedings*, no. 63, p. 306, The Post Graduate Committee in Veterinary Science, The University of Sydney.

6 McMillan F. D. 1995, 'The animal mind and veterinary nursing', in: *Vet Tech*, Part 1, vol. 16, no. 8.

Chapter 3, What Do Dogs Eat?

7 Rohrs M., September 1987, 'Domestication of wolves and wild cats: Parallels and differences in nutrition, malnutrition and dietetics in the dog and cat', Proceedings of an international symposium. Hanover; English version, Edney A. T. (ed.), Waltham Center for Pet Nutrition.

8 Markwell P J., Erk W., Parkin G. D. and others 1990, 'Obesity in the dog', *J. Sm. Anim. Pract*, vol. 31, pp. 533–7, and Markwell P. J., Butterwick R. F., Wills J. M. and Raiha M. 1994, 'Clinical studies in the management of obesity in dogs and cats', *International Journal of Obesity*, vol. 19, suppl. 1, s. 39–43.

9 Dodds J. W. 1998, 'Pet food preservatives and other additives', in: *Complementary and Alternative Veterinary Medicine*, Mosby, St Louis Missouri.

10 Brown G. and Park J. 1968, 'Control of dental calculus in experimental beagles', *Lab. An. Care*, vol. 18, no 5.

Chapter 4, What Do Dogs Need?

11 Energy need is calculated from body weight in kilograms, multiplied to the power of 0.75, and then multiplied by 110. Maintenance energy =110 x bwt (kg)0.75. This is then rounded for simplicity.

12 Adapted from: *Feeding the Dog and Cat*, 1997, Uncle Ben's of Australia.

13 Ross M. H. 1972, 'Length of life and calorie intake', *Am. J. Clin. Nutr.*, vol. 25, pp. 834–8.

14 Lewis L. D, Morris M. L., Hand M. S. 1987, 'Dogs: Feeding and care'. In: *Small Animal Clinical Nutrition*, Mark Morris Associates, Topeka Kansas, ch. 3, pp. 1–32.

15 Leibetseder J. F. and Neufeld K. W. 1991, 'Effects of medium protein diets in dogs with chronic renal failure' *J. Nutr.*, vol. 121, s. 145–9.

16 Kronfeld D. S. 1983, in: 'Nutrition', *Proceedings*, no. 63, p. 190, The Post Graduate Committee in Veterinary Science, The University of Sydney.

17 Burger I. 1993, *The Waltham Book of Companion Animal Nutrition*, p. 10, Pergamon Press, Oxford.

18 Ibid., p. 11.

19 Kronfeld D. S. 1983, in: 'Nutrition', *Proceedings*, no 63, p. 140, The Post Graduate Committee in Veterinary Science, The University of Sydney.

20 Kronfeld D. S. 1989, 'Vitamins and mineral supplementation for dogs and cats', *Veterinary Practice*.

Chapter 5, Home-made Diets for Dogs

21 Costa N. 1996, *A Short Supplement in the Nutrition of the Dog and Cat*, Murdoch University School of Veterinary Studies, Murdoch, WA.

22 Hanssen M. 1984, *Additive Code Breaker: Everything You Should Know about Additives in Food*, Lothian Publishing, Sydney.

23 Burger I. 1993, *The Waltham Book of Companion Animal Nutrition*, p. 48, Pergamon Press, Oxford.

24 Ibid.

25 Schunemann C., Muhlum A. and Meyer H., September 1987, 'Precaecal and post ileal digestibility of various carbohydrates in dogs in nutrition, malnutrition and dietetics in the dog and cat', Proceedings of an international symposium. Hanover; English version Edney A. T. (ed.), Waltham Center for Pet Nutrition.

26 Quoted in Kronfeld D.S. 1983, in: 'Nutrition', *Proceedings*, no. 63, p. 204, The Post Graduate Committee in Veterinary Science, The University of Sydney.

27 Ibid., p. 219.

28 Costa N. 1996, *A Short Supplement in the Nutrition of the Dog and Cat*, Murdoch University School of Veterinary Studies, Murdoch, WA.

29 Adapted from Costa N., op. cit., and Kronfeld D. S. 1983, in: 'Nutrition', *Proceedings*, no. 63, p. 184, The Post Graduate Committee in Veterinary Science, The University of Sydney, and Burger I. 1993, *The Waltham Book of Companion Animal Nutrition*, Pergamon Press, Oxford.

Chapter 6, Supplements

30 Heanes D. L., Aug. 1990, 'Vitamin A concentrations in commercial foods for dogs and cats', *Aust. Vet. J.*, vol. 67 (8), pp. 291–4.

31 Costa N. 1996, *A Short Supplement in the Nutrition of the Dog and Cat*, Murdoch University School of Veterinary Studies.

32 Ibid.

33 Schoen A. and Wynn S. (eds) 1997, *Complementary and Alternative Veterinary Medicine*, Mosby, New York.

34 Rivera P. 1996, 'Antioxidants: The missing link for the treatment of degenerative processes', *AHVMA Proceedings*, Annual Conference, Portland, Oregon.

35 Costa N. 1996, *A Short Supplement in the Nutrition of the Dog and Cat*, Murdoch University School of Veterinary Studies, Murdoch, WA.

36 Schoen A. and Wynn S. (eds) 1997, *Complementary and Alternative Veterinary Medicine*, Mosby, New York.

37 Belfield W. O. 1967, 'Vitamin C in the treatment of canine and feline distemper complex', *Veterinary Medicine of the Small Animal Clinic*, vol. 62, p. 345.

38 Scott D. W., Sheffy B. E. 1987, 'Dermatosis in dogs caused by vitamin E deficiency', *Comp. Anim. Pract.*, vol. 1, pp. 42–6.

39 Figueriredo C. 1985, 'Vitamin E serum contents, erythrocyte and lymphocyte counts, PCV and heamoglobin determinations in normal dogs, dogs with scabies and dogs with demodicosis', *Proc. Annual Am. Acad. Vet. Derm. and Am. Coll. Vet. Derm.*, p. 8, and Miller W. H. 1989, 'Nutritional considerations in small animal dermatology', *Vet. Clin.. North Am. Sm. Anim. Pract.*, vol. 19, pp. 497–511.

40 Ayres S., Mihan R., March 1978, 'Is vitamin E involved in the autoimmune mechanism?', *Cutis*, vol. 21 (3), pp. 321–5, and Scott D. W., Walton D. K. 1985, 'Clinical evaluation of oral vitamin E for the treatment of primary canine acanthosis nigricans', *J. Am. Anim. Hosp.*, vol. 21, pp. 345–50.

41 Schoen A. and Wynn S. (eds) 1997, *Complementary and Alternative Veterinary Medicine*, Mosby, New York.

42 Davenport D. 1996, 'Nutraceuticals: Food, medicine or witchcraft?', *Proceeding of Small Animal Sessions, Veterinary Continuing Education*, no. 169, pp. 179–93, Massey University, New Zealand.

43 Schoen A. and Wynn S. (eds) 1997, *Complementary and Alternative Veterinary Medicine*, p. 101, Mosby, New York.

44 Ibid., pp. 54–61.

45 Burger I. 1993, *The Waltham Book of Companion Animal Nutrition*, p. 20, Pergamon Press, Oxford.

46 Schoen A. and Wynn S. (eds) 1997, *Complementary and Alternative Veterinary Medicine*, pp. 56–8, Mosby, New York.

47 Steel, R. S., Oct 1997, 'Thiamine deficiency in a cat associated with the preservative of "pet meat" with Sulphur dioxide', *AVJ*, vol. 75, no. 10, pp. 719–21.

48 Ibid.

49 From Costa N. 1996, *A Short Supplement in the Nutrition of the Dog and Cat*, Murdoch University, School of Veterinary Studies, Murdoch, WA.

50 McCluggage D. 1997, Proceedings of the Am. Hol. Vet. Med. Assoc.

51 Murray M. 1996, *Encyclopedia of Nutritional Supplements*, Prima Publishing, California.

52 Balch J. F, Balch P. A. 1990, *Prescription for Nutritional Healing*, Avery Publishing, New York.

53 Ibid.

54 Codner E. C., Thatcher C. D. 1990, 'The role of nutrition in the management of dermatoses', *Semin. Vet. Surg. (Sm. Anim.)*, vol. 5, pp. 167–77, and Van der Broek A. H. M., Thoday K. L. 1986, 'Skin disease in dogs associated with zinc deficiency: A report of five cases', *J. Sm. Anim. Pract.*, vol. 27, pp. 313–23.

55 Burger I. 1993, *The Waltham Book of Companion Animal Nutrition*, Pergamon Press, Oxford.

56 Lloyd D. H. 1989, 'Essential fatty acids and skin disease', *J. Sm. Anim. Pract.*, vol. 30, pp. 207–12.

57 Schoen A. and Wynn S. (eds). 1997, *Complementary and Alternative Veterinary Medicine*, Mosby, New York.

58 Bauer J. E. 1994, 'The potential for dietary polyunsaturated fatty acid supplements in domestic animals', *Aust. Vet. J.*, vol. 71, pp. 342–5.

59 *Nutrition in Practice*, edition 4/1995, Uncle Ben's of Australia.

60 Bauer J. E. 1994, 'The potential for dietary polyunsaturated fatty acid supplements in domestic animals', *Aust. Vet. J.*, vol. 71, pp. 342–5.

61 *Nutrition in Practice*, edition 4/1995, Uncle Ben's of Australia.

62 Ibid.

63 Bauer J. E. 1994, 'The potential for dietary polyunsaturated fatty acid supplements in domestic animals', *Aust. Vet. J.*, vol. 71, pp. 342–5.

64 Ibid.

65 Schoen A. and Wynn S. (eds) 1997, *Complementary and Alternative Veterinary Medicine*, Mosby, New York.

66 Janti J. 1989, 'Evening primrose oil in rheumatoid arthritis: Changes in serum lipids and fatty acids', *Annals Rheum. Dis.*, vol. 48, pp. 124–7, quoted in Murray M. 1996, *Encyclopedia of Nutritional Supplements*, Prima Publishing, California.

67 Buffington C. A. 1987, 'Nutrition and the skin', *Proceedings of the 11th Kal. Kan. Symposium*, pp. 11–16.

68 *Nutrition in Practice*, edition 4/1995, Uncle Ben's of Australia.

69 Landhmore E. W., Cameron C. A, Sheridan B. L., et al. 1986, 'Reduction of intimal hyperplasia in canine autologous vein grafts with cod liver oil and dipyridamole', *Canadian J. Surgery*, vol. 29, pp. 357–8.

70 Scott D. W. and Buerger R. G. 1988, 'Nonsteroidal anti-inflammatory agents in the management of canine pruritis', *J. Amer. Anim. Hosp. Assoc.*, vol. 24, pp. 425–8.

71 Costa N. 1996, *A Short Supplement in the Nutrition of the Dog and Cat*, Murdoch University, School of Veterinary Studies, Murdoch, WA.

72 Kronfeld D. S. 1983, in: 'Nutrition', *Proceedings*, no. 63, p. 333, The Post Graduate Committee in Veterinary Science, The University of Sydney.

73 Murray M. 1996, *Encyclopedia of Nutritional Supplements*, Prima Publishing, California.

74 Logas D. 1993, 'Double blind crossover study with high dose eicosapentanoic supplementation for the treatment of canine allergic pruritis', *Proceedings of the Am. Acad. of Vet. Derm.*

75 Campbell K. L. 1993, 'Clinical use of fatty acid supplements in dogs', *Veterinary Dermatology*, vol. 4, pp. 167–73, and Lloyd D. H. 1989, 'Essential fatty acids and skin disease', *J. Small Animal Practice*, vol. 30, pp. 207–12.

76 Lloyd D. H, Thomsett L. R. 1989, 'Essential fatty acid supplementation in the treatment of canine atopy', *Vet. Dermatol.*, vol. 1, pp. 41–4, and Bond R., Lloyd D. H. 1992, 'A double blind comparison of olive oil and a combination of evening primrose oil and fish oil in the management of canine atopy', *Vet. Rec.*, vol. 131, pp. 558–60.

77 Some forms of epilepsy in people can be associated with an elevated level of prostaglandin series 1.

78 Hamdan I. 1974, 'Acidolin, an antibiotic produced by acidophilus', *Journal of Antibiotics*, vol. 8, pp. 631–6.

79 Reddy G. 1983, 'Antitumor activity of yoghurt components', *Journal of Food Protection*, vol. 46, pp. 8–11.

80 *Handbook of Natural Medicine*, 1996, Health World Ltd, pp. 67–73.

81 Chaitow L. and Trenev N. 1990, *Probiotics*, Thorsons/Harper Collins.

82 Murray M. 1996, *Encyclopedia of Nutritional Supplements*, Prima Publishing, California.

83 Ibid.

84 McCluggage D. 1997, in: *Am. Hol. Med. Assoc. Annual Proceedings*.

85 McEntee K. and others 1995, 'Clinical electrocardiographic and echocardiographic improvements after L-carnitine supplementation in a cardiomyopathic Labrador', *Canine Pract.*, vol. 20, pp. 12.

86 Kelly N. and Wills J. (eds) 1996, *Manual of Companion Animal Nutrition and Feeding*, British Small Animal Veterinary Association.

87 Keene B. 1991, 'L-Carnitine supplementation in the therapy of canine dilated cardiomyopathy', *Vet. Clin. North Am.*, vol. 21, pp. 1005–10.

88 Murray M. 1996, *Encyclopedia of Nutritional Supplements*, Prima Publishing, California.

89 Schoen A. and Wynn S. (eds) 1997, *Complementary and Alternative Veterinary Medicine*, Mosby, New York.

90 *Coenzyme Q10*, Veterinarian product brochure, Vetri-Science Laboratories, Vermont USA.

91 Murray M. 1996, *Encyclopedia of Nutritional Supplements*, Prima Publishing, California.

92 Schoen A. and Wynn S. (eds). 1998, *Complementary and Alternative Veterinary Medicine*, Mosby, New York.

93 Howell. E. (MD) 1985, *Enzyme nutrition: The food enzyme concept*, Avery Publishing Group, Wayne NJ, USA.

94 Schoen A. and Wynn S. (eds). 1998, *Complementary and Alternative Veterinary Medicine*, Mosby, New York.

95 Ibid.

96 Adapted from Kronfeld D. S. 1983, in: 'Nutrition', *Proceedings*, no. 63, p. 194, The Post Graduate Committee in Veterinary Science, The University of Sydney.

97 Adetumbi M. A. 1983, '*Allium sativum*—a natural antibiotic', *Med. Hypotheses*, vol. 12 (3), pp. 227–37..

98 McCluggage D. 1997, *Am. Hol. Med. Assoc. Annual Proceedings*.

99 daCamara C. C. and Dowless G. V. 1998, 'Glucosamine sulphate for osteoarthritis', *Annals of Pharmacotherapy*, vol. 32 (5), pp. 580–7, School of Pharmacy, Campbell University, NC, USA.

Barclay T. S., Tsourounis C., McCart G. M. 1998, 'Glucosamine', *Annals of Pharmacotherapy*, vol. 32 (5), pp 574–9, School of Pharmacy, University of California, San Francisco.

Kelly G. S., Feb.1998, 'The role of glucosamine sulphate in the treatment of degenerative joint disease', *Alternative Medicine Review*, vol. 3 (1), pp. 27–39.

100 Murray A. 1994, *Arthritis*, Prima Publishing Company, California.

101 Kronfeld D. S. 1983, in 'Nutrition', *Proceedings*, no. 63, p. 158, The Post Graduate Committee in Veterinary Science, The University of Sydney.

102 Ballarini G., 'Animal psychodietetics. in pet nutrition and practice', *Waltham Symposium*, no. 13.

103 Schoen A. and Wynn S. (eds) 1997, *Complementary and Alternative Veterinary Medicine*, Mosby, New York.

104 McCluggage D. 1996, 'Applied clinical nutrition: Healing with nutrition', *AHVMA Proceedings*, pp. 77–91.

Chapter 7, Medicinal Herbs

105 Farnsworth N. et al. 1985, 'Medicinal plants in therapy', *Bull. World Health Org.*, vol. 63, pp. 965–81.

106 Schoen A. 1994, *Veterinary Acupuncture: Ancient Art to Modern Medicine*, Mosby, Sydney.

107 Davis Rh., Dec. 1994, 'Aloe vera, hydrocortisone and sterol influence on wound tensile strength and anti-inflammation', *J. of Am. Podiatric Medical Assoc.*, vol. 84 (12), pp. 614–19.

108 Schmidt J. M. and Greenspoon J. S. 1991, 'Aloe vera dermal wound gel is associated with a delay in wound healing', *Obstet. Gynecol.*, vol. 78, pp. 115–17, cited in Murray M. 1995, *The Healing Power of Herbs*, p. 41, Prima Publishing, California.

109 Florence T. M., Setright R. T. 1994, *The Handbook of Preventive Medicine*, Kingsclear Books, Sydney.

110 Racz-Kotilla E., Racz G. and Solomon A. 1974, 'The action of *Taraxacum officinale* extracts on the body weight and diuresis of laboratory animals', *Planta Medica*, vol. 26, pp. 212–17, cited in Murray M. 1995, *The Healing Power of Herbs*, Prima Publishing, California.

111 Murray M. 1995, *The Healing Power of Herbs*, pp. 95–103, Prima Publishing, California.

112 Ibid., pp. 102–3.

113 Hitoshi, Ito, 1986, *Jap. J. Pharmacol.*, vol. 40, pp. 435–43.

114 Middle C., July 1996, 'The use of essiac in the treatment of cancer as an alternative to chemotherapy in small animal practice', in *Chiron*, Newsletter of the Australian Assoc. Holistic Veterinarians, vol. 2, no. 3.

115 Murray M. 1995, *The Healing Power of Herbs*, pp. 122–5, Prima Publishing, California.

116 Olsen J. 'Synopsis of the 1995 AHMA conference: The changing face of healing', *J. Am. Holistic Vet. Med. Assoc.*, vol. 14, no. 4, pp. 15–16.

Chapter 8, Acupuncture

117 Schoen A. 1994, *Veterinary Acupuncture: Ancient Art to Modern Medicine*, pp. 5–19, Mosby, Sydney.

118 Maciocia G. 1989, *The Foundations of Chinese Medicine: A Comprehensive Text for Acupuncturists and Herbalists*, pp. 127–43, Churchill Livingston, Melbourne.

119. Schoen A. 1994, *Veterinary Acupuncture: Ancient Art to Modern Medicine*, pp. 20–1, Mosby, Sydney.

120 International Veterinary Acupuncture Society course notes, 1997.

121 Bossut D. F. B. and others 1983, 'Plasma cortisol and B-endorphins in horses subjected to electro acupuncture for cutaneous analgesia', *Proc. Intl. Vet. Acup. Soc.*, vol. 4, p. 501, cited in: Schoen A. and Wynn S. 1998, *Complementary and Alternative Medicine*, Mosby, Sydney.

122 Schoen A. 1994, *Veterinary Acupuncture: Ancient Art to Modern Medicine*, Mosby, Sydney.

123 Frank E., June 1996, 'Myofascial pain syndromes due to trigger points', in: *Australian Veterinary Acupuncture Association Annual Proceedings*, NZVA–AVA Conference, Christchurch.

124 Schoen A. 2001, *Veterinary Acupuncture: Ancient Art to Modern Medicine* (2nd ed.), Mosby, Sydney.

125 Ibid.

Chapter 10, Homeopathy

126 Day C. 1990, *The Homoeopathic Treatment of Small Animals: Principles and Practice*, The C. W. Daniel Company Ltd, UK.

127 25 per cent of German physicians use homeopathy, 32 per cent of French doctors use it, 42 per cent of UK doctors refer patients to homoeopaths and in India it is practised in the National Health Service. Micozzi M. S. (MD) 1996, *Fundamentals of Complementary and Alternative Medicine*, Churchill Livingston, Melbourne.

128 Vithoulkas G. 1980, *The Science of Homeopathy*, Grove Weidenfeld, New York.

129 Boericke W. (MD) 1993, Materia Medica *with Repertory B*, Jain Publishers Ltd, New Delhi.

130 Also called the Law of Similars, Vithoulkas G., *The Science of Homeopathy*.

131 Delinicl A. N. 1991, 'A hypothesis on how homoeopathic remedies work on the organism', *Berl. J. Res. Homeopath.*, vol. 1, pp. 249–53.

132 Gerber R. (MD) 1996, *Vibrational Medicine*, Bear and Company, New Mexico.

133 Schoen A., Wynn S. 1998, *Complementary and Alternative Medicine: Principles and Practice*, Mosby, Sydney.

134 Day C. 1990, *The Homoeopathic Treatment of Small Animals: Principles and Practice*, The C. W. Daniel Company Ltd, UK.

135 Day C. 'Veterinary homeopathy: Principles and practice', in: Schoen A., Wynn S. 1998, *Complementary and Alternative Medicine: Principles and Practice*, Mosby, Sydney.

136 Schoen A., Wynn S. 1998, *Complementary and Alternative Medicine: Principles and Practice*, p. 499, Mosby, Sydney.

Chapter 11, Aromatherapy

137 Micozzi M. S. (ed.) 1996, *Fundamentals of Complementary and Alternative Medicine*, pp. 140–7, Churchill Livingstone, Melbourne.

138 Ibid., pp. 145–7.

139 Battaglia S. 1995, *The Complete Guide to Aromatherapy*, p. 329, The Perfect Potion Pty Ltd, Sydney.

140 Ibid., pp. 231–43.

141 Ibid.

142 Villar D. et al. 1994, 'Toxicity of melaleuca oil and related essential oils applied topically on dogs and cats (review)', *Vet. Human Toxicol.*, vol. 36 (2), p. 139.

143 Battaglia S. 1995, *The Complete Guide to Aromatherapy*, p. 347, The Perfect Potion Pty Ltd, Sydney.

Chapter 12, Chiropractic, Physical Therapy and Massage

144 Willoughby S. L. 1994, 'Veterinary chiropractic care', In: Schoen A., *Med. veterinary acupuncture*, p. 687, Sydney.

145 Volhard W. and Brown K. 1995, *The Holistic Guide for a Healthy Dog*, Howell Book House, New York.

146 Willoughby S. 'Chiropractic care', in: Schoen A. M. and Wynn S. 1998, *Complementary and Alternative Veterinary Medicine: Principles and Practice*, p. 195, Mosby, Sydney.

147 Willoughby S. L. 'Veterinary chiropractic care', in: Schoen A.M. (ed.) 1994, *Veterinary Acupuncture*, p. 690, Sydney.

148 Rivera P. L. 1996, 'Introduction to veterinary chiropractic', *Proceedings of the American Holistic Veterinary Medical Association, Annual Conference*, Burlington Vermont, USA.

Chapter 13, Tellington Touch and Hands-on Healing

149 Tellington Jones L., Taylor S. 1992, The Tellington Touch—A Holistic Approach to Training, Healing and Communicating with Animals, Cloudcraft Books, England.

150 Gerber R. 1996, *Vibrational Medicine: New Choices for Healing Ourselves*, Bear & Company, New Mexico, USA.

151 Brennan B. A. 1988, *Hands of Light: A Guide to Healing Through the Human Energy Field: A New Paradigm for the Human Being in Health, Relationship, and Disease*, Bantam, New York.

152 Heidi P. 1988, 'Effect of therapeutic touch on anxiety level of hospitalised patients', *Nurs. Res.*, vol. 30, pp. 32–7.

Kramer N. A. 'Comparison of therapeutic touch and casual touch on stress reduction of hospitalised children', *Pediatri Nurs.*, vol. 16, pp. 483–5.

Kreiger D., Peper E., Ancoli A., 'The therapeutic touch: Searching for evidence of physiological change', *Am. J. Nurs.*, vol. 79, pp. 660–2.

Meehan M. T., 'The effect of therapeutic touch on the experience of acute pain in postoperative patients', *Dissertation Abstracts Int.*, vol. 46, p. 795B.

Wetzel W. S., 'Reiki healing: A physiological perspective', *J. Holis. Nurs.*, vol. 7, pp. 47–54.

153 Wirth D. P. 'The effect of non-contact therapeutic touch on the healing rate of full thickness dermal wounds', *Subtle Energies*, vol. 1 (1), pp. 1–20.

Chapter 14, Chronic Disease

154 Marsden S. 1996, 'Resolving dermatitis: A naturopathic approach', *Proceedings*, AHVMA Annual Conference, pp. 150–2.

155 Halliwell R. E. 1995, 'Dietary allergy and intolerance in the dog: New concepts', *ASAVA Dermatology*, AVA Annual Conference Proceedings.

156 Nagata M. 1999, 'Efficacy of commercial hypoallergenic diets in canine allergic dermatosis', *The Japanese Journal of Veterinary Dermatology*, vol. 5, pp. 25–9.

157 Fratkin J. P. 1996, 'Leaky Gut Syndrome: Treating intestinal candidiasis and dysbiosis', in: *Proc. Am. Hol. Vet. Med. Assoc. Conference Proceedings*, pp. 188–95.

158 Ibid., 1997.

159 Scanlan N. 1996, 'Toxic detox', *Am. Hol. Vet. Med. Assoc. Annual Proceedings*.

Chapter 15, Skin and Coat

160 McDonald R. K. and Langston V. C. 1995, in: Ettinger S. J. and Feldman E. C. (eds), *Textbook of Veterinary Internal Medicine*, 4th ed., p. 284, Saunders, Philadelphia.

161 Ibid.

162 White S., March 1998, *Food Allergy in Dogs*, The Compendium, Philadelphia.

163 Emily J. W., Conroys J. D., 'Contact dermatitis in dogs and cats: Pathogenesis, histopathology, experimental induction and case reports', *Veterinary Dermatology*, vol. 5, no. 4, pp. 149–62.

164 Outlined in Codner E. C. and Griffin C. E. 1996, 'Serologic allergy testing for dogs', *The Compendium Small Animal*, vol. 18 (3), pp. 237–48.

165 Reported in Chalmers S. A. and Medieau L. 1994, 'An update on atopic dermatitis in dogs', in: *Symposium on Atopy in Dogs and Cats, Vet. Med.*, pp. 326–41.

166 Mueller R. S., Bettenay S.V. 1996, 'Long-term immunotherapy of 146 dogs with atopic dermatitis: A retrospective study', *Aust. Vet. Pract.*, vol. 26 (3).

167 Cited in Paterson S. 1995, 'Additive benefits of EFAS in dogs with atopic dermatitis after partial response to antihistamine therapy', *J. of Small Animal Practice*, vol. 36, pp. 389–94.

168 Stewart J. C. M., Morse P. F., Moss M. et al., cited in: Mills S. and Bone K. 2000, *Principles and Practice of Phytotherapy*, Churchill Livingstone, Sydney.

169 Mills S. and Bone K. 2000, *Principles and Practice of Phytotherapy*, pp. 320–7, Churchill Livingstone, Sydney.

170 Cowling, BHMA 1983, *British Herbal Pharmacopoeia*, pp. 224–5.

171 Leung A. 1980, *Encyclopedia of Common Ingredients Used in Food, Drugs and Cosmetics*, pp. 80–1, J. Wiley and Sons, New York.

172 Scarff D. H., Lloyd D. H. 1992, *Veterinary Record*, vol. 131 (5), pp. 97–9.

173 Schoen A. and Wynn S. 1997, *Complementary and Alternative Medicine: Principles and Practice*, p. 343, Mosby, Sydney.

174 Kwochka K. W. 1993, 'Infectious diseases', in: Griffin C. E., Kwochka K. W., Macdonald J. M. (eds), *Current Veterinary Dermatology*, Section I, pp. 3–21, Mosby Editions, St Louis, USA.

Kwochka K. W. 1998, 'Rational shampoo therapy in veterinary dermatology', in: Campfield W. W. (ed.), *Proceedings of the 11th annual Kal Kan Symposium for the Treatment of Small Animal Diseases*, p. 87, Kal Kan Foods, Vernon CA, USA.

Kwochka K. W. 1993, 'Keratinisation disorders', in: Griffin C. E., Kwochka K. W., Macdonald J. M. (eds), *Current Veterinary Dermatology*, Section V, pp. 167–202, Mosby Editions, St Louis, USA.

175 Kwochka K. W. 1993, 'Infectious diseases', in: Griffin C. E., Kwochka K. W., Macdonald J. M. (eds), *Current Veterinary Dermatology*, Section I, pp. 3–21, Mosby Editions, St Louis; and

Kwochka K. W. 1998, 'Rational shampoo therapy in veterinary dermatology', in: Campfield W. W. (ed.), *Proceedings of the 11th Annual Kal Kan Symposium for the Treatment of Small Animal Diseases*, p. 87, Kal Kan Foods, Vernon CA, USA; and

Kwochka K. W. 1993, 'Keratinisation disorders', in: Griffin C. E., Kwochka K. W, Macdonald J. M. (eds), *Current Veterinary Dermatology*, Section V, pp. 167–202, Mosby Editions, St Louis, USA.

176 Stewart J. C. M., Morse P. F., Moss M. et al., cited in: Mills S. and Bone K. 2000, *Principles and Practice of Phytotherapy*, Churchill Livingstone, Sydney.

177 Deans S. G. and Ritchie, G. 1987, 'Antibacterial properties of plant essential oils', *Int.J. Food Microbiology*, vol. 5, p. 165.

178 Wagner H., Weirer M., Bauer R. 1986, cited in: Mills S. and Bone K. 2000, *Principles and Practice of Phytotherapy*, Churchill Livingstone, Sydney.

179 Morris D. O. 1999, 'Malassezia dermatitis and otitis', *Vet. Clinics of North America, Small Anim. Pract.*, vol. 29 (6), pp. 1303–10.

180 Ibid.

181 Amer M., Taha M., Tosson Z. 1980, 'The effect of an aqueous garlic extract on the growth of dermatophytes', *Int. J. Dermatol.*, vol. 19, pp. 285–7.

Chapter 16, Digestive System

182 *Tooth Brushing and Canine Oral Hygiene*, Waltham Researcher, May 1997.

183 Simpson J. W. 1993, 'Nutritional management of intestinal disease focus on gastroenterology', *BSAVA Congress*, Berlin.

184 Dillon R. 1989, 'Effects of corticosteroids on the gastrointestinal system', in: Kirk R. W. (ed.), *Current Vet. Therapy*, vol. X., p. 897, W. B. Saunders, Philadelphia.

185 August J. R. 1985, 'Dietary hypersensitivity in dogs: Cutaneous manifestations, diagnosis and management', *Compendium of Continuing Education*, vol. 7, pp. 469–77.

White S. D., April 1986, 'Food hypersensitivity in 30 dogs', *J. Am. Vet. Med. Assoc.*, vol. 188 (7), pp. 695–8.

186 Diehl K. J., 'Inflammatory bowel disease', in: Tilley L. P. and Smith F. W. 1997, *The 5-minute Veterinary Consult*, Williams and Wilkins, Sydney.

187 Macleod R. J. 1995, 'Inhibition of intestinal secretion by rice', *Lancet*, vol. 346, pp. 75–81.

188 Adapted from Belfield W. O. 1998, 'Orthomolecular medicine: A practitioner's perspective', in: Schoen A. and Wynn S., *Complementary and Alternative Medicine Principles and Practice*, pp.122–3, Mosby, Sydney.

189 Dillon R. 1989, 'Effects of corticosteroids on the gastrointestinal system', p. 897, in: Kirk R. W. (ed.). *Current Vet. Therapy*, vol. X., W. B. Saunders, Philadelphia.

190 McCluggage D. 1997, 'An introduction to clinical nutrition: Healing with nutrition', *AHVMA Annual Conference Proceedings*, Vermont. USA.

191 Murray M. 1995, *The Healing Power of Herbs*, Prima Publishing, California.

192 Simpson J. W. et al. 1993, 'Dietary management of clinical disease', in: *Clinical Nutrition of the Dog and Cat*, p. 56, Blackwell Scientific Publications, Oxford.

193 Hall E. J. and Batt R. M. 1988, 'Challenge studies to demonstrate gluten sensitivity of a naturally occurring enteropathy in Irish Setter dogs', *Gasteroenterology*, vol. 94 (A), p. 167.

194 Mills S. Y. 1988, *The Dictionary of Modern Herbalism*, Healing Arts Press, Rochester VT, USA.

195 McCluggage D. 1996, 'Applied clinical nutrition healing with nutrition', *AHVMA Proceedings*, pp. 77–91.

196 Mertz W., May 1975, 'Effects of metabolism of glucose tolerance factors', *Nutrition Review*, vol. 33, no. 5, pp. 129–35.

197 Allen F. M. 1927, 'Blueberry leaf extract: Physiologic and clinical properties in relation to carbohydrate metabolism', *JAMA*, vol. 89, pp. 1577–81.

198 Murray M. T. 1995, *The Healing Power of Herbs* (2nd edn), p. 56, Prima Publishing, California.

199 Ribes G. et al. 1984, 'Effects of fenugreek seeds on endocrine pancreatic secretions in dogs', *Ann. Nutr. Metab.*, vol. 28, pp. 37–43.

200 Sheela C. G. and Augusti K. T. 1992, 'Antidiabetic effects of S-1llyl cysteine sulphoxide isolated from garlic (*Allium sativum* Linn.)', *Indian J. Exp. Biol.*, vol. 30, pp. 523–6.

201 McCluggage D. 1997, 'An introduction to clinical nutrition: Healing with nutrition', in: *AHVMA Annual Conference Proceedings*, Vermont.

202 Murray M. T. 1995, *The Healing Power of Herbs* (2nd edn), p. 187, Prima Publishing, California.

203 Ibid., p. 359.

Chapter 17, Ears andEyes

204 Atkinson D. 1952, 'Malnutrition as an etiological factor in the senile cataract', *Eye Ear Nose and Throat Monthly*, vol. 31 pp. 79–83. Cited in: Murray M. and Pizzorno J. 1991, *Encyclopedia of Natural Medicine*, p. 193, Prima Publishing, California.

205 Murray M. and Pizzorno J. 1991, *Encyclopedia of Natural Medicine*, p. 193, Prima Publishing, California.

206 *Experimental Eye Research*, 1984, vol. 39, pp. 745–9.

Chapter 18, The Immune System

207 Robinson W. F. and Huxtable C. R. 1990, *Clinicopathologic Principles for Veterinary Medicine*, Cambridge University Press, Sydney.

208 Ibid.

209 Gerber R. 1996, *Vibrational Medicine*, pp. 433–5, Bear and Company, Santa Fe, New Mexico, USA.

210 Ibid., p. 445.

211 Ibid., pp. 433–5.

212 Schoen A. and Wynn S. (eds) 1997, *Complementary and Alternative Veterinary Medicine*, Mosby, New York.

213 Lewis L. D., Jan. 1996, 'Nutrition for recovery', *Vet. Forum*, pp. 58–9.

214 Schoen A. and Wynn S. (eds) 1997, *Complementary and Alternative Veterinary Medicine*, Mosby, New York.

215 Balch J. F, Balch P. A. 1990, *Prescription for Nutritional Healing*, Avery Publishing, New York.

216 Ibid.

217 Schoen A. and Wynn S. (eds) 1997, *Complementary and Alternative Veterinary Medicine*, Mosby, New York.

218 McCluggage D. 1997, 'Applied clinical nutrition: Clinically effective protocols', *AHVMA Proceedings*, pp. 60–71.

219 Reddy G. 1983, 'Antitumor activity of yoghurt components', *Journal of Food Protection*, vol. 46, pp. 8–11.

220 *Handbook of Natural Medicine*, 1996, pp. 67–73, Health World Ltd.

221 Schoen A. and Wynn S. (eds) 1997, *Complementary and Alternative Veterinary Medicine*, Mosby, New York.

222 Murray M. 1995, *The Healing Power of Herbs*, Prima Publishing, California.

223 Ibid.

224 Bone K. 1997, *Clinical Applications of Ayurvedic and Chinese Herbs*, Phytotherapy Press, Queensland.

225 Ibid.

226 McCluggage D. 1996, 'Applied clinical nutrition: Healing with nutrition', *AHVMA Proceedings*.

227 Murray M. 1995, *The Healing Power of Herbs*, Prima Publishing, California.

228 Brown C., Armstrong P., Globus H., May 1995, 'Nutritional management of food allergy in dogs and cats', *Small Animal Compendium*, pp. 637–58.

229 Duval D., Giger U. 1996, 'Vaccine-associated immune-mediated haemolytic anaemia in the dog', *JVIM*, vol. 10, pp. 290–5.

230 Schoen A. and Wynn S. (eds) 1997, *Complementary and Alternative Veterinary Medicine*, Mosby, New York.

231 Ibid.

232 Ibid.

233 Ramesh G. et al., Sept–Oct 1992, 'Effect of essential fatty acids on tumor cells', *Nutrition*, vol. 8 (5), pp. 343–7.

234 Murray M. 1995, *The Healing Power of Herbs*, Prima Publishing, California.

235 Murray M. and Pizzorno J. 1991, *Encyclopedia of Natural Medicine*, pp. 60–1, Prima Publishing, California.

236 Ibid.

237 Murray M. and Pizzorno J. 1991, *Encyclopedia of Natural Medicine*, p. 191, Prima Publishing, California.

238 Murray M. 1995, *The Healing Power of Herbs*, Prima Publishing, California.

239 Ibid.

240 Ibid.

241 Bone K. 1997, *Clinical Applications of Ayuvedic and Chinese Herbs*, Phytotherapy Press.

242 McCluggage D. 1996, 'Applied clinical nutrition: Healing with nutrition', *AHVMA Proceedings*.

243 Murray M. 1995, *The Healing Power of Herbs*, Prima Publishing, California.

Chapter 19, Glandular Health

244 Evans F. Q. 1958, 'The rational use of glycyrrhetinic acid in dermatology', *Br. J. Clin. Pract.*, vol. 12, pp. 269–79.

245 Mills S. and Bone K. 2000, *Principles and Practice of Phytotherapy*, pp. 313–17, Churchill Livingstone, Sydney.

246 Dodds J. 1997, 'Immune thyroiditis', from lecture notes taken at American Holistic Veterinary Association Conference.

Chapter 20, Pain and Inflammation

247 Rollin B. E. 1989, *The Unheeded Cry: Animal Consciousness, Animal Pain and Science*, Oxford University Press, Oxford.

248 *Aust. Vet. Practitioner* 1996, vol. 26 (4), pp. 206–9.

249 Australian College of Veterinary Scientists, 'Guidelines for the management of pain in veterinary practice', *Aust. Vet. Pract.*, vol. 26 (4), 1996.

250 Murray M. and Pizzorno J. 1991, *Encyclopedia of Natural Medicine*, p. 191, Prima Publishing, California.

251 Chandra D. and Gupta S. 1972, 'Anti-inflammatory and antiarthritic activity of volatile oil of *curcuma longa*', *Ind. J. Med. Res.*, vol. 60, pp. 138–42; and
Arora R., Basu N. and Jan A. 1971, 'Anti-inflammatory studies on curcuma longa (turmeric)', *Ind. J. Med. Res.*, vol. 59, pp. 1289–95, cited in: Murray M. and Pizzorno J. 1991, *Encyclopedia of Natural Medicine*, Prima Publishing, California.

252 Leung A. Y. 1980, *Encyclopedia of Common Natural Ingredients Used in Food*, John Wiley & Sons, New York.

253 Lewith G. T. and Machin D. 1983, *On the Evaluation of the Clinical Effects of Acupuncture Pain*, vol. 16, pp. 111–27.

254 Murray M. 1995, *The Healing Power of Herbs*, Prima Publishing, California.

Chapter 21, Muscles, Bones and Joints

255 Johnston S., Fox S. 1997, 'Mechanisms of action of anti-inflammatory medications used for the treatment of osteoarthritis', *JAVMA*, vol. 210, no. 10, pp. 1486–96.

256 Ibid.

257 Isaacs J. P. 1996, 'Adverse effects of non-steroidal anti-inflammatory drugs in the dog and cat', *Aust. Vet. Pract.*, vol. 26 (4).

258 Kealy R. D. et al. 1997, *J. Am. Vet. Med. Assoc.*, vol. 21, pp. 222–5.

259 Drovanti A. et al. 1980, 'Therapeutic activity of oral glucosamine sulfate in osteoarthritis: A placebo-controlled double-blind investigation', *Clin. Ther.*, vol. 3 (4), p. 260.

260 Chandra D. and Gupta S. 1972, 'Anti-inflammatory and antiarthritic activity of volatile oil of curcuma longa', *Ind. J. Med. Res.*, vol. 60, pp. 138–42; and
Arora R., Basu N., and Jan A. 1971, 'Anti-inflammatory studies on *curcuma longa* (turmeric)', *Ind. J. Med. Res.*, vol. 59, pp. 1289–95, cited in: Murray M. and Pizzorno J. 1991, *Encyclopedia of Natural Medicine*, Prima Publishing, California.

261 Durkes T. E. 'Gold bead implants', in: Schoen A. 1994, *Veterinary Acupuncture: Ancient Art to Modern Medicine*, pp. 285–6, Mosby, Sydney.

262 Janssens L. A. 1994, 'Trigger point therapy', in: Schoen A., *Veterinary Acupuncture: Ancient Art to Modern Medicine*, Mosby, Sydney.

263 Janssens L. A. 1997, 'Acupuncture for thoracolumbar and cervical disc disease', in International Veterinary Acupuncture Society course notes.

264 Janssens L. A. 1989, 'Treatment of thoracolumbar disc disease in dogs by means of acupuncture: A comparison of two techniques', *J. Small Animal Hosp. Assoc.*, vol. 25, pp. 169–74.

265 Janssens L. A. 1985, 'The treatment of canine cervical disc disease by acupuncture: A review of 32 cases', *J. Small Animal Practice*, vol. 26, p. 203.

266 Janssens L. A. 1997, 'Acupuncture for thoracolumbar and cervical disc disease', in International Veterinary Acupuncture Society course notes.

267 Ibid.

Chapter 22, The Cardiovascular System

268 Smith F. 1994, 'Acupuncture for cardiovascular disorders', in: Schoen A., *Veterinary Acupuncture: Ancient Art to Modern Medicine*, Mosby, Sydney.

269 Duke J. A. 1985, *Handbook of Medicinal Herbs*, CRC Press, Boca Raton FL, USA.

Chapter 23, The Nervous System, Epilepsy and Strokes

270 Frey H. H. 1986, 'Use of anticonvulsants in small animals', *Vet. Rec.*, vol. 118, pp. 484–6.

271 Collins J. R., July 1994, 'Seizures and other neurological manifestations of allergy', *Vet. Clin. North Amer. Small Anim. Pract.*, vol. 24 (4), p. 735–48.

272 Roach E. S. N., 21 Oct 1982, 'N-Dimethylglycine for epilepsy', *The New England Journal of Medicine*, vol. 307 (17), pp. 1081–2.

273 Redaksie A. D., March 1988, 'The use of acupuncture in canine epilepsy', *J. South African Vet. Assoc.*

Chapter 25, Behavioural Problems

274 Ballarini G., 'Animal psychodietetics in pet nutrition and practice', Waltham Symposium, no. 13.

275 DeNapoli J. S, Dodman N. H. et al., 15 Aug 2000, 'Effect of dietary protein content and tryptophan supplementation on dominance aggression, territorial aggression and hyperactivity in dogs', *JAVMA*, vol. 217 (4), pp. 504–8.

276 Ballarini G., 'Animal psychodietetics in pet nutrition and practice', Waltham Symposium, no. 13.

277 Blake S., 'Show no fear when it comes to Bach flowers and homeopathy', *J. Hol. Vet. Med. Asoc.*, vol 16, pp. 4, 35.

Chapter 26, Urinary Tract

278 Sobota A. E. 1984, 'Inhibition of bacterial adherence by cranberry juice: Potential use for the treatment of urinary tract infections', *J. Urol.*, vol. 131, pp. 1013–16.

Chapter 28, Health Maintenance

279 T. Phillips and R. Shultz. 1992, 'Canine and feline vaccines', in: *Current Veterinary Therapy*, vol. XI, W. B. Saunders, Philadelphia; and
Smith P. A and C. 1995, 'Are we vaccinating too much?', *JAVMA*, vol. 207 (4), pp. 421–5.

280 Frick O., Brooks D. 1981, 'Immunoglobulin E antibodies to pollens augmented in dogs by virus vaccines', *Am. J. Vet. Res.*, vol. 44, p. 440.

281 Duval D., Giger U. 1996, 'Vaccine-associated immune mediated hemolytic anaemia in the dog', *J. Vet. Int. Med.*, vol. 10, p. 290.

282 Littman V. D. M. M., May–July 1995, 'Why I don't vaccinate for Lyme disease', *Journal of AHVMA*, vol. 14, no. 2, pp. 11–12.

283 Wynn S. and Dodds W. 1995, 'Vaccine-associated disease in a family of young Akita dogs', *Proc. Am. Hol. Vet. Med. Assoc.*, p. 81; and
Dodds W. 1995, 'Vaccine-associated disease in young Weimaraners', *Proc. Am. Hol. Vet. Med. Assoc.*, pp. 85–6.

284 Day C. 1984, *The Homeopathic Ttreatment of Small Animals*, Wigmere Publishers, London.

285 Murray M. 1995, *The Healing Power of Herbs*, Prima Publishing, California.

286 Hooser S. B. et al. 1986, 'Effects of an insecticidal dip containing d-limonene in the cat', *JAVMA*, vol. 189, no. 8.

287 Dryden M. W. 1989, 'Effects of ultrasonic flea collars on Ctenocephalides felis on cats', *JAVMA*, vol. 195, no. 12.

288 Delmar D. 1994, 'Natural predator enters flea war', *Veterinary Product News*, vol. 6, no. 1.

289 Baker N. 1983, 'Failure of brewer's yeast as a repellent to fleas on dogs', *JAVMA*, vol. 183, no. 2.

290 Adapted from Table 9.2 in: *Manual of Companion Animal Nutrition and Feeding*, edited by Noel Kelly and Josephine Wills, BSAVA, 1996. Based on maintenance energy requirements for target weight multiplied by 45 per cent to allow a weight loss of approximately 1 per cent per week.

Index

AAFCO (American Association of Food Control Officials) 16, 31
acupressure 83–6
acupuncture 77–86, 101, 132, 135, 137, 140, 141, 142, 146, 147, 151, 191
  health 118
  how it works 78–9
  pain 185–6
  precautions 79
  success 83
  uses 79–82
    behavioral problems 81, 218
    cancer 81, 175
    digestive tract disorders 80–1, 152, 153, 155, 156
    eyes and ears 82, 158, 160, 161
    heart disorders 81
    immune disorders 81, 167, 168, 171
    muscle and bone problems 80, 192–3
    nervous system and spinal problems 80, 208
    reproduction 82
    respiratory disorders 82, 212, 213, 214
    skin disorders 80, 187
    urinary tract problems 82, 228
  veterinary 77, 79, 83
  what to expect 82–3
Addison's disease 180
adrenal gland 150, 179
adult dogs 23
aggression, see behavioural problems
ageing dogs 6, 23–4, 50, 54, 55, 56, 59, 62, 72–3, 91–2, 96, 108, 244–5, see also supplements
alcohol 67
allergies 45, 63, 120, 129–33, 167–70, see also herbs, supplements
  food, 149–50
alternative medicine, see medicine
anaemia 205–6
anal glands 138, 152
antibiotics 120, 121, 145, 177–8

antioxidants 43, 47, 54, 60, 72–3
anxiety, see behavioural problems
aromatherapy 103–5, 118, 128
  guidelines 103–4
  how it works 103
  suggested use 104–5
  toxicity 103–4
arthritis 60, 69, 70, 75–6, 78, 80, 94, 190–3, see also herbs, homeopathy, massage, supplements
ataxia 208

Bach flower remedies 87–96, 118, 124, 132, 135, 137, 140, 141, 145, 146, 148, 151
bacteria
  beneficial 29, 52, 53, 126
  harmful 52, 87, 120, 126, 133–6, 234
barking 219–20
behavioural problems 216–23, see also herbs, supplements, Tellington touch
  aggression 93, 221–2
  anxiety 93, 113, 219
  depression 75–6, 92, 94
  fear 220–1
  nerves 61, 63, 70, 75, 76, 113, 219
  obsessive–compulsive disorder 139, 222
  remedies, see Bach flower remedies
  separation anxiety 7, 94, 95, 96, 220
  urinating inappropriately 222–3
biochemical salts, see flatulence, homeopathy
bladder, see also diet
  incontinence 227–9
  infection or cystitis 224–5
  stones—Urolithiasis 226–9
blood, see also anaemia
  flow and clots 72–3, 76, 79
  hyperlipidaemia 20
bones 190–202, see also diet: food, hip dysplasia
bowel 12, 65, 69, 73, 121, 124–5, 138–9,

148, 149, see also constipation, diarrhoea
  detoxification 124–5, 150, 151, 176
  dysbiosis 121, 123, 125, 126
brain problems 210
breeding 8, see also pregnancy
bronchitis 212–14
burns 69, 71

cancer 53, 56, 57, 62, 71, 72, 74, 81, 100, 172–5, see also herbs, supplements
canned foods, see diet: food
carbohydrates, see energy
cataracts 161–2
chemicals 120, see medicine
Chinese Traditional Medicine,
chiropractic, 106–7, see also physical therapy and massage
  arthritis, for 193
  subluxation 106–7
cigarette smoke 6, 12
circulation, see heart
complementary medicine, see medicine
conjunctivitis 162
constipation 51–2, 150–1
contacts, useful 249–50
conventional medicine, see medicine
coprophagy 25
corticosteroids 123, 128, 132, 141, 181–2
  herbal treatment, with 181–2
Cushing's disease
cystitis, see bladder

dachshunds 200
dandruff, see skin and coat
deafness, see ears
death and dying, see euthanasia
depression, see behavioural problems
detoxification, see bowel, naturopathy
diabetes 46, 51, 58, 67, 72, 155–6, see also herbs, supplements
diarrhoea 44, 51, 53, 62, 73–4, 81, 98, 142
  acute 145–7
  chronic 147–8

recipes to aid, 146, *see also* recipes
under diet
diet 8, 13–41, 117, 133, 138, 139, 140,
141, 142–4, 143, 145, 146, 147, 150,
151, 152, 153, 154
allergies, for 168
arthritis 191–2
balanced 26
behavior control, for 217
bladder 226
cancer 173
elimination diet 149–50, 152, 169–70
eyes, for 161, 163
fibre 25, 51, 139, 150, 155
food
bones 17–18
canned food 16–17, 21
commercial food 15
cooked food 30, 32
dry food 15–16, 21, 150
home–made food 18, 27–41, 133,
150
beans and lentils 29
cereals 29, 30, 39
chicken 28, 38, 40–1, 146
eggs 30
fish 28, 40, 62, 146
fruits 30, 36–7, 53, 141, 143,
145
meat 27–8, 33, 38–9, 40, 41, 46,
57, 141
milk and dairy 28–9
organic food 31
raw food 30, 31, 32, 55
seeds 30
tofu and soy 29
vegetables 29–30, 36–7, 53, 141,
143, 145
immune system 165, 171
nutrition 7–8, 9, 12, 26, 31–2
oils 31, 37, 49, *see also* fatty acids
recipes
alternatives 33–6
basic 32
exchanges 36–7
carbohydrate 36
liver 37
meat 33
oil 37
vegetable or fruit 36–7
growth 34
low–fat 35, 147
low–protein 36
other
carrot soother 146
chicken and rice recovery 38,
146
chicken wing dinner 38
chicken wing teeth cleaner 38
dog dinner loaf 40
dog oat surprise biscuits 39
lamb crockpot 38
mutley muesli breakfast 39
soup 124
chicken broth 41

chicken soup 40–1
mutton or lamb broth 41
liver disease, for 153
nervous system, for 207
pain, for 185
pancreatic problems, for 154
vomiting, for 152
weight loss diet 247
digestion 29–30, 51, 52, 55, 60, 64, 70,
74, 75, 80–1, 85, 103, 124, 142–56, *see
also* teeth
domestication 5, 9, *see also* wild dogs
dry eye 162–3
dry foods 15
dysbiosis, *see* bowel, naturopathy

ears 157–60, *see also* herbs, massage,
supplements, Tellington touch
aural haematoma 160
deafness 160
middle and inner ear problems 159
vestibular syndrome 208
elimination diet, *see* diet
emotion 7, 78, 81, 87–96, *see also*
behavioural problems
energy 5, 8, 9, 19–24, 29, 31, 54, 78,
113–15
body 5, 77, 87, 111, 246
carbohydrates 24–5, 36
fat 24, 28, 44, 54
protein 23, 147, 148
environment 9–10, 130
life-style 8, 9
epilepsy and seizures 209–10
euthanasia and the dying process 115
exercise 9, 145, 146, 150, 247–8
liver disease, for 154
eyes 160–3, *see also* cataracts, conjunctivitis, diet, dry eye, glaucoma,
herbs, supplements

family 248
fasting, *see* bowel detoxification
fat, *see* energy
fatty acids 48–9, 58, 131, 141, 155, *see
also* diet: oils
evening primrose oil 50–1, 131, 134
flax seed oil 50, 153, 155
fish oil 50
fear, *see* behavioural problems
fibre 51, *see also* diet
flatulence 151–2
Bach flowers 151
biochemical salts 152
diet 151
herbs 151
homeopathy 151
recommendations 151
supplements 151
fleas 104, 129, 240, 241–3
flowers, *see* Bach flower remedies
food, *see* diet
free radicals 6–7, 47, 54, 57–8

glands 179–83

adrenal gland 179–80
glaucoma 163
gum disease, *see* teeth

hands–on healing 113–15, *see also*
Tellington touch
head
ears, nose, mouth and eyes 70, 76,
82, 85, 113
injuries and brain problems 210
tilt 208
health 8, 11–12, 237–48, *see also* Bach
flower remedies
problems
chronic 7, 25, 82, 102
longstanding 4–5
heart 73, 81, 85, 203–6
heartworm 205
herbs, medicinal 64–76, 117–18, 131–2,
134, 138, 140, 141, 142, 144, 145, 146,
147, 151
allergies, for 168
arthristis 192
behavioural disorders, for 217
cancer, for 174
diabetes, for 155
ears, for 158, 159, 160
eyes, for 161–3
guidelines 66–7
health 117–18
immune system, for 166, 171
infusion and decoction 67
liver disease, for 153
nervous system 207–8
pain 185
pancreatic problems, for 154
safety 65–6
tablets and capsules 67
tinctures 67
types of
alfalfa 69, 137, 142
aloe vera 69, 132, 147
bladderwrack/kelp 61, 69
burdock 69, 122, 126, 132, 137
calendula, marigold 69
celery 70
chamomile 70, 144, 151
cleavers 70, 122, 123, 132
comfrey 70
dandelion 70–1, 122, 137, 142, 145
echinacea 71, 123, 134, 135, 141,
144
essiac 71–2, 151
fennel 145, 151
fresh
herbs 67
plant cream 68
garlic 72–3, 137
ginger 72, 137, 148
gingko 72–3
ginseng
panex 74, 134
Siberian 75
hawthorn 73

liquorice 73, 122, 123, 125, 134, 137, 147, 151
nettle 73, 122, 132
oak bark 73–4, 147
parsley 145, 151
peppermint 74, 131, 142, 145, 147, 151
pumpkin 74
red clover 74, 75, 122, 126, 131, 137
red raspberry 74–5, 147
saw palmetto berries 75
skullcap 75
St Johns Wort 75–6, 144
St Mary's thistle, milk thistle 76, 122, 123, 126, 137, 141
thyme 76, 131, 135, 136, 137, 144
valerian 76
yellow dock 76, 122, 132, 151
use 65
vomiting, for 152
wound repair 186–7
hip dysplasia 193–5
holistic veterinarian 116–17, see also chiropractic, homeopathy
home-made diets 18
homeopathy 97–102, 118, 133, 135, 138, 139, 144, 145, 147, 148, 151
allergies 168
arthritis 193
behavioural disorders, for 218–19
cancer, for 175
choosing 102
diabetes, for 156
ears, for 158, 159
eyes, for 162, 163
dosing 102
guidelines 101–2
liver disease, for 153–4
nosodes 99–100, 239
pain 186
pancreatic problems, for 155
potency 101
principles 97–9
responses 102
Schüssler biochemic salts 100, 133, 135, 138, 138, 139, 140, 145, 146, 148, 152
veterinarian 100, 101
vomiting, for 152
when not to use 100
when to use 100–1
wound repair 187
hydrotherapy 134
hyperlipidaemia 51

immune system 63, 72, 81, 84–5, 103, 134, 164–78, see also diet, herbs, skin: immunotherapy, supplements
auto–immune disease 170–2
incontinence 227–9
infections 177–8, 234–5
inflammation 184–9
information 249–50
injuries 108, see also pain, wounds
infusion and decoction, see herbs

itching, see skin

joints 190–202

kidney disease 229–30

lactation, see pregnancy
large dogs 22, 33
leaky gut syndrome 120–1, 123, 133, 149
lick granulomas, see skin and coat
liver disease 153–4, see also herbs, naturopathy, supplements
Lyme disease 195
lymphatic system 64, 70, 175–6

massage 83, see also chiropractic, physical therapy and massage
arthritis, for 193
ear 158
mastitis, see Reproductive, female
medication 133
medicine, 117
alternative 147, 239–40, 242
Chinese, Traditional 77–9
Complementary 2, 249–50
conventional 10–11, 50, 65, 73, 79, 147
medicinal herbs, see herbs, medicinal
minerals 25, 46
calcium 44, 46
chromium 46
copper 47, 154
salt 47
selenium 47, 130, 148
zinc 47, 126, 141, 153, 154
muscles 190–202
trigger points 190, 195–6

naturopathy 120, 122–6, 133
alteratives 122–3
detoxification 122–3, 132
liver detoxification 125, 126
plan 125–6
correction of dysbiosis 125–6
correct nutritional deficiencies 126
short-term modified fast 125
program, the 124
repair 123
tonification 123
nerves, see behavioural problems
nervous system 207–10, see also herbs, supplements
nerve paralysis 208–9
neutraceuticals and supplements 117
nose, see respiratory system
nutrition, see diet

oats 135
obesity, see weight
obsessive–compulsive disorder, see behavioural problems
oils, see diet, fatty acids
older dogs, see ageing dogs

oxidative stress 6

pain 75–6, 77, 80, 108, 175, 184–9, see also herbs, supplements
pancreatic problems 154–5, see also herbs, supplements
parasites 8, 120, see also fleas, ticks, worms
physical therapy and massage 108–9, see also chiropractic, massage
pneumonia 214–15
pregnancy 19–20, 22–3, 74–5, 79, 83, 101, 104, 108, 231–2
false 233–4
lactation 76, 231–2
whelping 231–2
prostate 236
protein 27, 28, see also energy
low–protein recipe 36
puppies 15, 17–18, 19, 21–2, 46, 73, 99
recipes for 34–5
pyoderma, see skin: bacterial skin disease
pyometra, see reproductive system, female

reading, further 251–3
recipes, see diet
recovery, see surgery
Reiki 114
relaxation 110, 114, 219, see also Tellington touch
reproductive system 82, 231–6
female 231–5
infertility 232–3
mastitis 234
pyometra or infection 234–5
male 75, 82
infertility 235
prostate disorders 236
respiratory system 211–15
nasal discharge 211–12

Schüssler biochemic salts, see homeopathy
scratching, see skin
seizures and epilepsy 209–10
separation anxiety, see behavioural problems
show dogs 92, 93, 94
skin and coat 1, 8, 15, 43, 47, 61, 64, 69, 71, 73, 74, 80, 85, 92, 127–41
allergic skin disease 129–33
anal glands 138–9
aromatherapy oils 128
atopy 130, 132
bacterial skin disease 133–6
bathing 131,134
chronic skin problems 128
diet 129
guidelines 128–9
compresses 134
demodectic mange 141
dermatologist, veterinary 128
doggy odour 136, 140

dry skin and dandruff 137–8
  recommendations 137
hair loss and shedding 138
hotspots 135–6
immunotherapy 130
itching 131
lick granulomas 139–40
  topical applications 140
moisturising agents
recurrent skin infections 133
rinses and washes 127, 131
scratching 130–1
shampoo 127, 134, 138
topical agents 134–5, 136
yeast or Malassezia dermatitis 136–7
  acupuncture 137
  conventional therapy 136
  diet 136
  naturopathic approach 136
  supplements 136
  systemic 137
  topical agents 136
snakebite 71,187
spine 197–9
  degenerative myelopathy 201–2
  disc disease 199–200
  Wobbler syndrome 200–1
spleen, see lymphatic system
stings 186–7
stress 7–8, 43, 45, 54, 55, 75, 121, 128
  immune system 164–5
subluxation, see chiropractic
supplements 42–63, 129, 131, 136, 137,
  138, 139, 140, 141, 142, 144, 145, 146,
  148, 150, 151, 153, 154, 155
  allergies, for 168
  arthritis, for 192
  behavioural disorders, for 217
  cancer, for 174
  diabetes, for 155
  ears, for 157, 159, 160
  eyes, for 160, 161, 162163
  health, for 117
  immune system, for 165, 171
  liver disease, for 153
  nervous system, for 207
  pain, for 185
  pancreatic problems, for 154
  types of
    bioflavinoids 57
    carnitine 54
    choline 63
    coenzyme Q 54–5
    dimethylglycine 55, 141
    enzymes 55, 59, 126, 140, 141, 142,
      145, 146, 148, 151, 154
    garlic 58, 72–3
    glandular products 59
    glucosamine 59–60, 123, 142, 148,
      155
    glutamine 60, 123, 126, 142, 146,
      148
    grape seed extract 57–8
    green foods 60–1
    honey 56, 144

bee propolis 56
kelp 61, 69, 140, 141
lecithin 61–2, 126, 140, 153
liver 57, 59
mushrooms: shiitake, maitake,
  cordyceps and reishi 62–3
perna mussel 62
prebiotics 53, 123, 142
probiotics 29, 52–3, 123, 126, 142,
  145, 146, 148, 151
shark and bovine cartilage 62
slippery elm 75, 123, 125, 142, 144,
  146, 147, 151
wheat germ 63
yeast 63
vomiting, for 152
wound repair, for 186
surgery 187–9

tea 134
teeth, see also digestion
  bad breath 144–5
  gum disease and periodontal dis-
    ease 142–4
  gum rubs 144
  tooth brushing 143–4
Tellington touch 110–13, see also
  hands–on healing
  behavioural disorders, for 218
  belly 113
  ear 113
  how it works 110
  how to breathe 112
  how to use your hands 111
  mental attitude 111
  mouth 113
  pressure 112
  tail 113
thyroid 182–3
ticks 241–3
tinctures, see herbs
TLC (tender loving care) 109
toxins 6, 9, 25, 31, 42, 50, 53, 61, 62, 65,
  68, 76, 103–4, 119–20
Traditional Chinese Medicine (TCM),
  see medicine
trauma 187–9

urinary tract 224–30
urinating 222–3, see also behavioural
  problems

vaccination 121–2, 237–40
  alternatives 239–40
veterinary care 10, 16, 66, 77, 98, 116,
  see also acupuncture
vitamins 25, 33, 42
  vitamin A 43, 137, 148, 154
  vitamin B complex 45, 63, 71, 76, 140,
    142, 146, 148, 151, 153
  vitamin C 43–4, 57, 126, 130, 140, 144,
    145, 148, 153, 155
  vitamin D 44, 154
  vitamin E 44, 126, 130, 144, 145, 148,
    153, 154, 155

vitamin K 69 , 154
vomiting, chronic 152

water 25, 134
weight 19–20, 245–8
  control 245
  gain 4, 5, 32
  low-fat recipes 35, 247
  obesity 69, 245
whelping, see pregnancy
wild dogs 5, 13, see also domestication
Wobbler syndrome, see spine
worms 74, 126, 240–1
  heartworm 205
wounds 70, 71, 92, 186–7